Britain and the Intellectual Origins of the League of Nations, 1914–1919

In this innovative account of the origins of the idea of the League of Nations, Sakiko Kaiga casts new light on the pro–League of Nations movement in Britain in the era of the First World War, revealing its unexpected consequences for the development of the first international organisation for peace. Combining international, social and intellectual history and international relations, she challenges two misunderstandings about the role of the movement: that their ideas about a league were utopian and that its peaceful ideal appealed to the war-weary public. Kaiga demonstrates how the original post-war plan consisted of both realistic and idealistic views of international relations and shows how it evolved and changed in tandem with the war. She provides a comprehensive analysis of the unknown origins of the League of Nations and highlights the transformation of international society and of ideas about war prevention from the twentieth century to the present.

Sakiko Kaiga is a research fellow at the Institute of Social Science, University of Tokyo.

T0345467

Britain and the Intellectual Origins of the League of Nations, 1914–1919

Sakiko Kaiga

University of Tokyo

CAMBRIDGE
UNIVERSITY PRESS

CAMBRIDGE
UNIVERSITY PRESS

Shaftesbury Road, Cambridge CB2 8EA, United Kingdom

One Liberty Plaza, 20th Floor, New York, NY 10006, USA

477 Williamstown Road, Port Melbourne, VIC 3207, Australia

314–321, 3rd Floor, Plot 3, Splendor Forum, Jasola District Centre, New Delhi – 110025, India

103 Penang Road, #05–06/07, Visioncrest Commercial, Singapore 238467

Cambridge University Press is part of Cambridge University Press & Assessment, a department of the University of Cambridge.

We share the University's mission to contribute to society through the pursuit of education, learning and research at the highest international levels of excellence.

www.cambridge.org
Information on this title: www.cambridge.org/9781108733540

DOI: 10.1017/9781108774130

First published 2021
First paperback edition 2022

A catalogue record for this publication is available from the British Library

ISBN   978-1-108-48917-1   Hardback
ISBN   978-1-108-73354-0   Paperback

Cambridge University Press & Assessment has no responsibility for the persistence or accuracy of URLs for external or third-party internet websites referred to in this publication and does not guarantee that any content on such websites is, or will remain, accurate or appropriate.

Contents

Acknowledgements

This study originates with the events of 11 September 2001, which had strong impacts on many humanities and social science scholars of my generation. As a teenager who grew up in a country that embraced Article 9 and pacifist education that tended to argue that you should not support war under any circumstances, witnessing widespread support for the US military actions by the press, politicians and the public opinion of my home country left a striking impression. It led me to pursue an academic career, with a focus on how war has historically been regulated in international society and how people discussed it in the past.

This book is largely based on my PhD thesis submitted to the Department of War Studies, King's College London. The greatest debt undoubtedly goes to my PhD supervisor, Joe Maiolo, to whom I would like to express my gratitude and admiration both as a scholar and teacher. I have always been convinced that if I had not been lucky enough to be his supervisee, I could not have learned as much as I have and this book would not be as it is now. I am also deeply grateful to Patricia Clavin and Gaynor Johnson for constantly giving me generous, warm support that has helped me continue my research. For offering advice, encouragement, commentary on drafts of the manuscript and/or sharing unpublished work and sources, I would like to thank John Bew, Martin Ceadel, Hilary Davies, Seung-Young Kim, Hatsue Shinohara, Jan Stöckmann, Takahiko Tanaka and Corinna Unger. For their valuable insight, I am particularly grateful to Michael Watson, Emily Sharp and the production team at Cambridge University Press. I would also like to thank the two anonymous readers of the manuscript for their encouraging and helpful comments, which strengthened the book.

I wish to acknowledge the institutions that have sponsored this project since I defended my thesis. I owe thanks to friends, colleagues and staff at each of these places. Special thanks must go to the Max Weber team of the European University Institute, who allowed me to spend a memorable and beautiful time in Florence, and to the Peace Research Institute at International Christian University, especially Norie Takazawa and Kei

Nasu, who accommodated me in a warm academic base in Tokyo when it was really needed.

This project became possible thanks to invaluable financial assistance. In particular, I am grateful to King's College London, the Gilbert Murray Trust, the Canon Foundation, the Panasonic Foundation, the Rotary Foundation and Japan Student Services Organisation. Earlier versions of chapters were presented in London, Birmingham, Bristol, Dublin, Lisbon, Florence, Niigata and Tokyo. I would also like to thank the audiences in these places.

My friends, some of whom also helped this study by commenting on the drafts and providing useful references, have been sources of inspiration and motivation. I would especially like to thank Pablo Marcello Baquero, Takahiro Chino, Amparo Fontaine, Jens van 't Klooster, Misun Lim, Joy Peng, Bilyana Petrova, Danilo Scholz, Christopher Roberts, James Lee, Sophia Moesch, Kanako Morishita, the late Klaus Neuberg, Annie Morley-Slinn and Koji Yamamoto.

My final and most important thanks go to my grandparents for their incredible amount of love and to my family, Toshihiko, Keiko and Yuta Kaiga, for supporting me as I finished the book and for raising me in such a happy family. To them this book is dedicated.

Abbreviations

ALLPP	Abbott Lawrence Lowell Peace Papers (Harvard University, Houghton Library)
BL	British Library, London
BLEPS	British Library of Economic and Political Science
CKC	Cambridge, King's College Archives
CNC	Cambridge, Newnham College Archives
HUHL	Harvard University, Houghton Library
LEPR	League to Enforce Peace Records (Harvard University, Houghton Library)
LPL	Lambeth Palace Library
NAS	The National Archives of Scotland
NLW	The National Library of Wales
OBL	Oxford, Bodleian Library
PA	Parliamentary Archives
TNA	The National Archives

Introduction

> The high contracting parties,
> In order to promote international co-operation and to achieve international peace and security
> by the acceptance of obligations not to resort to war,
> by the prescription of open, just and honourable relations between nations,
> by the firm establishment of the understandings of international law as the actual rule of conduct among Governments, and
> by the maintenance of justice and a scrupulous respect for all treaty obligations
> in the dealings of organised peoples with one another,
> Agree to this Covenant of the League of Nations.[1]

Thus begins the Covenant of the League of Nations of 1919. At the outset of the preamble, the Covenant stipulated the obligation of states not to resort to war as a means to preserve peace. For the first time, war – more precisely, initiating war – was in effect made illegal and the idea of collective security was institutionalised.[2] It was, historians have tended to suggest, achieved due to war-weariness, the horrors of the long, grinding war, great-power diplomacy or the personal project of the US President Woodrow Wilson.[3] While all these factors played important roles in

---

[1] *The Covenant of the League of Nations*, the Avalon Project, http://avalon.law.yale.edu/20th_century/leagcov.asp.

[2] Martin Ceadel, 'Enforced Pacific Settlement or Guaranteed Mutual Defence? British and US Approaches to Collective Security in the Eclectic Covenant of the League of Nations', *The International History Review*, vol. 35, no. 5 (2013), pp. 993–1008.

[3] Henry R. Winkler, *The League of Nations Movement in Great Britain, 1914–1919* (Rutgers University Press, 1952); Peter J. Yearwood, *Guarantee of Peace: The League of Nations in British Policy, 1914–1925* (Oxford University Press, 2009); George W. Egerton, *Great Britain and the Creation of the League of Nations: Strategy, Politics, and International Organization, 1914–1919* (Scolar Press, 1978); Tony Smith, *Why Wilson Matters: The Origin of American Liberal Internationalism and Its Crisis Today* (Princeton University Press, 2017); Thomas J. Knock, *To End All Wars: Woodrow Wilson and the Quest for a New World Order* (Oxford University Press, 1992); Ross A. Kennedy (ed.), *A Companion to Woodrow Wilson* (Wiley-Blackwell, 2013); Ross Kennedy, *The Will to Believe: Woodrow Wilson, World War I, and America's Strategy for Peace and Security* (Kent State University Press,

founding the first international organisation for peace, this book reveals that the League originated intellectually from the little-appreciated pro-league movement in Britain and the unexpected development and consequences of its idea during the Great War.

In war-time Britain,[4] the development of the league of nations movement from a small circle of elite intellectuals to a mass movement was never smooth, straightforward or driven by purely utopian ideals. Because historians have largely neglected the contribution of this expanding movement to post-war peacemaking, two misunderstandings persist about the role of the movement. The first is that scholars have labelled it utopian. Historians and international relations theorists have tended to dismiss the leading pro-league thinkers as starry-eyed idealists.[5] This book challenges that received wisdom by tracing the ideas of the leading members of the pro-league movement, especially those of the Bryce Group, one of the first pro-league circles in Britain, and its successor, the League of Nations Society, up to the Paris Peace Conference of 1919. This analysis offers a fresh assessment of liberal internationalism in the early twentieth century – the intellectual foundation of the pro-league movement in Britain and the League of Nations, which defied such clear-cut categories as utopian or realist. To reveal the neglected evolution of ideas during the war, this book mainly examines the thinkers who invented the post-war idea and initiated the movement in 1914.[6]

The second misunderstanding is that the movement promoted a purely peaceful ideal and thereby succeeded in receiving the support of the war-weary public at the end of the war.[7] In the actual course of developing the pro-league movement, the more popular and influential

---

2009); Lloyd E. Ambrosius, *Wilsonian Statecraft: Theory and Practice of Liberal Internationalism during World War I* (Scholarly Resources Books, 1991).

[4] In this book, 'the Great War', 'the war' and 'war time' refer to the First World War.

[5] E. H. Carr, *The Twenty Years' Crisis, 1919–1939: An Introduction to the Study of International Relations* (Macmillan, 2001), pp. 97–98; Martin Ceadel, *Thinking about Peace and War* (Oxford University Press, 1987); Paul Laity, *The British Peace Movement, 1870–1914* (Oxford University Press, 2001), introduction and chapter 8; Helen McCarthy, *The British People and the League of Nations: Democracy, Citizenship and Internationalism, c. 1918–45* (Manchester University Press, 2011), p. 135.

[6] Hence, the book focuses on intellectual leaders of the pro-league movement who were mostly highly educated, liberal internationalists such as Cambridge classicist Goldsworthy Lowes Dickinson, Liberal MP Willoughby Dickinson and renowned international lawyer James Bryce, rather than those who became associated with the league project later in the war including Liberal MP David Davies, Conservative MP Robert Cecil or political scientist Alfred Zimmern.

[7] For example, Yearwood has indicated that in Britain 'liberals, conservatives, and socialists had united in the war effort' and 'wanted guarantees of an enduring peace'. See, Yearwood, *Guarantee of Peace*, p. 364.

it became, the less control the original leadership enjoyed over its direction. In popularising their ideas for mass consumption, the pro-leaguers'
original proposal about a post-war organisation lost its nuance and
sophistication. Previous works have missed this crucial process of
change. The story of the League cannot be understood without recognising the remarkable extent to which the movement transformed its official
thinking about a league into something different and unforeseen because
of the pressures of public opinion and war-time politics. At the outbreak
of the war in 1914, pro-league thinkers identified the divisive international politics of anarchy, the balance of power and rival alliance blocs
as the primary causes of war.[8] The goal of founding a league of nations
was therefore to reform international relations by introducing a new and
cooperative international institution *inclusive* of all the great powers. Yet,
by the end of the war in 1918, the pro-league leaders came to promote
what they had originally opposed: the league as a *continuation* of the war-
time alliance against Germany and its allies into the post-war peace.[9] The
key driver behind this shift in 1917–1918 was the successful 'self-
mobilisation' of civil society, which, as John Horne has argued,
reinforced the argument to fight until Germany fell and the widely shared
belief that the league should be formed as a coalition of democratic
states.[10] This book examines why and how this shift unfolded by exploring how post-war ideas were elaborated inside the movement and promoted in public and thereby reassesses the ideas as well as the evolution
of the pro-league movement in Britain from 1914 to 1919 – a crucial
period that framed the power and limitations of the League of Nations.

The shift of the league of nations idea to a continuation of the war-time
alliance will also show the little-debated background of the Paris Peace
Conference that eventually determined the formation of the League of
Nations. Despite the fact that John Maynard Keynes, the economist and
a British delegate at Versailles, famously criticised the reparation clauses
as unjustified and unworkable,[11] the Peace Settlement imposed harsh

---

[8] The pro-league thinkers also discussed some of the other causes of war, for example,
secret diplomacy, the arms industry and lack of democratic control of foreign policy, but
this book examines the thinkers' main foci, the balance of power and rival alliance blocs,
as the key to reforming the international system for future war prevention.

[9] As Chapter 5 will show, the league as a continuation of the war-time alliance against
Germany was not unanimously upheld by all the pro-league activists. Yet, as this book
will demonstrate, as one united movement for the creation of a new organisation, the
pro-league movement promoted exclusivity at the end of the war.

[10] John Horne (ed.), *State, Society and Mobilization in Europe during the First World War*
(Cambridge University Press, 1997), pp. 195, 198, 209–11.

[11] Zara Steiner, *The Lights That Failed: European International History, 1919–1933* (Oxford
University Press, 2005), pp. 63–66; John Maynard Keynes, *The Collected Writings of John*

and antagonistic terms on Germany. While most of the literature focuses on the diplomacy of peacemaking among the Big Four victors and the question of reparations, the punitive nature of the peace arose from more than just flawed negotiations or poor leadership. As reflected in the peacemaking, there were great domestic demands, at least in Britain, for punishing the enemy country severely and excluding it from a new world order. The prevailing hostile attitude towards Germany – one crucial factor that shaped what historians have evaluated as the defective treaty – was mirrored in the pro-league movement and then at the Peace Conference. Analysis of non-governmental actors, such as the public and popular movements, in addition to high-level policy-making and diplomacy, will yield profound insights into how such actors influenced decision-making and international relations.

In this book, I employ the lower case 'a league of nations' to refer to the ideas and movement for such an organisation during the First World War. For the international organisation set up in 1920 in Geneva, I use the customary capitalised 'League of Nations'. This distinction speaks directly to one of the core themes of this book – the distinction between the foundational ideas of a league and the fate of those ideas in war-time domestic politics and post-war international politics.

Historical interest in the League of Nations has recently revived and expanded to study a whole range of international and transnational themes,[12] in particular, the economic and social spheres of the League's development.[13] While the establishment of the League paved new ways of conceiving the legality and the legitimacy of war in the

Maynard Keynes, Volume 2, The Economic Consequences of the Peace (Cambridge University Press, 2013).

[12] Patricia Clavin, *Securing the World Economy: The Reinvention of the League of Nations, 1920–1946* (Oxford University Press, 2013); Susan Pedersen, *The Guardians: The League of Nations and the Crisis of Empire* (Oxford University Press, 2015); Stephen Wertheim, 'The League of Nations: A Retreat from International Law?', *Journal of Global History*, vol. 7, no. 2 (2012), pp. 210–32; Elisabetta Tollardo, *Fascist Italy and the League of Nations, 1922–1935* (Palgrave Macmillan, 2016); Simon Jackson and Alanna O'Malley (eds.), *The Institution of International Order: From the League of Nations to the United Nations* (Routledge, 2018).

[13] Susan Pedersen, 'Back to the League of Nations: Review Essay', *The American Historical Review*, vol. 112, no. 4 (October 2007), pp. 1091–117; Patricia Clavin and Jens-Wilhelm Wessels, 'Transnationalism and the League of Nations: Understanding the Work of Its Economic and Financial Organization', *Contemporary European History* (2005), pp. 465–92; Daniel Laqua (ed.), *Internationalism Reconfigured: Transnational Ideas and Movements between the World Wars* (Tauris Academic Studies, 2011); Daniel Gorman, *International Cooperation in the Early Twentieth Century* (Bloomsbury Academic, 2017); Karen Gram-Skjoldager and Haakon A. Ikonomou, 'The Construction of the League of Nations Secretariat: Formative Practices of Autonomy and Legitimacy in International Organizations', *The International History Review*, vol. 41, no. 2 (2019), pp. 257–79.

international system, scholarly attention has tended to be deflected away from the organisation's central founding purpose: the prevention of war.[14] Most studies have focused on the period *after* the Paris Peace Conference of 1919–1920 and only explored the question of how the League was planned for the maintenance of peace from certain angles, especially the diplomacy between the victorious great powers.

When scrutinising the establishment of the first international organisation, it is not surprising that the first strand of scholarship focused on high politics and diplomacy. How the politicians of Britain and the United States negotiated the creation of the League during and after the war, for example, has been thoroughly investigated by Peter Yearwood and George Egerton.[15] These rich and detailed accounts have helped us understand the League as a product of political manipulation, since it was undoubtedly politicians who had the ultimate power to decide what the League would be like in reality.[16] According to Yearwood, the establishment of the League was predominantly 'a product of British war-time diplomacy'. The formation of the idea and the institution were 'part of, not apart from, British policy'.[17] His work therefore mostly underestimates how pro-league groups constructed and popularised the idea of a league before it became a central subject in the negotiation of the peace settlement. Yet, in international relations, as Akira Iriye has argued, the issue of peace and world order are very frequently closely related to popular movements, interests, values and

---

[14] Many studies on war prevention in international society of the early twentieth century have focused on the Kellogg-Briand Pact of 1928. See Oona A. Hathaway and Scott J. Shapiro, *The Internationalists: How a Radical Plan to Outlaw War Remade the World* (Simon & Schuster, 2017); Oona A. Hathaway and Scott J. Shapiro, 'International Law and Its Transformation through the Outlawry of War', *International Affairs*, vol. 95, no. 1 (January 2019), pp. 45–62; Robert H. Ferrell, *Peace in Their Time: The Origins of the Kellogg-Briand Pact* (Yale University Press, 1952); John E. Stoner, *S. O. Levinson and the Pact of Paris: A Study in Techniques of Influence* (University of Chicago Press, 1943); Harriet Hyman Alonso, *The Women's Peace Union and the Outlawry of War, 1921–1942* (University of Tennessee Press, 1989).

[15] Both Yearwood's and Egerton's work have also given much more weight to the inter-war period rather than war time. See, Yearwood, *Guarantee of Peace*; Egerton, *Great Britain and the Creation of the League of Nations*.

[16] While concentrating on British high politics and diplomacy, Egerton's book has demonstrated awareness of the relation between the pro-league movement and high politics. For example, the book has indicated that 'it is necessary to place British debate on the league question in its broader social and strategic context. Not only did the League of Nations movement see the realisation of its immediate goal in the creation of the league at the Paris peace conference, but the ideas of war-time dissenters and proleaguers had a powerful impact on the political attitudes and values of postwar British society'. See Egerton, *Great Britain and the Creation of the League of Nations*, p. xiii.

[17] Yearwood, *Guarantee of Peace*, pp. 4.

norms as well as power politics.[18] While it is true that politicians eventually decided to build the League, it was the league of nations movement led by the Bryce Group and the League of Nations Society, rather than politicians, that devised the post-war plan for a new order, obtained popular support for it and pushed the league onto the political agenda in Britain and the United States. Interactions with other actors should also be included, given that the movement not only involved some politicians as leading members but also loosely kept some politicians as supporters of the idea. For instance, Willoughby Dickinson, the Liberal MP, was one of the founding members of the pro-league groups; renowned politicians such as Robert Cecil and Edward Grey favoured a broadly defined post-war organisation from the early years of the war.[19] Moreover, the Phillimore Committee, the Foreign Office's official study group on the creation of a league of nations, examined the plans by the pro-league groups and reflected them in its official reports of 1918, which provided the basis for the discussion on the League of Nations Covenant at the Paris Peace Conference.[20] Thus, the analysis of policy-making alone cannot reveal the whole picture of how the idea of the post-war organisation developed during the war and in what ways this development contributed to the resulting League of Nations.

In studies of popular movements in Britain, the main attention of historians has been devoted to the Union of Democratic Control, the most well-known radical group active during the war.[21] The Union, which called for an end to secret diplomacy as well as for the democratic control of foreign policy by Parliament,[22] has aroused scholarly interest due to its primarily political ambitions. Led by politically active journalist E. D. Morel and Labour MP Ramsay MacDonald, the Union of Democratic Control was not only a part of what A. J. P. Taylor has described as the 'trouble makers' of foreign policy dissenters but was also

---

[18] Akira Iriye, *War and Peace in the Twentieth Century* (Tokyo University Press, 2009) [in Japanese], chapter 1; Hedley Bull, *The Anarchical Society: A Study of Order in World Politics* (Columbia University Press, 2002), p. xxxiii.

[19] See Chapter 5.

[20] Winkler, *The League of Nations Movement*, p. 57; TNA: CAB29/1, The Committee on the League of Nations, Interim Report, 20 March 1918 and Final Report, 3 July 1918.

[21] Marvin Swartz, *The Union of Democratic Control in British Politics during the First World War* (Clarendon Press, 1971). Also see Stuart Wallace, *War and the Image of Germany: British Academics 1914–1918* (Donald, 1988); A. J. P. Taylor, *The Trouble Makers: Dissent over Foreign Policy, 1792–1939* (H. Hamilton, 1957); Sally Harris, *Out of Control: British Foreign Policy and the Union of Democratic Control, 1914–1918* (University of Hull Press, 1996); Jan Stöckmann, 'The First World War and the Democratic Control of Foreign Policy', *Past & Present* (forthcoming).

[22] Wallace, *War and the Image of Germany*, p. 90; Swartz, *The Union of Democratic Control in British Politics*, p. 25.

firmly set against the Liberal cabinet at the point of the group's foundation in 1914.[23] The League of Nations Union, the largest pro-league
group in Britain, formed in 1918 as a consequence of the amalgamation
of two pro-league groups, the League of Nations Society and the League
of Free Nations Association, has been examined by Donald S. Birn and
Helen McCarthy. Both authors, however, focus on the Union's main
activities in the inter-war period rather than its emergence during the
First World War.[24] Although some scholars, such as Henry R. Winkler
and Keith Robbins, have studied the war-time league movement, they
have tended to overlook how the movement interacted with domestic and
international politics.[25] Such interactions were, in fact, pivotal to the
building of ideas about a post-war organisation and the public attitudes
towards it. In a transnational context, the pro-league movement as a
network of several countries' intellectuals and activists has been analysed
by Carl Bouchard, Stephen Wertheim and Warren Kuehl.[26] Although
these works have suggested the importance of the transnational dimen-
sion, we still know little about how and to what extent pro-league activists
and their post-war plans influenced those beyond borders and led to
collaboration with others. As Chapter 4 will show, exploring such aspects
of the pro-league movement will illuminate how ideas and ideals simultaneously provided inspiration and generated friction across boundaries.

The founding thinkers behind the league have frequently been dis-
missed by scholars as 'utopian' or 'pacifist' – in other words, ivory-tower
thinkers who had no sense of how politics worked in reality. This asser-
tion, that pro-league thinkers were detached from political realism, in
part explains why the role of the movement has been long discounted.[27]
As Martin Ceadel has noted, however, such conceptual categories are

---

[23] Taylor, *The Trouble Makers*.
[24] Donald S. Birn, *The League of Nations Union, 1918–1945* (Oxford University Press, 1981); McCarthy, *The British People and the League of Nations*; Helen McCarthy, 'The League of Nations, Public Ritual and National Identity in Britain, c. 1919–1956', *Historical Workshop Journal* (2010), pp. 108–32.
[25] Winkler, *The League of Nations Movement*; Keith Robbins, *The Abolition of War: The 'Peace Movement' in Britain, 1914–1919* (University of Wales Press, 1976).
[26] Carl Bouchard, *Le Citoyen et L'ordre Mondial (1914–1919). Le Rêve D'une Paix Durable au Lendemain de la Grande Guerre (France, Grande-Bretagne, États-Unis)* (Pédone, 2008); Warren Kuehl, *Seeking World Order: The United States and International Organization to 1920* (Vanderbilt University Press, 1969). The American pro-league of nations movement has been studied by Ruhl Bartlett, *The League to Enforce Peace* (University of North Carolina Press, 1944); Wertheim, 'The League of Nations: A Retreat from International Law?', *Journal of Global History*, vol. 7, no. 2 (2012), pp. 210–32.
[27] Carr, *The Twenty Years' Crisis*, pp. 97–98; Ceadel, *Thinking about Peace and War*; Laity, *The British Peace Movement*, introduction and chapter 8; McCarthy, *The British People and the League of Nations*, p. 135.

ideal types and do not capture the complexity and dilemmas that thinking about international politics must confront.[28] Political theorists, such as Lucian Ashworth and Peter Wilson, in their work on the inter-war years have also argued that those who were labelled realists or idealists held a variety of perspectives and opinions that ranged across the very conceptual divide.[29] As we shall see in Chapter 2, even concepts that appear to be opposing – realism and idealism – are inseparably entwined in the pro-leaguers' post-war plan for preventing war.[30] Hence, rather than avoiding these categories, this book employs them to understand inconsistencies and the fragile balance incorporated in the ideas about the post-war order. To appreciate how idealism and realism are common core concepts rather than opposing ideas, it is important to study not only what the pro-league thinkers published – something most international relations scholars do – but also their private discussions and correspondence.[31] Building on a study of this private conversation among the leading league activists, this book investigates the ambiguity and ambivalence in early twentieth century thought about international order and particularly the prevention of war. Such ambiguity and ambivalence, as this book will suggest, are inherently part of the original thinking that continues to shape the way in which we think about international politics to this very day.

Even though the pro–league of nations movement has usually been categorised as a peace movement,[32] most of the pro-league activists were

---

[28] Ceadel, *Thinking about Peace and War*, p. 19. Also see Martin Ceadel, *Pacifism in Britain, 1914–1945: The Defining of a Faith* (Oxford University Press, 1980); Martin Ceadel, *Semi-Detached Idealists: The British Peace Movement and International Relations, 1854–1945* (Oxford University Press, 2000).

[29] L. M. Ashworth, 'Did the Realist-Idealist Great Debate Really Happen? A Revisionist History of International Relations', *International Relations*, vol. 16, no. 1 (2002), pp. 33–51; L. M. Ashworth, 'Where Are the Idealists in Inter-War International Relations?', *Review of International Studies*, vol. 32, no. 2 (2006), pp. 291–308. A similar argument can be found in Jeremy Weiss, 'E. H. Carr, Norman Angell, and Reassessing the Realist-Utopian Debate', *The International History Review*, 2013, vol. 35, no. 5, pp. 1156–84; Peter Wilson, *The International Theory of Leonard Woolf: A Study in Twentieth Century Idealism* (Palgrave Macmillan, 2003); David Long and Peter Wilson (eds.), *Thinkers of the Twenty Years' Crisis: Inter-War Idealism Reassessed* (Clarendon Press, 1995); John Bew, *Realpolitik: A History* (Oxford University Press, 2016); Peter Jackson, *Beyond the Balance of Power: France and the Politics of National Security in the Era of the First World War* (Cambridge University Press, 2013), pp. 520–21.

[30] See Chapter 2. Also see Sluga's analysis of 'the national and international' in Glenda Sluga, *Internationalism in the Age of Nationalism* (University of Pennsylvania Press, 2013), p. 150.

[31] For instance, Wilson, *The International Theory of Leonard Woolf*; Long and Wilson (eds.), *Thinkers of The Twenty Years' Crisis*.

[32] Robbins, *The Abolition of War*; Winkler, *The League of Nations Movement*.

neither pacifists nor opposed to war in all circumstances.[33] Since it aimed to devise a new system to prevent future wars, the pro-league movement should be better understood as a movement for international reform. In Paul Schroeder's term, the evolution of the pro-league movement embodied the 'emergence of the new order'.[34] Yet, as he has indicated, this emergence depended on a widespread, collective recognition of the need for it.[35] As this book will illustrate, this recognition was initially shared only among the pro-league activists and a few political figures. By the end of the war, this idea had become sufficiently widespread to bring about a new international order; but in so doing, it took the post-war plan out of the original pro-leaguers' hands.

A larger transition in international politics was also highlighted by the shift of the pro-league movement's idea into a league that excluded enemy countries – from the diplomacy of the Concert of European Great Powers in the nineteenth century to the ideological, polarised international politics of the years between the two World Wars and of the Cold War in the twentieth century.[36] A stable order and universal peace were rarely sought beyond European politics. This was true from the nineteenth century to the beginning of the Great War and was grounded in the politics of the balance of power and the notion that war was 'the continuation of politics by other means'.[37] From the First World War onwards, as Woodrow Wilson and Bolshevik leader Vladimir Lenin called for 'new diplomacy',[38] a world peace constructed upon an ideological framework began to be a central concept in the discussion of

---

[33] See Chapter 3.

[34] Paul W. Schroeder, *Systems, Stability, and Statecraft: Essays on the International History of Modern Europe* (Palgrave Macmillan, 2004), pp. 249, 258. This book also aims to show how a new international order after the Great War was already laid down before the 'after victory'. See G. John Ikenberry, *After Victory: Institutions, Strategic Restraint, and the Rebuilding of Order after Major Wars* (Princeton University Press, 2019), pp. 4, 7.

[35] Schroeder, *Systems, Stability, and Statecraft*, pp. 249, 258.

[36] For the Concert of Europe of the nineteenth century, see Paul W. Schroeder, *The Transformation of European Politics, 1763–1848* (Clarendon Press, 1996); Schroeder, *Systems, Stability, and Statecraft*. For the shift to ideological polarity in the twentieth century, see Alan Cassels, *Ideology and International Relations in the Modern World* (Routledge, 1996), pp. 139–56; Mark Mazower, 'Violence and the State in the Twentieth Century', *The American Historical Review*, vol. 107, no. 4 (October 2002), pp. 1158–78. For the shift of international politics from the nineteenth century to the outbreak of the Great War, also see Cohrs, *The Unfinished Peace after World War I*, p. 26.

[37] Carl von Clausewitz, *On War* (Start Pub. LLC, 2013); F. H. Hinsley, *Power and the Pursuit of Peace: Theory and Practice in the History of Relations between States* (Cambridge University Press, 1967), chapter 14; Michael Eliot Howard, *War and the Liberal Conscience* (Oxford University Press, 1981).

[38] Alan Sharp, 'The New Diplomacy and the New Europe, 1916–1922', in Nicholas Doumanis (ed.), *The Oxford Handbook of European History, 1914–1945* (Oxford University Press, 2016); Robert W. Tucker, 'Woodrow Wilson's "New Diplomacy"',

international affairs.[39] Whilst military force remained a vital tool of international politics, how that force would be employed would, as the book demonstrates, never be the same again.[40]

The Great War, producing as it did changes in so many spheres,[41] also left a legacy of what David Stevenson has described as a 'deeper transformation of western attitudes towards armed conflict'[42] – in other words, values about the legitimacy of war. Contrary to the accepted narrative,[43] the long, horrible experience of the Great War neither transformed the public attitude into opposition to war in and of itself nor accelerated the development of the pro-league movement. Instead, this book suggests that the experience of the war led not to opposition of war itself but to the conviction that legitimate reasons must be provided for going to war in the future. Before 1914, the reasons for going to war could be varied – conquest, defence and sometimes honour. Fuelled by jingoism and war's image as something short, heroic and rewarding, the public was not particularly inclined to consider whether there were 'righteous' reasons for waging war.[44] As this book illustrates in the case of Britain, but the point is applicable elsewhere too, the experience of the First World War elevated the preservation of peace as the most legitimate moral and ideological reasons for war.[45]

This book investigates the overlooked history of the intellectual origins of the league as an idea and political goal in Britain. The study of intellectuals and their role in 'the production and circulation' of values and ideas are vital in the study of the Great War and international relations.[46] It was because the war was 'a battle of ideas' from the outset and mobilised intellectuals on an unprecedented scale[47] that their interactions with politicians and the public beyond their borders influenced

---

World Policy Journal, vol. 21, no. 2 (Summer, 2004), pp. 92–107; Arno J. Mayer, *Wilson vs. Lenin: Political Origins of the New Diplomacy 1917–1918* (Meridian Books, 1969).

[39] Iriye, *War and Peace in the Twentieth Century*, pp. 60–61; William Mulligan, *The Great War for Peace* (Yale University Press, 2014), pp. 376–77.

[40] Kosaka, *International Politics*, pp. 8–10.

[41] Jay Winter (ed.), *The Cambridge History of the First World War*, vol. 2 (Cambridge University Press, 2013); Mulligan, *The Great War for Peace*, pp. 10, 375; Jackson, *Beyond the Balance of Power*, p. 207.

[42] D. Stevenson, *Cataclysm: The First World War As Political Tragedy* (Basic Books, 2004), p. 244; Jackson, *Beyond the Balance of Power*, p. 207.

[43] For example, Bouchard, *Le Citoyen et L'ordre Mondial*, p. 16.

[44] I. F. Clarke, *Voices Prophesying War, 1763–1984* (Oxford University Press, 1966), pp. 131, 162.

[45] Ceeclia Lynch, *Beyond Appeasement: Interpreting Interwar Peace Movements in World Politics* (Cornell University Press, 1999), pp. 61–62.

[46] John Horne, 'End of a Paradigm? The Cultural History of the Great War', *Past & Present*, vol. 242, no. 1 (February 2019), pp. 158.

[47] Ibid., pp. 158, 169.

the development of norms in international relations.[48] Thus, tracing intellectuals' groups and ideas also illustrates how the Great War was 'part of a remaking of the global, as well as the European, order'.[49] The chapters are structured chronologically to show how the pro-league movement developed and how its original ideas about an international organisation changed: from one that a small intellectual circle envisaged into one that reflected public concerns such as victory, democracy and anti-militarism. To observe how post-war ideas were shaped and reshaped in response to larger social, political and international changes, this book for the first time exploits in depth and in detail the rich unpublished manuscripts and private papers of key original pro-league thinkers and activists in addition to official and published records.

This book starts with the background of the pro–league of nations movement and its thinking about the causes of war and the conditions of peace. Previous research about the movement has focused on its activity predominantly during the inter-war period, despite the fact that the post-war plan emerged from an older European intellectual trad-ition.[50] Chapter 1, therefore, contextualises the pro-league movement within this rich legacy by exploring two broader contexts: the immediate backdrop to the evolution of the movement and the history of ideas about war and peace up to the outbreak of the Great War. In the pre-1914 period, the future pro-league activists already had networks of influence that became the basis of a pro-league movement. Even though they drew upon an intellectual legacy from the fourth century to the eve of the First World War, the problems they faced differed from those of their prede-cessors – the breakdown of the Concert of Europe and the rise of nationalism. These problems led the pro-leaguers to not only develop fresh perspectives on the causes of war but also conclude that a new world order should be established. By revealing the background of the pro-league movement, this chapter introduces the deep intellectual foun-dation that shaped war-time thought.

Turning to how the pro–league of nations movement began at the outbreak of the Great War, Chapter 2 focuses on the Bryce Group, one of the first pro-league circles formed in Britain in 1914, and its discussion about future war prevention in 1914–1915. The Bryce Group was the forerunner of the war-time pro-league movement and its post-war plan,

---

[48] Mulligan, *The Great War for Peace*, p. 10; Schroeder, *Systems, Stability, and Statecraft*, pp. 263–64.
[49] Mulligan, *The Great War for Peace*, p. 10.
[50] Hinsley, *Power and the Pursuit of Peace*, introduction.

Proposals for the Avoidance of War in 1915,[51] provided the springboard for the subsequent debate about a new world order. The *Proposals* was the first scheme for an international organisation to be advanced during the war that would became the prototype of the Covenant of the League of Nations.

While scholars have tended to associate the pro-league activists, including the Bryce Group members and their ideas, with utopianism, some focused studies of the group have mostly depicted its post-war plan as a product of realistic thinking. Drawing on the under-used manuscripts of the intellectual founders of the League of Nations, this chapter reveals that their early thinking defies simple categorisation. Not only was their war prevention plan realistic about the role of armed force, it also depended critically on idealistic expectations about the moral force of public opinion. Realistic and idealistic views could rarely be separated,[52] and both of them developed the group's plan for peace that incorporated the collective use of force as a crucial element of the post-war order. Although the group attempted to maintain a balance between the two views, the result was inconsistencies and contradictions. The paradox of collective security discussed by the group in 1914–1915 – that peace at least in part rested on the threat of force – was unresolved by the foundation of the League and remains so to this day.

Building on the Bryce Group's *Proposals for the Avoidance of War*, the League of Nations Society was founded in May 1915 to promote a post-war organisation to the public. Chapter 3 analyses the early pro-league movement with all its challenges and complexities by examining how the League of Nations Society came to organise a 'successful' first public meeting. In 1915–1916, the Society had worked undercover in order to avoid being denounced as pacifists. Only after its first public meeting in May 1917 did the Society publicly start promotional activity and succeed in pushing the league as an important item on the political agenda in Britain. As a result, previous studies have regarded May 1917 as a positive turning-point of the movement and mainly focused on widespread support for the league thereafter.

Chapter 3 provides a more nuanced assessment of the war-time development of the pro-league movement. It is notable that in 1917 the movement successfully evolved from a small, private elite circle to a mass

---

[51] *Proposals for the Avoidance of War, with a Prefatory Note by Viscount Bryce, As Revised up to 24 February 1915* (hereafter *Proposals for the Avoidance of War*), Edwin Cannan Papers 970, British Library of Political and Economic Science.

[52] As Chapter 2 will note, pro-league thinkers and their contemporaries did not employ the terms 'realism' and 'idealism'. These categories were created and imposed after the First World War.

movement that mobilised the public to establish a peace organisation. The evolution was necessary to make the 'emergence of a new order' possible after the war. Yet, the year 1917 also marked the time when the originators of the movement began to lose control of defining what the league would be like. Whereas the first public meeting did give the Society popularity for pressing the league as a critical issue, that popularity came at the cost of losing the complexities of the league plan for the prevention of war prepared by the Bryce Group. The increased public profile of the league also had the consequence that the movement lost a firm grip on the debate about the post-war order. To communicate to the general public, the League of Nations Society simplified its ideas by underscoring only the creation of an international organisation without going into details. This led the pro-league movement to abandon its original, sophisticated discussions about a new order, such as a possible mechanism for preventing war and its problems, which became accelerated in the following years.

Chapter 4 examines the influence of the Bryce Group's *Proposals for the Avoidance of War* more broadly, scrutinising the relationship between the League of Nations Society and its counterpart in the United States, the League to Enforce Peace. Most scholars have analysed these two pro-league groups in the English-speaking world separately by drawing heavily upon sources kept in their respective national archives. Even though a few studies have touched upon their relationship, it is still largely unknown how they interacted with each other. This chapter, therefore, explores how the Bryce Group's post-war plan inspired not only cooperation but also, more importantly, disagreements across the Atlantic, by investigating at a greater length *both* American and British records for the first time.[53]

Both groups in Britain and the United States sprang from liberal internationalist traditions, had a lot in common in terms of social and educational background and worked for the same broad aim of reforming the global order.[54] Nonetheless, such similarities did not enable them to

---

[53] As Chapter 4 will mention, this book focuses on pro-league activists in Britain and their interaction with a group in the United States, because British thinkers not only initiated discussion about the league in 1914 but also influenced the ideas of the actual League set up in 1920. Although this book will touch on French ideas about the post-war order, the French discussion was more government-led and only intensified after 1917. See Chapter 4 for more details.

[54] As Chapter 4 will show, this book will analyse liberal internationalism as something embedded in certain political and cultural contexts. Also see Glenda Sluga and Patricia Clavin (eds.), *Internationalisms: A Twentieth-Century History* (Cambridge University Press, 2017); Duncan Bell, *Reordering the World: Essays on Liberalism and Empire* (Princeton University Press, 2016), chapter 10.

establish a constructive collaboration, let alone a transnational movement. In reality, both groups sought political support for their own post-war schemes and regarded their counterpart merely as a medium for approaching statesmen on the other side of the Atlantic. Moreover, the differences in their domestic contexts and in the British and American liberal internationalist traditions hindered the two groups from building mutual trust and a joint lobbying strategy. By constructing the story of cooperation and disagreement between the US and British pro-leaguers, this chapter illustrates the power and the limitations of an ideal as a mobilising and unifying force in a transnational context.

Lastly, Chapter 5 demonstrates how the league of nations became an important political issue in the final years of the war. While the pro-league movement succeeded in attracting public attention for the plan of a post-war organisation, pro-leaguers came to promote a conception of the league that the Bryce Group membership in 1914–1915 had opposed: a league of victorious powers aligned against Germany. Begun as a reaction against anti-German jingoism and the politics of the balance of power, the pro-league movement initially aspired to change the norms of international relations by creating a new institution comprising all the great powers. Yet by 1918, the activists had come to promote the league as a continuation of the war-time alliance against Germany, backed by a powerful argument both to defeat Germany and to form the league as a coalition of democratic states. From the standpoints of the public, politicians and even the pro-league activists, the League of Nations was not a product of the yearning for peace as scholars have supposed but an extension of the politics of the Great War. Many pro-league leaders expected the league would evolve to conform to their idea of a perfectly functioning organisation with universal membership at some point in the future. Despite such an expectation, many supporters of a league in 1918 did not anticipate German admission to a league at all, at least in the foreseeable future. As the chapter will show, they did not set out any specific conditions or roadmaps for universal membership other than vaguely repeating the need of 'democratisation'. Whereas the idea of an exclusive league of nations as a coalition of victors helped increase the popularity of the movement, it simultaneously marked a break with the original vision of world order discussed at the Bryce Group. Indeed, it also marked the beginning of the ideological divide in the era of mass politics between democracy and autocracy. That divide became one of the underlying patterns of twentieth-century international politics. The Conclusion brings together the historical findings of the book and reviews the consequence of the war-time league of nations movement and its ideas at the Paris Peace Conference. It then draws

out the wider implications for international history, international relations and the studies of the Great War.

Because of the unprecedented scale of the war and loss of life, the
fighting of the First World War had to be justified by aims beyond
national defence, interests or security. Governments thus framed the
war as a struggle for a peaceful new order.[55] This higher cause, paradox-
ically, served to intensify the violence[56] and also to legitimise the continuation of the war until victory. The only way the idea of a league of
nations could become popular, legitimate and a practical political project
in Britain was if it was consistent with the defeat of Germany and its
allies. Tracking how ideas about a league developed in tandem with the
war, this book will highlight the reality of people and nations at war. Even
though the pro-leaguers hoped for a new peaceful organisation and
fought for a higher cause such as 'a war against war', in reality they
fought for victory over enemy states. Fighting against states entailed
seeking military victory as well as political and ideological supremacy
and that required the mobilisation of the public and their hatred of the
enemy. The truth that war involved hate and violence was an essential
problem that pro-league activists had to acknowledge during the war for
their purpose of achieving a new order.

This book, by exploring the dynamism and the problems of the establishment of the first international organisation, will also illuminate the
limits of liberal internationalism – a recently challenged and re-examined
concept[57] – in the world order. The creation of the League led liberal
internationalism to take centre stage for the first time in the international
arena. It legitimatised new norms such as peaceful conflict resolution,
disarmament, democracy and international cooperation; yet the establishment of the League simultaneously posed the fundamental conun-
drum of liberal internationalism. For instance, while one of the key
characters of liberal internationalism, especially of the time, was a trust
in the gradual progress and the evolution of society and humans, pro-
leaguers' views on international relations did not significantly progress
from the one held in the previous century. The war-time ideas about a
league rarely questioned a Eurocentric post-war order and by the end of
the war, they endorsed a plan of an organisation of only the civilised and

---

[55] Mulligan, *The Great War for Peace*, pp. 7–9.   [56] Ibid., pp. 8–9.
[57] For example, see 'Ordering the World? Liberal Internationalism in Theory and
Practice', *International Affairs*, vol. 94, no. 1 (January 2018), pp. 1–172; 'Rising Powers
and the International Order', *Ethics & International Affairs*, vol. 32, no. 1 (Spring 2018),
15–101; 'Out of Order? The Future of the International System', *Foreign Affairs*, vol. 96,
no. 1 (January/February 2017); 'Is Democracy Dying? Global Report', *Foreign Affairs*,
vol. 97, no. 3 (May/June 2018).

democratic states.[58] Similarly, international lawyers in the nineteenth century presumed that international law as 'le droit public d'Europe' would only apply to 'civilized, European and Christian peoples'.[59] Stressing civilisation as a core concept, international law offered a 'moral justification' for European expansion into non-Christian/European regions.[60] Resting on the assumption that the civilisation of these regions would not reach a satisfactory degree in the near future, the great imperial powers justified the persistence of empire in the colonial world as civilising missions of 'education and enlightenment'.[61] Whereas such a discriminatory boundary of civilisation provided a criterion of belonging to the West or the rest in the nineteenth century,[62] the boundary of 'civilised/uncivilised', as this book will suggest, began to be replaced by that of 'democratic/undemocratic' and/or 'liberal/non-liberal' in international politics from the First World War onwards.[63]

The League of Nations, although aimed to prevent war, was designed to prevent only certain types of war, not *all* wars. Collective security did

---

[58] Alison Duxbury, *The Participation of States in International Organisations: The Role of Human Rights and Democracy* (Cambridge University Press, 2011).

[59] Antony Anghie, *Imperialism, Sovereignty and the Making of International Law* (Cambridge University Press, 2004), pp. 59–60, 103; Samantha Besson and Jean d'Aspremont (eds.), *The Oxford Handbook of the Sources of International Law* (Oxford University Press, 2018), pp. 132, 148–49; Gunther Hellman (ed.), *The Transformation of Foreign Policy: Drawing and Managing Boundaries from Antiquity to the Present* (Oxford University Press, 2016), pp. 144–45, 151; Thomas Hippler and Miloš Vec (eds.), *Paradoxes of Peace in Nineteenth Century Europe* (Oxford University Press, 2015), p. 38; Martti Koskenniemi, *The Gentle Civilizer of Nations: The Rise and Fall of International Law 1870–1960* (Cambridge University Press, 2004), p. 63. While an argument in favour of extending the application of international law to non-Christian nations such as Japan and China existed in the nineteenth century, it remained a minority opinion among European elites. See, Besson and d'Aspremont (eds.), *The Oxford Handbook*, pp. 148–49.

[60] Hippler and Vec (eds.), *Paradoxes of Peace*, pp. 245–46, 249; Hellman (ed.), *The Transformation of Foreign Policy*, p. 150; Benjamin Allen Coates, *Legalist Empire: International Law and American Foreign Relations in the Early Twentieth Century* (Oxford University Press, 2016), chapters 1–2.

[61] Arnulf Becker Lorca, *Mestizo International Law: A Global Intellectual History 1842–1933* (Cambridge University Press, 2014), pp. 43–44, 48–49, 51; Anghie, *Imperialism, Sovereignty and the Making of International Law*, pp. 5–6; Hippler and Vec (eds.), *Paradoxes of Peace*, pp. 248, 280.

[62] Hellman (ed.), *The Transformation of Foreign Policy*, pp. 150, 289; Hippler and Vec (eds.), *Paradoxes of Peace*, pp. 178, 220–21; Duncan Bell (ed.), *Victorian Visions of Global Order: Empire and International Relations in Nineteenth-Century Political Thought* (Cambridge University Press, 2007). See also Ian Clark, *Legitimacy in International Society* (Oxford University Press, 2005), pp. 4, 7, 248–49; Martin H. Geyer and Johannes Paulmann, *The Mechanics of Internationalism: Culture, Society, and Politics From the 1840s to the First World War* (Oxford University Press, 2001), chapter 9.

[63] Hippler and Vec (eds.), *Paradoxes of Peace*, pp. 219, 220–21. See also Mulligan, *The Great War for Peace*, p. 10.

not exclude the use of force but rather incorporated another kind of war – military, as well as economic, sanctions – into the system for the maintenance of peace.[64] It also bolstered the system of war prevention and conflict resolution that ultimately hinged upon military force, as the last, yet valid and indispensable measure for the maintenance of peace. As this book demonstrates, the possibility of triggering or escalating war by relying on the use of force as a final resort was intensely debated by the war-time pro-leaguers.[65] They nonetheless ended up envisaging a league that they simply anticipated would evolve over time, however imperfect the original form had been. In practice, the vagueness of the pro-leaguers' proposals was both a strength and a limitation. Publicly abandoning the detailed ideas about a post-war order meant that they lost control of the league project. Nevertheless, avoiding a dogmatic approach to the creation of a league also enabled the idea to be interpreted widely and to develop politically, thereby helping to achieve the pro-leaguers' ultimate goal of creating a new organisation, despite its flaws. Their liberal internationalist thought assumed that military sanctions would be replaced in the future by a viable alternative that would underpin a peaceful, stable international society. Even though this optimistic expectation was not an idea unique to the pro-leaguers but was widely shared by the contemporary league supporters and liberal internationalists,[66] it remained unclear how they would further develop their vision of world order after the war or how the next generation would tackle this issue. While almost a century has passed since the establishment of the League of Nations, we are faced with the same dilemma of how force could and should be used to secure peace that troubled the pro-league activists at the outbreak of the Great War.

---

[64] As for ideas about economic sanctions from war time to the Paris Peace Conference, see Nicholas Mulder, *The Economic Weapon: Interwar Internationalism and the Rise of Sanctions, 1914–1945* (Columbia University PhD Dissertation, 2019), chapters 2–3. Also see Nicholas Mulder, *The Economic Weapon: Interwar Internationalism and the Rise of Sanctions, 1914–1945* (forthcoming).

[65] See Chapter 2.

[66] See Chapter 4 regarding Wilson's expectation that the League would evolve in the future. Also see Steiner, *The Lights That Failed*, pp. 40, 69 and a letter from Dwight Morrow to Jean Monnet, 10 November 1919, Dwight Morrow Papers, JMAS/2, Historical Archives of EU.

1   Precursors

Thinking about War and Peace before 1914

Introduction

This chapter investigates the background of the British pro-league movement and its ideas. In previous studies of the pro-league movement and the prehistory of the League of Nations, the principal concern has been with the later years of the First World War to the 1930s.[1] Although research into the movement has often neglected its social and intellectual backgrounds, pro-league activists already had networks of influence that they could exploit to form and promote the movement prior to the war. The pro-league activists also drew upon a rich intellectual tradition of thought regarding how war could be prevented: for example, the necessity for the legal regulations for the conduct of war and an understanding of structural causes of war.[2] In order to fully appreciate the origins of the ideas and activities behind the first international organisation for peace, we need to analyse them within a wider historical context.

This chapter, therefore, examines both the short- and the long-term developments that led to the pro–league of nations movement and thereby weaves its network and ideas into a more expansive story. The chapter first traces the evolution of the pro-league movement immediately before the war and then investigates how the intellectual legacy, which liberal internationalism inherited in Western Europe beginning in the fourth century and embraced up to the eve of the Great War, influenced that development. While rooted in the accumulated tradition of thought, the problems that pro-leaguers confronted – specifically, the legacy of the Concert of Europe, its breakdown and the rise of nationalism – differed from those of their predecessors. These new

---

[1] See Introduction, nn. 15 and 24.
[2] F. H. Hinsley, 'Introduction', in *Power and the Pursuit of Peace: Theory and Practice in the History of Relations between States* (Cambridge University Press, 1967), pp. 1–9; Alan Sharp, 'The New Diplomacy and the New Europe, 1916–1922', in Nicholas Doumanis (ed.), *The Oxford Handbook of European History, 1914–1945* (Oxford University Press, 2016), p. 123.

challenges brought fresh perspectives on the origins of war and the conditions for peace, which prompted the pro-leaguers to think about a new way to organise peace through an institution – specifically, a league of nations.

The project of the league of nations was an attempt to reform international politics. By creating an organisation based on the principles of cooperation and the peaceful resolution of disputes, the pro-league activists sought to replace the old order of great power rivalries. One could argue that the pro-leaguers were trying to initiate what Paul Schroeder has described as the normative transformation of international politics. The war-time activists presumed that 'the old order is no longer sustainable or tolerable and that something new and different must replace it'.[3] While this recognition was limited to the pro-league thinkers in 1914–1915, it later became sufficiently widespread to bring about a new order. Revealing the prehistory of the pro-league movement will illuminate how an international change could be planned and introduced at the non-governmental level and how deep the roots of the ideas about a peaceful order were.

Networks As the Basis of the Movement

The pro–league of nations movement came into existence not only as a reaction to the outbreak of the Great War but also as a consequence of exploiting the close pre-war network of British intellectuals. In this network, which Noel Annan has described as an 'intellectual aristocracy',[4] pro-leaguers were bound together 'by ties of kinship and shared assumptions based on intermarriage and common educational background'.[5] Most of them were liberal in their political outlook and were highly educated professional elites, such as academics, MPs or journalists. By the outbreak of the First World War, they were around forty to fifty years old and therefore too old to go to the battlefield. Staying at home led them to think not only about the current war but its future implications for their lives.[6]

---

[3] Paul W. Schroeder, 'The Cold War and Its Ending in "Long-Duration" International History', in P. W. Schroeder et al. (eds.), *Systems, Stability, and Statecraft: Essays on the International History of Modern Europe* (Palgrave Macmillan, 2004), p. 248.

[4] J. H. Plumb (ed.), *Studies in Social History: A Tribute to G. M. Trevelyan* (Longmans, 1955), chapter VIII.

[5] Stuart Wallace, *War and the Image of Germany: British Academics 1914–1918* (Donald, 1988), p. 3.

[6] See Chapter 3.

These elite networks had three crucial features: personal links, overlapping organisational ties and, most significantly, the common intellectual ground of liberal internationalism.[7] First, most of the leading activists were male and retained personal links from their university days, predominantly at either Oxford or Cambridge, where many of them studied from the late 1870s to 1880s. Some of them were professional academics at Oxford or Cambridge or taught at universities such as the London School of Economics and Political Science, which was founded by the Fabians in 1895. For instance, the political scientist Graham Wallas and the economist John A. Hobson, both of whom participated in one of the first pro-league circles, the Bryce Group, knew each other from their Oxford days and resumed contact in 1887 when Hobson came to London.[8] In the universities, future pro-leaguers built close links through student societies, such as the Apostles in Cambridge, in which the members debated topics such as ethics and politics. Members of the Apostles met regularly with undergraduate students and occasionally with former members to cultivate their acquaintance with one another. Leonard Woolf, the author of *International Government* (1916), which became one of the critical pro-league books during the war, received his formative education largely through the Apostles.[9] The Apostles had an impact on Woolf's political writings and put him in contact with leading pro-league intellectuals such as Goldsworthy Lowes Dickinson and Bertrand Russell.[10]

Second, pro-leaguers maintained organisational ties that connected them in the pre-1914 period. Building on the personal links they had formed during their university days, future pro-league activists belonged to the same social circles, which frequently had overlapping memberships. Four meeting places became the main hubs of their intellectual networks: the Fabian Society, the Rainbow Circle, the offices of the *Nation* and the National Liberal Club. The Fabian Society, which was associated with eminent names such as the Webbs, George Bernard Shaw and Leonard Woolf, was one of the most notable meeting places; it had been founded in 1884 for 'the reconstruction of Society in accordance with the highest moral possibilities'.[11] Many key figures of the war-

---

[7] Donatella Della Porta and Mario Diani, *Social Movements: An Introduction* (Wiley-Blackwell, 2005), pp. 112, 116, 127.

[8] Peter Clarke, *Liberals and Social Democrats* (Cambridge University Press, 1978), p. 51.

[9] S. P. Rosenbaum, 'Woolf, Leonard Sidney (1880–1969)', in *Oxford Dictionary of National Biography* (Oxford University Press, 2004). www.oxforddnb.com/view/article/37019?docPos=1.

[10] Ibid.

[11] Edward R. Pease, *The History of the Fabian Society* (E. P. Dutton & Company, 1916), p. 31.

time pro-league or anti-war movement, such as Graham Wallas, John
A. Hobson, Ramsay MacDonald, Leonard Woolf and Henry Brailsford,
met through their Fabian connections. Although some like Wallas left the
Fabian Society before the war, their unbroken contact with members
perhaps fostered collaboration between the League of Nations Society
and the Fabian Society for a league plan by 1916.[12] Similarly, the
political and social discussion group, the Rainbow Circle, served as a
meeting place for like-minded liberal intellectuals in London. Between
1894 and 1931, regular members included Hobson, MacDonald and the
Fabian essayist Sydney Olivier. Furthermore, prominent figures such as
Wallas, Brailsford, Noel Buxton MP, Fabian educationalist Leonard
Hobhouse and Charles Trevelyan MP were occasional attendees. They
were mostly social reformers who pursued common ground among
progressives of different political perspectives. The third hub formed
around the *Nation*, a liberal weekly magazine edited by the journalist
Henry William Massingham from 1907. The *Nation*'s business manager
was Richard Cross, the secretary of the pro-league Bryce Group as well as
the solicitor of the Yorkshire entrepreneurial Rowntree family who
owned the *Nation*. Massingham inaugurated a weekly lunch at the
Nation for the magazine's staff and some guests. As Peter Clarke has
described it, this lunch was 'not a meal but a seminar' where they
discussed various contemporary issues such as women's suffrage.[13]
Contributors, including Hobson, Hobhouse and Brailsford, were regular
attendees, whereas some, such as Goldsworthy Lowes Dickinson, were
invited as guests. The *Nation* lunch was usually held at the National
Liberal Club, which was another networking site. Founded by
Gladstone as a social venue for the liberals in 1882, the club was frequently used as a meeting place for liberal intellectuals as well as MPs,
providing opportunities for future pro-leaguers to 'meet in friendly intercourse, and interchange information and views'.[14] Indeed, with prominent individuals such as the former American ambassador Viscount James
Bryce, the club helped forge important links for the pro-league activities
during the war.

More significantly, the pro-league activists were liberal
internationalists who, as Casper Sylvest has argued, had grappled in the
late nineteenth and early twentieth centuries with the problem of

---

[12] George W. Egerton, *Great Britain and the Creation of the League of Nations: Strategy,
Politics, and International Organization, 1914–1919* (Scolar Press, 1978), p. 18.
[13] Clarke, *Liberals and Social Democrats*, p. 108.
[14] BL, General Reference Collection 8139.a.48, 'The National Liberal Club – a
Description with Illustrations' (London, 1894), pp. 7–8.

international politics, including the causes of war, morality, progress and how to secure peace.[15] In the words of Sandi Cooper, these liberal thinkers at the beginning of the twentieth century believed in human nature as well as progress, and 'provided an energetic counter-argument to the international anarchy and the status-quo of alliances, balance of power and the attendant arms race'.[16] In fact, this third feature of elite networks – liberal internationalism – was built upon the European history of thinking about the origins of war and the conditions of peace. To understand how this intellectual common ground formed the foundation for the notion of the first international peace organisation, we need to understand the tradition of ideas about international relations in a larger historical context.

From the Just War to Morality in the Renaissance Period

The long-term historical context for the emergence of the pro–league of nations movement was the rich European intellectual legacy of thought regarding the nature of war and peace. Reviewing this tradition and the trajectory of liberal internationalism, common ground that pro-leaguers shared for the post-war planning, this section aims to show how ideas that accumulated over many centuries were also highly relevant to the contemporary views on international relations.

We begin with the idea of just war, the oldest tradition that continues to be an influential approach to the issue of using force in the modern day. During the First World War, one of the core beliefs that buttressed the pro-leaguers' war prevention plan was the necessity for *just* war in order to maintain peace. In the League of Nations Covenant established after the war, wars of aggression were outlawed but wars for collective security were legal; it distinguished between acceptable and unacceptable, that is, just and unjust, wars. To understand the origin of just war theory and its influence, we should look to its original advocate in the fourth century, St Augustine. *Jus ad bellum*, as it is called, regulated the waging of war without just reasons and defined the distinction between justified and unjustified wars. Augustine condemned war as a

---

[15] Casper Sylvest, *British Liberal Internationalism, 1880–1930: Making Progress?* (Manchester University Press, 2009), pp. 3–4, 11, 26, 139, 197.

[16] Sandi E. Cooper, 'Liberal Internationalists before World War I', *Peace & Change* 1, no. 2 (April 1973), p. 12. In addition, liberal internationalists discussed a wide range of subjects such as rights, law and society. See David Boucher, 'The Recognition Theory of Rights, Customary International Law and Human Rights', *Political Studies* 59, no. 3 (2011); Matt Hann, *Egalitarian Rights Recognition: International Political Theory* (Palgrave Macmillan, 2016).

disturbance to the social order and an affront to Christian morality. By introducing the ideas of what later became known as just war theory, he sought to warn against war without limits, to regulate war through law and to lay down the ethical foundations for permissible violence. For a religious leader such as Augustine, the law amounted to religious precepts and a just war was a 'Holy War'.[17] While asserting that war within Christendom was sinful both from a religious and a social point of view, Augustine admitted that war against heathens could be justified since wars against external peoples were necessary to restore peace and protect the unity of the Roman Empire.[18] Just war had to be fought under legitimate authority and only as a last resort to obtain peace – out of necessity and not out of choice.[19] Having advocated certain sorts of wars, he drew the line between just wars and unjust wars – in a way similar to that of the pro-league activists as they developed their post-war plan.

In Europe, just war theory continued to be the dominant thinking about war and peace well into the sixteenth century. While morally objecting to war in and of itself, the philosophers of this period also recognised the need for some types of war. The Dutch humanist Desiderius Erasmus, however, declared that 'there is scarcely any peace so unjust, but it is preferable, upon the whole, to the just(est) war'.[20] Erasmus denied that war could be justified under some circumstances and remained pacifistic because his Christian faith urged him to associate peace with Christ and war with 'unlike Christ' and with the grand destroyer.[21] In his work *Complaint of Peace* (1517), Erasmus appealed to all Christians 'to unite with one heart and one soul, in the abolition of war, and the establishment of perpetual and universal peace'.[22]

In this period, the modern concept of war – a necessary political instrument for preserving an orderly system of interstate relations – began to appear in the work of the Italian statesman Niccolo Machiavelli.[23] This rising trend to consider war as a necessary evil

---

[17] John Langan, 'The Elements of St. Augustine's Just War Theory', *Journal of Religious Ethics* 12, no. 1 (Spring, 1984), p. 25.

[18] Ibid., pp. 27–28; Sophia Moesch, *Augustine and the Art of Ruling in the Carolingian Imperial Period: Political Discourse in Alcuin of York and Hincmar of Rheims* (Routledge, 2019), pp. 194–95.

[19] Michael Howard, *War and the Liberal Conscience* (Oxford University Press, 2008), p. 9; Langan, 'The Elements of St. Augustine's Just War Theory', pp. 26–27.

[20] Desiderius Erasmus, *The Complaint of Peace* (Chicago, 1917), p. 44.

[21] Richard Tuck, *The Rights of War and Peace: Political Thought and the International Order from Grotius to Kant* (Oxford University Press, 2001), pp. 29–30; Erasmus, *The Complaint of Peace*, pp. 18, 77; Howard, *War and the Liberal Conscience*, p. 8.

[22] Erasmus, *The Complaint of Peace*, pp. 18, 77.

[23] Howard, *War and the Liberal Conscience*, p. 8.

seemed to have exerted little influence on Erasmus.[24] The concept of just war, or law to justify war, also divided Erasmus from his contemporary English scholar Thomas More. Although he regarded war as brutal, detestable and inhumane, More agreed with Machiavelli that war could be a continuation of politics.[25] In his famous work *Utopia*, the people of Utopia also utterly loathe war, yet they reluctantly conduct war for the following reasons:[26]

either to protect their own territory or drive an invading enemy out of their friends' country, or when in pity for a nation oppressed by tyranny they seek to deliver them by force of arms from the yoke and bondage of a tyrant, a course prompted merely by human sympathy. Though they oblige their friends with help, not always indeed to defend them, but sometimes also to avenge and requite injuries previously done to them, they only do it if they are consulted before any step is taken, and recommend that war should be declared only after they have approved the cause and demand for restitution has been made in vain.[27]

These reasons were, according to Michael Howard, derived from medieval legal texts that stated war could be waged to help friends, to protect territories, to avenge injuries or in self-defence.[28] Renaissance humanists, while condemning war on moral grounds, mostly affirmed that war could be legally upheld under certain conditions or circumstances.

Jus ad Bellum and *Jus in Bello*: International Lawyers after the Peace of Westphalia

In the seventeenth century, a normative base for discussion of war and peace began to shift from the moral-theological conception of the ancient and medieval periods to a conception of legal order.[29] Until the outbreak of the First World War in 1914, international lawyers' ideas about war, which developed after the Peace of Westphalia, remained crucial in legal texts regarding issues of war and peace. The Thirty Years War and the ensuing Peace of Westphalia of 1648 caused international lawyers to tackle the question of how to prevent war through the law. In 1625, one of the most famous international lawyers of this period, Hugo Grotius, published *On the Law of War and Peace* (*De Jure Belli ac Pacis*). While proposing that the rights and wrongs of war might be judged by universal moral standards, Grotius' book addressed three justifiable

---

[24] Ibid.   [25] Ibid., pp. 8–9.   [26] Thomas More, *Utopia* (Oxford, 1923), p. 94.
[27] Ibid. Also see, Thomas More, *Utopia*, George M. Logan (ed.), Robert M. Adams (trans.) (Cambridge University Press, 2016), pp. 89–90.
[28] Howard, *War and the Liberal Conscience*, p. 9.
[29] Ian Clark, *Legitimacy in International Society* (Oxford University Press, 2005), pp. 4, 7, 248–49.

causes of wars: defence, indemnity and punishment.[30] Just as for Augustine, Grotius' principles were formulated in order to avert war as something essentially irrational. As Frédéric Mégret has described, among international lawyers Grotius was an 'idealist' – to him the law of nations (*jus gentium*) was mandated by natural law and therefore should rest on what 'ought' to be rather than what 'is'.[31]

By contrast, Grotius' eighteenth-century successor, Emmerich de Vattel, focused more narrowly on *jus in bello* – the law of war. He not only set out the conditions for initiating war, which were less critical for him than questions regarding *the ways to conduct war*, but also clearly highlighted a weakness of just war theory itself.[32] Whereas in war time both fighting parties would claim to act justly, international society had no superior authority to adjudicate one side right and the other wrong. Hence, the reasoning of justifiable war was bound to be irrelevant and useless in practice, except as an expedient means to rally opinion in favour of war. This, in effect, undermined just war theory's distinction between acceptable and unacceptable wars. Any war *could be* interpreted as acceptable. Concentrating on the law of war, Vattel sought to minimise the possible damage caused by warfare and to end conflict at the earliest opportunity.[33] Admittedly, in the nineteenth century, the great powers at the Concert of Europe had come to mutual understandings about 'acceptable' and 'unacceptable' state actions, such as war for the settlement of disputes.[34] In international law, however, Vattel's critique of just war theory prevailed on the eve of the Great War and remained central until the League of Nations Covenant once again drew the line between justifiable and unjustifiable wars.

A Decision-Making Structure As a Cause of War

In the seventeenth and eighteenth centuries, another strand of thinking about the cause of war became prevalent in Europe, which would later

---

[30] Hugo Grotius, *The Rights of War and Peace: Including the Law of Nature and of Nations*, A. C. Campbell (trans.) (M. W. Dunne, 1901), p. 75. Also see, Hugo Grotius, *Hugo Grotius on the Law of War and Peace*, Stephen C. Neff (ed.) (Cambridge University Press, 2012), p. 82.

[31] Frédéric Mégret, 'International Law As Law', in James Crawford and Martti Koskenniemi (eds.), *The Cambridge Companion to International Law* (Cambridge University Press, 2012), p. 75.

[32] Emer de Vattel, *The Law of Nations: Or, Principles of the Law of Nature, Applied to the Conduct and Affairs of Nations and Sovereigns*, Joseph Chitty (ed.) (Cambridge University Press, 2011), pp. 304–5.

[33] Michael Howard, *Invention of Peace* (Profile Books, 2000), p. 25.

[34] John Ikenberry, *After Victory: Institutions, Strategic Restraint, and the Rebuilding of Order after Major Wars* (Princeton University Press, 2001), p. 107.

have a profound impact on ideas about the league of nations.[35] European political thinkers began to focus on the domestic decision-making system of states as the prime cause of war and on public opinion as a powerful tool to prevent wars. Dynastic elites who dominated the decision-making process were war-prone, while public opinion tended to be pacific and resisted war. As Hidemi Suganami has called, in reference to democratic confederalism, 'state executives are often autocratic, and reflect the popular will far less accurately than do (representative) legislatures'.[36]

In the seventeenth century, the close connection between war and the structure of domestic society was highlighted by the French monk Eméric Crucé. He asserted that 'neither international obstacles, nor differences of religion, nor diversity of nationality are legitimate causes for war'.[37] His book, the New Cyneas, was addressed to the monarchy and the ruling class, 'not to men who are subject to a master', and assumed the former made 'the decision of whether there shall be peace or war'.[38]

As an answer to the problem of war, Crucé encouraged peaceful occupations, such as agriculture and commerce, instead of becoming a warrior.[39] Especially, he valued free trade that would make 'countries more interdependent' and consequently 'cause wars to grow less frequent'.[40] By increasing the wealth and power of the peace-loving population, free trade would put people of different nations into constant contact with one another. It could raise people's awareness of the community of interests in shared prosperity, thereby helping promote international understanding.[41] As a promoter of international peace, the notion of free trade became widely embraced in subsequent generations.

Thinkers in the eighteenth century, such as Montesquieu and Rousseau, similarly addressed the problem of decision-making as the main cause of war. Opposing Hobbes' theory that men were born in a state of war, Montesquieu professed peace, not war, to be 'the first law of nature',[42] because individuals in a state of nature were defenceless and

---

[35] See Chapter 2.
[36] Hidemi Suganami, *The Domestic Analogy and World Order Proposals* (Cambridge University Press, 1989), p. 166.
[37] Eméric Crucé, *The New Cyneas of Émerie Crucé* (Philadelphia, 1909), pp. xv.
[38] Howard, *War and the Liberal Conscience*, p. 11; Crucé, *The New Cyneas of Émerie Crucé*, p. x.
[39] Howard, *War and the Liberal Conscience*, p. 11.
[40] Ibid., p. xii. Also see, Béla Kapossy, Isaac Nikhimovsky and Richard Whatmore (eds.), 'Introduction', in *Commerce and Peace in the Enlightenment* (Cambridge University Press, 2017), pp. 1–19.
[41] Howard, *War and the Liberal Conscience*, pp. 11–12.
[42] Charles-Louis de Montesquieu, *The Spirit of Laws* (London, 1758), p. 5; Also see, Charles-Louis de Montesquieu, *The Spirit of the Laws*, Anne M. Cohler, Basia Carolyn Miller and Harold Samuel Stone (trans. and eds.) (Cambridge University Press, 1989).

too timid to start war.[43] Nonetheless, when individuals formed a society, war became possible:

as soon as mankind enter into a state of society, they lose the sense of their weakness; the equality ceases, and then commences the state of war. Each particular society begins to feel its strength, whence arises a state of war betwixt different nations. The individuals likewise of each society become sensible of their strength; hence the principal advantages of this society they endeavour to convert to their own emolument, which constitutes between them a state of war.[44]

For Montesquieu, war was the product of social organisation, not of individual human nature. Although war might be waged if required, for instance, for self-defence, states must provide compelling reasons that would satisfy the principles of justice.[45] To Rousseau as well, war was a social evil that arose from the social order and could only be cured by severing the bonds holding society together. Identifying the wilful machinations of decision-makers as a major cause of war,[46] he denied war could be abolished or controlled by law.[47] Rather, Rousseau expected public opinion to be a powerful mechanism for discouraging statesmen from commencing wars. As Mark Mazower has noted, to thinkers such as Rousseau, 'it is politicians who entangle men in wars, and special interests that corrupt man's innate selflessness'.[48] Public opinion, according to this theory, will always choose peace and be hostile to the elites who determine foreign policy.[49]

This fundamental thinking about the causes of war was shared by the Prussian philosopher Immanuel Kant in the late eighteenth century. First, Kant rejected the concept of just war and of a law of war as self-contradictory. Any justification for war was the antithesis of the moral law, since perpetual peace was the highest good that people should strive to achieve.[50] In the sense of refusing to 'draw a neat distinction between morality and law', Kant, as well as Grotius, was an idealist who supposed that 'international law is law *because* it is moral or because it is moral for it to be so'.[51] Moreover, Kant also considered the ways in domestic

---

[43] Howard, *War and the Liberal Conscience*, p. 12.

[44] Montesquieu, *The Spirit of Laws*, p. 7. Also see, Montesquieu, *The Spirit of the Laws*, Cohler, Miller, Stone (trans. and eds.), p. 7.

[45] Stephen J. Rosow, 'Commerce, Power and Justice: Montesquieu on International Politics', *The Review of Politics* 46, no. 3 (July 1984), p. 363.

[46] Howard, *War and the Liberal Concience*, p. 15.   [47] Ibid., pp. 13–14.

[48] Mark Mazower, *Governing the World: The History of an Idea* (Penguin Books, 2012), p. 45.

[49] Ibid., *Governing the World*, p. 45.   [50] Howard, *War and the Liberal Conscience*, p. 17.

[51] Mégret, 'International Law As Law', in Crawford and Koskenniemi (eds.), *The Cambridge Companion to International Law*, p. 75.

policy-making could lead to war and how public opinion could be an effective means to prevent statesmen from going to war. In his *Perpetual Peace* of 1795, Kant called for the creation of republican constitutions, the gradual abolition of standing armies and a federation of free states.[52] According to him, non-republican government could 'decide on war for the most trifling reasons, as if it were a kind of pleasure party', while people 'should weigh the matter well' because of the high costs of war.[53] Such a stance, along with that of Montesquieu and Rousseau, influenced the pro-leaguers' expectation that public opinion would play a pivotal role in their war prevention plan. This assumption was transmitted to the architects of the League of Nations and shaped their idea that it could serve as one of the principal sanctions of the League.[54]

Developments in the Nineteenth Century

The pro–league of nations movement was also the product of events in Europe from the nineteenth century to the First World War. Particularly significant issues were the growth of peace movements, the rise of nationalism and the development of international law and of international organisations. First, fledgling peace movements gained impetus during the Napoleonic Wars, driven by a strong moral reaction against war. Not only did many people suffer from the wars, but the middle class also began to obtain education, wealth and influence, which allowed popular movements to evolve.[55] Notably, the Society of Friends, known as Quakers, were a leading peace-lobbying group inspired by a new strain of evangelism. By the beginning of the nineteenth century, some Quaker families, such as the Frys, Cadburys and Lloyds, were becoming prosperous and politically influential in Britain and the United States. In 1816, the Quaker William Allen founded the first Peace Society in London and called it the Society for the Promotion of Permanent and Universal Peace; a similar body was established in the United States. A variety of peace groups, including women's organisations, began to be formed and held several international conferences throughout the

---

[52] Toshiki Mogami, *International Organisations* (Tokyo University Press, 2006) [in Japanese], p. 22; Suganami, *The Domestic Analogy and World Order Proposals*; Kapossy, Nikhimovsky and Whatmore (eds.), *Commerce and Peace in the Enlightenment*, introduction.

[53] Immanuel Kant, *Perpetual Peace: A Philosophical Essay, 1795* (London, 1903), pp. 122–23.

[54] Mazower, *Governing the World*, p. 45.

[55] Martin Ceadel, 'Pacifism', in Jay Winter (ed.), *The Cambridge History of the First World War*, vol. 2 (Cambridge University Press, 2013).

nineteenth century.[56] Their activities were strengthened by a newly founded movement for free trade initiated by the English political reformer Richard Cobden. Following Cruce's approach, Cobden reiterated that free trade, along with disarmament and international arbitration, could eliminate the barriers between nations that incited hatred and triggered wars.[57]

Although many peace movements appeared in the late nineteenth century, they also encountered a great obstacle: the upsurge of nationalism. Chiefly after the French Revolution and in reaction to the Napoleonic conquests, nationalism grew as a foundation of the modern state.[58] In Europe from the late nineteenth century to the outbreak of the Great War, nationalism evolved rapidly with xenophobic sentiments, encouraging both the state and the public to become more bellicose. Eric Hobsbawm has described the emergence of nationalism as follows:

For the period 1880 to 1914 was also that of the greatest mass migration yet known, within and between states, of imperialism and of growing international rivalries ending in world war. All these underlined the differences between 'us' and 'them'. And there is no more effective way of bonding together the disparate sections of restless peoples than to unite them against outsiders ....[59]

From the ruling classes' point of view, a wave of nationalism was convenient for creating the public's loyalty to the nation-state.[60] Exploiting rampant nationalism, governments presented war as a defence against foreign threats and as a national policy that served the whole nation not just elite interests.[61] Even Cobden, faced with chauvinist hatred, realised that not only the aristocracy but also 'entire peoples could be belligerent'.[62] The Crimean War, in particular, shocked him in that he learnt that 'the press and the public opinion they had been accustomed to appealing to [promote peace] could turn to aggression so easily'.[63] In light of nationalism's impact on nation-states' relations, the assumption that public opinion would always be rational and oppose war became increasingly doubtful.

---

[56] Howard, *War and the Liberal Conscience*, pp. 29–31.   [57] Ibid., pp. 34–35.

[58] James Mayall, *Nationalism and International Society* (Cambridge University Press, 1990), pp. 43, 152.

[59] Eric J. Hobsbawm, *Nations and Nationalism Since 1780: Programme, Myth, Reality* (Cambridge University Press, 1992), p. 91.

[60] Ibid., p. 83; Benedict Anderson, *Imagined Communities: Reflections on the Origin and Spread of Nationalism* (Verso, 2006), chapters 6 and 8.

[61] Hobsbawm, *Nations and Nationalism Since 1780*, p. 89; Anderson, *Imagined Communities*, chapters 6 and 8.

[62] Howard, *War and the Liberal Conscience*, p. 37.

[63] Mazower, *Governing the World*, p. 46.

The convening of the Hague Peace Conferences in 1899 and 1907 attracted fresh attention to war prevention by law.[64] The political nature of the conferences was highlighted by the initiative of the Czar of Russia, Nicholas II, who proposed to stop the arms race so that Russia, suffering from financial difficulties, could spend less on armaments. Nevertheless, 'the sincerity of the Czar in seeking to halt the arms race', and the efforts of peace groups should perhaps not be underestimated.[65] As a result of the two Hague Conferences, where topics including the peaceful settlement of disputes, arms control and arbitration procedures were discussed, a permanent court of arbitration was established and many of the laws of warfare were codified. A lawyer and a French delegate to the Conferences, Léon Bourgeois, declared that the Conferences were 'a tangible illustration of solidarism in action' and could be recognised as an early feature of a league of nations.[66] Still, the thrust of the Conferences was on the law of war – in other words, the manner of conducting war – and not on the regulation or prevention of war itself.[67] While some agreements such as the Bryan Treaties of 1913–1914 sought to renounce war between individual states, most discussions of war and law, echoing Vattel's thought, concentrated on the conduct of war rather than on the adjudication of war's rightness.

In the nineteenth century, several international organisations also gradually evolved for facilitating communication and coordination in Europe.[68] These organisations, or the 'public international unions' in Inis Claude's phrase, arose as a consequence of the increasing flow of goods, services, people and ideas across national frontiers.[69] Some of the first organisations were, for instance, the various international river commissions of Europe, the International Telegraphic Union in 1865 and the Universal Postal Union in 1874. Through international administration, these organisations fostered genuine international cooperation and set a precedent as well as a model for a league of nations.[70]

---

[64] Martti Koskenniemi, *The Gentle Civilizer of Nations: The Rise and Fall of International Law, 1870–1960* (Cambridge University Press, 2002), p. 87; Maartje Abbenhuis, *The Hague Conferences and International Politics, 1898–1915* (Bloomsbury Academic, 2019).

[65] Scott A. Keefer, 'Great Britain and Naval Arms Control: International Law and Security 1898–1914', the London School of Economics and Political Science PhD thesis, 2011, p. 87. See also, Scott Andrew Keefer, *The Law of Nations and Britain's Quest for Naval Security: International Law and Arms Control, 1898–1914* (Palgrave Macmillan, 2016).

[66] Koskenniemi, *The Gentle Civilizer of Nations*, pp. 286–87.

[67] Keefer, *Great Britain and Naval Arms Control*, pp. 13, 235; Keefer, *The Law of Nations and Britain's Quest for Naval Security*.

[68] Inis L. Claude, *Swords into Plowshares: The Problems and Progress of International Organization* (Random House, 1987), p 34.

[69] Ibid., p. 34.   [70] Mogami, *International Organisations*, pp. 31–36.

Thinking about War on the Eve of the Great War

While the pro–league of nations activists inherited the legacy of European ideas about war and peace, their settings – especially the rise of nationalism and the breakdown of the Concert of Europe – were different from those of their predecessors. These developments prompted the pro-leaguers to re-examine the major causes of war and to think in new ways about how to organise peace. First, nationalism, which fuelled hostilities among European states and impeded the growing peace movements, divided the pro-leaguers from their predecessors regarding expectations about public opinion. Crucé and Kant had presumed the primary cause of international conflict was the domestic decision-making system dominated by the ruling classes. Under this assumption, public opinion would behave rationally and oppose war and thereby help preserve peace. Nationalism, however, made this assumption far less tenable, since both the elite and the public became bellicose, as the peace activists of the late nineteenth to the early twentieth century witnessed.[71]

Nevertheless, thinkers did not completely lose faith in public opinion as a promoter of peace. Instead of presupposing that public opinion would automatically turn to rational choices such as peace, thinkers now assumed that public opinion had to be educated and enlightened to do so.[72] The English author Norman Angell, for instance, stressed the education of public opinion in *The Great Illusion* (1910). This book argued that war between modern industrial states was economically unsustainable and pointless; military power had nothing to do with the prosperity of the people, nor would war be profitable even to the victors.[73] Meanwhile, Angell reminded readers that 'war is not impossible ... it is not the likelihood of war which is the illusion, but its benefits'.[74] War was possible unless people were convinced of war's futility: 'so long as his notions of what war can accomplish in an economic or commercial sense remain what they are, the average man will not deem that his prospective enemy is likely to make the peace ideal a guide of conduct'.[75] As a solution to this problem of war, Angell

---

[71] Howard, *War and the Liberal Conscience*, p. 37; Mazower, *Governing the World*, p. 46; Casper Sylvest, 'Continuity and Change in British Liberal Internationalism, c. 1900–1930', *Review of International Studies*, vol. 31, no. 2 (2005), pp. 281–82.

[72] See Chapter 2; also see Stephen Wertheim, 'Reading the International Mind: International Public Opinion in Early Twentieth Century Anglo-American Thought', in Daniel Bessner and Nicolas Guilhot (eds.), *The Decisionist Imagination: Democracy, Sovereignty, and Social Science in the 20th Century* (Berghahn Books, 2018).

[73] Norman Angell, *The Great Illusion: A Study of the Military Power to National Advantage* (London, 1913), p. x.

[74] Ibid., p. 387.   [75] Ibid., p. 372.

proposed the education of public opinion.[76] If the public recognised the futility of war, they would act to avoid it. During the Great War, the education of public opinion arose as a crucial task of the pro-league groups. Overwhelming public support for war founded on nationalism became an impediment to the pro-league movement, a trend that compelled activists to be careful and covert in the early years of the war. Even so, the goal of transforming public opinion was never forgotten. Despite the war-time jingoism, they produced educational leaflets to improve the public's understanding of international relations as well as of the need for a new international organisation to promote peace.[77]

Another issue that divided the pro-leaguers from their predecessors was their perception of the Concert of Europe. On the eve of the Great War, the most dominant thoughts on war and peace from the nineteenth century derived from the British Prime Minister, William Ewart Gladstone. The pro-league activists mostly accepted Gladstone's theory of international relations, especially regarding intervention. Gladstone was neither an unrestrained interventionist nor a war-mongering statesman; he believed that war or any military intervention 'needed to be justified by reference to a common interest of mankind over and above the maintenance of the security state or the maintenance of a stable balance of power'.[78] For instance, at the outbreak of the Crimean War, Gladstone was convinced that Britain and France had the right, if not the duty, to intervene. He 'believed it to be morally justified, because Russia had unilaterally applied force against Turkey in breach of "international law", or the diplomatic conventions of the "Concert of Europe"'.[79] In order to protect the European order, intervention was necessary.

Gladstone's stance on intervention was shared with the pro–league of nations activists during the Great War. Most of the war-time pro-leaguers also affirmed that intervention could be justified if it would restore a stable and legitimate peace and undo an injustice. On the eve of the war, most pro-leaguers were against British entry. The German invasion of Belgium, however, convinced many of them that defending the sanctity of international law and the rights of small nations justified British intervention.[80] During the war, the pro-league groups adopted Gladstone as a central reference point for their public education campaign. For example, Prime Minister Asquith's speech in 1914, which mentioned Gladstone's phrase 'public right', was frequently

---

[76] Howard, *War and the Liberal Conscience*, p. 60.   [77] See Chapter 3.
[78] Howard, *War and the Liberal Conscience*, pp. 47–48.
[79] Eugenio F. Biagini, *Gladstone* (Macmillan, 2000), p. 35.   [80] See Chapter 2.

quoted in the war-time pro-league pamphlets. In this speech, Asquith proclaimed that:

[Gladstone] said 'The greatest triumph of our time will be the enthronement of the idea of public right as the governing idea of European politics.' … The idea of public right, what does it mean when translated into concrete terms? … And it means, finally, or it ought to mean, perhaps by a slow and gradual process, the substitution for force, for the clash of competing ambitions, for groupings and alliances and precious equipoise, the substitution for all these things of a real European partnership, based on the recognition of equal right and established and enforced by a common will.[81]

In 1914, British statesmen also adopted the Gladstonian view of just war in order to defend Britain's entry into the war. The Foreign Secretary, Edward Grey, for instance, announced that Britain had to go to war due to the German invasion of Belgium and the need to uphold Britain's own honour and trust in Europe. Accordingly, the Gladstonian approach was employed as a rhetorical and logical device to justify both the current conflict and the prevention of future wars.

Although following Gladstone's line of intervention, the pro-leaguers disagreed about whether the Concert of Europe should be used as a system to preserve the European order. The Concert of Europe, a diplomatic practice and legal framework for great power cooperation that emerged after the Napoleonic Wars, aimed to prevent radical revolutions, to maintain the territorial status quo and resolve international disputes through negotiation.[82] Embracing the notion of the 'unity of Europe' in the Christian sense, Gladstone considered the Concert of Europe the fundamental European political system – potentially 'a secular proxy for the authority of the universal church'.[83] Intervention within the Concert, therefore, was endorsed by 'its moral authority as an agent of the divine will'.[84] As Martin Ceadel has noted, Gladstone deemed that 'the Concert was allowed to interfere in the affairs of other states and sometimes even coerce them only "because it represented the best

---

[81] British Library of Economic and Political Science, CANNAN 970, *Proposals for the Avoidance of War with a prefatory note by Viscount Bryce As revised up to 24 February 1915.*

[82] Biagini, *Gladstone*, p. 79; Paul W. Schroeder, *The Transformation of European Politics, 1763–1848* (Clarendon Press, 1996); Paul W. Schroeder, *Systems, Stability, and Statecraft: Essays on the International History of Modern Europe* (Palgrave Macmillan, 2004).

[83] Peter Clarke, *A Question of Leadership: British Rulers: Gladstone to Thatcher* (Penguin, 1991), p. 33.

[84] Martin Ceadel, 'Gladstone and a Liberal Theory of International Relations', in Peter Ghosh and Lawrence Goldman (eds.), *Politics and Culture in Victorian Britain: Essays in Memory of Colin Matthew* (Oxford University Press, 2006), p. 80.

available institutional representation of Christian morality in inter-national affairs'".[85] By emphasising the moral and humanitarian pur-poses of intervention such as the defence of innocent people, Gladstone was able to advocate his Christian faith, the expansion of the British Empire and its role in the world and international law altogether.[86]

By the outbreak of the war in 1914, the Concert of Europe had become associated with the balance-of-power system that the pro-leaguers iden-tified as the primary cause of arms races, international hostility and war. Indeed, this stand was related to the transformation of the focus of British liberal internationalists' argument from the late nineteenth cen-tury through the inter-war years. As Sylvest has pointed out, British liberal internationalism's focus gradually changed from moral arguments to institutional ones, a trend that became accelerated from the Great War onwards.[87] The moral arguments underscored the need for civilisational progress through the development of morality in the international domain.[88] The institutional arguments were based on international anarchy and the fallibility of human nature; liberal thinkers accordingly assumed that progress required not only morality but also institutional mechanisms that could help or even 'force people to act in ways deemed morally defensible'.[89] From the late nineteenth century to the beginning of the twentieth century, moral arguments were mainstream, and many Victorian liberals including Gladstone were moral internationalists who pursued the reform of international politics through the development of morality and rationality.[90] At the beginning of the Great War, moral arguments were still prevalent and were advocated by some pro-league leaders such as Goldsworthy Lowes Dickinson. Although he is known as an author of *European Anarchy* – a book that offered a framework for institutional arguments – when Britain entered the war in August 1914,

---

[85] Ibid.

[86] Brendan Simms and D. J. B. Trim (eds.), *Humanitarian Intervention: A History* (Cambridge University Press, 2011), pp. 271–72; Davide Rodogno, *Against Massacre: Humanitarian Interventions in the Ottoman Empire, 1815–1914: The Emergence of a European Concept and International Practice* (Princeton University Press, 2012), pp. 154–57.

[87] Sylvest, *British Liberal Internationalism*, pp. 198–99, 268–70; also see Nazli Pinar Kaymaz, 'From Imperialism to Internationalism: British Idealism and Human Rights', *The International History Review*, vol. 41, no. 6 (2019), pp. 1235–55.

[88] Ibid., pp. 267–68; Sylvest, 'Continuity and Change in British Liberal Internationalism', *Review of International Studies*, vol. 31, no. 2 (2005), pp. 266–67; Duncan Bell (ed.), *Victorian Visions of Global Order: Empire and International Relations in Nineteenth-Century Political Thought* (Cambridge University Press, 2007).

[89] Sylvest, *British Liberal Internationalism*, pp. 198–99, 268–70; Sylvest, 'Continuity and Change in British Liberal Internationalism', p. 268.

[90] Sylvest, 'Continuity and Change in British Liberal Internationalism', pp. 267–68.

he still put his faith in the morality of the public rather than in political institutions.

Not one of the men employed in this [war] work of destruction wants to perform it; not one of them knows how it has come about that he is performing it; not one of them knows what object is to be served by performing it. The non-combatants are in the same case. They did not foresee this, they did not want it, they did not choose it. They were never consulted. No one in Europe desires to be engaged in such work. We are sane people. But our acts are mad. Why? Because we are all in the hands of some score of individuals called Governments. Some score among the hundreds of millions of Europeans. These men have willed this thing for us over our heads. No nation has had the chance of saying No.[91]

Dickinson asserted that war was made not by the public but by a handful of 'men who have immediate power over other men',[92] as Rousseau and Kant had thought in the eighteenth century. Similarly, James Bryce, a renowned scholar and a key leading figure of the pro-league movement, criticised a few diplomats for determining Britain's entry into the war: 'how few are the persons in every state in whose hands lie issues of war and peace .... If they had decided otherwise than they did, the thing [the war] would not have happened'.[93] Thus, the moral arguments blamed conniving diplomats and cunning statesmen for making policy without consulting the general public and for precluding the possibility of international progress.[94] Bryce, who admired German culture,[95] could not believe that the German people he knew 'could possibly approve of the action of their Government'. By underscoring the British government's responsibility, he argued that their 'quarrel is with the German Government', not with the German people.[96] The distinction drawn between the government and the general public enabled Bryce and other liberal internationalists to support the war and to place a great deal of faith in the potential of public education and opinion.[97]

---

[91] G. Lowes Dickinson, 'Holy War', *The Nation*, 8 August 1914.

[92] G. Lowes Dickinson, *The War and the Way Out* (Chancery Lane Press, 1917), pp. 8–9. In 1914–1915, Lowes Dickinson explained the origin of the war by employing what he called 'the governmental theory'. See Lowes Dickinson, *After the War* (Fifield, 1915), pp. 7–8; G. Lowes Dickinson, 'Is War Inevitable?' *War and Peace*, vol. 1, no. 8 (May 1914), p. 221; Lowes Dickinson, 'Holy War'; Also see Wallace, *War and the Image of Germany*, pp. 18, 113–16.

[93] Wallace, *War and the Image of Germany*, p. 90.

[94] Sylvest, 'Continuity and Change', pp. 272–73, 281–82.

[95] Robbins, 'Lord Bryce and The First World War', p. 255; Sylvest, *British Liberal Internationalism*, p. 161.

[96] Sylvest, *British Liberal Internationalism*, p. 161; Richard Cross also wrote about a similar idea. See Cross, 'The Rights of the War', *The Nation*, pp. 791, 793.

[97] Wallace, *War and the Image of Germany*, p. 175.

The outbreak of the war, however, triggered the shift of the focus of internationalists' arguments towards institutional frameworks. Prior to the war, the Hague Conferences in 1899 and 1907 'stimulated interest in international law, arbitration, and other institutions in international politics'.[98] Yet, the major factors for this change were the shock of the war and its jingoistic public reception that refuted moral arguments.[99] For example, liberal internationalists such as John A. Hobson realised that his assumption based on moral arguments – most civilised men were rational in essence – was mere illusion.[100] In his 1915 pamphlet *Towards International Government*, Hobson admitted 'public opinion and a common sense of justice are found inadequate safeguards' against war. Hence, 'there must be an executive power enabled to apply an economic boycott, or in the last resort an international force'.[101] Equally, Lowes Dickinson, confronting the challenge of mobilising public opinion, came to perceive that the public were 'controlled more by passion than by reason'.[102] During the war, his pacifist reputation, especially in the face of widespread jingoism in 1914–1916, made him 'desperately pessimistic about the future of all civilization'[103] and led him to wonder 'whether it is worthwhile preaching to the insane'.[104] In his *European Anarchy* of 1916, Lowes Dickinson too shifted his emphasis to the international system; international politics had 'meant Machiavellianism' since 'the emergence of the sovereign State at the end of the fifteenth century':[105]

They [decision-makers] could not, indeed, practise anything else [other than Machiavellianism]. For it is as true of an aggregation of states as of an aggregation of individuals that, whatever moral sentiments may prevail, if there is no common law and no common force the best intentions will be defeated by lack of confidence and security.[106]

---

[98] Ibid., pp. 269–70.   [99] Ibid., pp. 274–75.

[100] John A. Hobson, *Confessions of an Economic Heretic* (G. Allen & Unwin, 1938), pp. 93–94, 104; Clarke, *Liberals and Social Democrats*, pp. 166, 170.

[101] John A. Hobson, *Towards International Government* (Macmillan, 1915), p. 6.

[102] Wallace, *War and the Image of Germany*, p. 120; Oxford, Bodleian Library, James Bryce Papers, MS. Bryce 58, 21, a letter from G. Lowes Dickinson to Bryce, 26 March 1915; OBL, Willoughby Dickinson Papers, MSEng.hist.c.403, a letter from G. Lowes Dickinson to W. H. Dickinson, 1917?; Parliamentary Archives, DAV325, 'Copies of Various Memoranda and Proposals for the League of Nations'.

[103] Arthur Ponsonby's diary (transcript), 23 July 1915.

[104] OBL, The Papers of Arthur Augustus William Harry Ponsonby, 1st Baron Ponsonby of Shulbrede, MS. Eng. hist. c.667, 183–84, a letter from G. Lowes Dickinson to Ponsonby, 22 January 1917.

[105] G. Lowes Dickinson, *The European Anarchy* (George Allen & Unwin, 1916), pp. 9–10; Sylvest, 'Continuity and Change in British Liberal Internationalism', *Review of International Studies*, p. 276.

[106] Dickinson, *The European Anarchy*, pp. 9–10.

Lowes Dickinson now acknowledged the necessity of solving the problem of anarchy – the prime cause of war, which bolstered institutional
arguments among liberal internationalists.[107]

During the Great War, the league of nations activists debated future
international order in the middle of this transition in liberal
internationalism from moral to institutional arguments and therefore
viewed international relations from both moral and institutional perspectives. Although the pro-leaguers, including Dickinson and Hobson, were
disillusioned about the rationality of human beings, they still supposed
the public, if appropriately informed, would become a powerful force to
prevent future war.[108] They called for the creation of a league of nations,
a new institution that could not only solve the problem of anarchy but
also provide the public with the focus, inspiration and education required
for moral progress.[109] While moral internationalists' arguments that war
was caused by a handful of aristocratic statesmen and that human rationality would promote international progress were on the wane, they identified a lack of authority in international society as the prime cause of war.
This shift in turn demanded the creation of an international institution.
The institution-driven framework 'became a precondition of the arguments for an international organisation for the prevention of war – a
league of nations – which soon became a cornerstone of liberal
internationalism'.[110]

Conclusion

Even though previous scholarship has little explored it, the questions of
how and why the league of nations movement emerged needs to be
discussed by contextualising its network and ideas in both short- and
long-term history. For the short term, the pro-league activists already had
pre-war networks of influence that they could exploit to organise the pro-
league movement. Their networks consisted in an 'intellectual aristocracy' who were closely bound by common educational background and
organisational ties.[111] Above all, most of them were liberal

---

[107] Sylvest, 'Continuity and Change in British Liberal Internationalism', *Review of
International Studies*, p. 276.
[108] See Chapter 2; Sylvest, 'Continuity and Change in British Liberal Internationalism',
Review of International Studies, pp. 281–82.
[109] Ibid.
[110] Sylvest, 'Continuity and Change in British Liberal Internationalism', pp. 274–77,
281–82.
[111] J. H. Plumb (ed.), *Studies in Social History: A Tribute to G. M. Trevelyan* (Longmans,
1955), chapter VIII; Wallace, *War and the Image of Germany*, p. 3.

internationalists who subscribed to a European legacy of thinking about war – the long-term context of the ideas about the league. Following the intellectual tradition, most of the pro-league activists objected to war on moral grounds, yet simultaneously recognised there were just and unjust wars – wars of aggression were unjust, and wars for collective security were just. In addition to the legal regulation of international conflicts as well as an understanding of the structural causes of war, they also regarded public opinion as a means to avert future wars. Whereas the growth of peace movements, international organisations and conferences fostered supportive environments for popular movements in the nineteenth century, the problems activists confronted in an age of nationalism and industrial total war were different in scale and kind from those encountered by their predecessors. To challenge the new problems – the Concert of Europe and its breakdown and the rise of nationalism – the pro-leaguers now devised a scheme of a new international order centred on the league of nations. This peaceful international organisation was designed with the legacy of thinking about war and peace in Europe and also shaped by the milieu of the beginning of the twentieth century. Indeed, the pro-leaguers' fundamental views about the post-war order consisted of both new and traditional thinking about war, as well as of both moral and institutional arguments of British liberal internationalism. The prehistory of the pro–league of nations movement and its ideas also suggests how the old intellectual traditions still have a pervasive influence on today's view on war and peace and how the nongovernmental movement could lead to the emergence of a new international order.[112]

---

[112] Schroeder, 'The Cold War and Its Ending in "Long-Duration" International History', in Schroeder and Wetzel et al. (eds.), *Systems, Stability, and Statecraft*, p. 248.

2　The Use of Force to Prevent War?

The Bryce Group's *Proposals for the Avoidance of War*, 1914–1915

Introduction

After the First World War, the League of Nations – as the first inter-national organisation to prevent future war – regulated initiating war in international law and institutionalised the idea of collective security.[1] The war-prevention functions of the League owed much to the Bryce Group, one of the first study circles in Britain that developed the idea of a post-war league. Although it was discussed by many organisations, such as the Union of Democratic Control and the Fabian Society, the Bryce Group and its offshoot, the League of Nations Society, were the first to present a fully worked out idea and to organise the popular movement for establishing the League of Nations.[2] From November 1914 to February 1915, the Bryce Group produced its first privately circulated draft scheme for a post-war order, *Proposals for the Avoidance of War*. In 1915, the *Proposals* led league advocates in Britain to found the League of Nations Society.[3] The Bryce Group also sent its *Proposals* to intellec-tuals in the United States, including the former ambassador to Belgium, Theodore Marburg, who organised an American pro-league group, the League to Enforce Peace, after studying the *Proposals* in 1915.[4] In 1918,

---

[1] See Introduction, nn. 1–2.
[2] Regarding the Union of Democratic Control, see Introduction, n. 21.
[3] Martin David Dubin, 'Toward the Concept of Collective Security: The Bryce Group's "Proposals for the Avoidance of War", 1914–1917', *International Organization*, vol. 24, no. 2 (Spring 1970), pp. 288–318; George. W. Egerton, *Great Britain and the Creation of the League of Nations: Strategy, Politics, and International Organization, 1914–1919* (Scolar Press, 1978), pp. 9–11; Henry R. Winkler, *The League of Nations Movement in Great Britain, 1914–1919* (Rutgers University Press, 1952), pp. 16–18.
[4] See Chapter 4; Warren Kuehl, *Seeking World Order: The United States and International Organization to 1920* (Vanderbilt University Press, 1969), p. 179; Ruhl J. Bartlett, *The League to Enforce Peace* (University of North Carolina Press, 1944), p. 35. One of the leaders of the League to Enforce Peace, A. Lawrence Lowell, admitted that the American group's plan was founded on the Bryce Group's *Proposals*; for example, see Lowell to Lowes Dickinson, 17 August 1915, Wallas Papers 4/5, British Library of Political and Economic Science (hereafter BLPES). The League to Enforce Peace was formally organised after reading and discussing the Bryce Group's proposal in meetings. See

the Phillimore Committee, the Foreign Office's official study group on the foundation of a post-war organisation, examined the plans by pro-league groups including the Bryce Group and its members; the committee reflected them in its official reports, which provided the basis for the discussion on the League of Nations Covenant at the Paris Peace Conference.[5] This chapter, therefore, explores the contents and the making of the group's *Proposals*, which became the springboard of wartime debates about future war prevention and ultimately influenced the authors of the 1919 Covenant of the League of Nations.

While International Relations (IR) scholars and historians have tended to associate pro-league of nations activists with utopianism, idealism or pacificism,[6] more focused studies on the Bryce Group have mostly depicted its *Proposals* as a product of realistic thinking.[7] These studies described the *Proposals* as a moderate and limited project by pointing to the fact that its authors did not advocate a world state or a federation[8]

Minutes, January–April 9, 30 March 1915, League to Enforce Peace Records (Int 6722.8.25*), box 4, Houghton Library, Harvard University. With lawyers such as former American President William Howard Taft as its leaders, the LEP's platform was legalistic in approach, based on its premise that states could form an international legal community. In contrast, the Bryce Group's *Proposals* aimed to be practical from politicians' point of view and rejected the assumption that the post-war world could be organised into one international community bound by law. See also Benjamin Allen Coates, *Legalist Empire: International Law and American Foreign Relations in the Early Twentieth Century* (Oxford University Press, 2016); Stephen Wertheim, 'The League of Nations: A Retreat from International Law?', *Journal of Global History*, vol. 7, no. 2 (2012), pp. 210–32; Stephen Wertheim, 'The League That Wasn't: American Designs for a Legalist-Sanctioned League of Nations and the Intellectual Origins of International Organization, 1914–1920', *Diplomatic History*, vol. 35, no. 5 (November 2011), pp. 797–836. As for the French side, intensified discussion about the league later in the war was led by the government, not private groups as in Britain and the United States. The French pro-league committee was appointed in June 1917, although its chairman, Léon Bourgeois, had already been thinking about a possible international organisation after the war. See Michael Clinton, 'The New World Will Create the New Europe: Paul-Henri d'Estournelles de Constant, the United States, and International Peace', *Journal of the Western Society for French History*, vol. 40 (2012); Peter Jackson, *Beyond the Balance of Power: France and the Politics of National Security in the Era of the First World War* (Cambridge University Press, 2013), pp. 178–82; Kuehl, *Seeking World Order*, pp. 234–36.

[5] Dubin, 'Toward the Concept of Collective Security', p. 305; Winkler, *League of Nations Movement*, p. 57; 'The Committee on the League of Nations, Interim Report', 20 March 1918, and 'Final Report', 3 July 1918, The National Archives (hereafter TNA), CAB 29/1.

[6] See Introduction, n. 5.

[7] Egerton, *Britain and the Creation of the League*, p. 10; Winkler, *League of Nations Movement*, p. 6; Roland N. Stromberg, 'Uncertainties and Obscurities about the League of Nations', *Journal of the History of Ideas*, vol. 33, no. 1 (January/March 1972), p. 144; Martin Ceadel, *Semi-Detached Idealists: The British Peace Movement and International Relations, 1854–1945* (Oxford University Press, 2000), p. 205.

[8] Winkler, *League of Nations Movement*, p. 18.

and that its recommendations included an enforced period of delay at the commencement of an armed conflict and the consideration of international disputes by a Council.[9] These accounts, however, rarely do more than comment on the internal logic of the *Proposals* completed in February 1915.[10] Apart from the brief accounts of Robbins and Ceadel, both of whom mention disagreements in the Bryce Group over international sanctions,[11] we know very little about what were in fact heated debates behind the drafting of the *Proposals*.[12]

This chapter redresses this imbalance by offering the first close examination of the drafting process of the *Proposals*. It reveals the group's intense debates and disagreements over the use of force to enforce peace – what is now called collective security.[13] The Bryce Group members were the first thinkers to propose collective action as a practical measure to prevent future war and it became the central pillar of their post-war scheme.[14] By analysing the rich yet underused manuscripts and correspondence of the group, this chapter illustrates how these early war-time debates culminated in the principle of collective security as enshrined by the League of Nations – with all its promises and problems.

---

[9] Egerton, *Britain and the Creation of the League*, p. 10; Winkler, *League of Nations Movement*, pp. 19–20.

[10] Dubin, 'Toward the Concept of Collective Security', pp. 288–318. Dubin's article has provided a detailed account of the Bryce Group's *Proposals* on the foundation of the League. It has not analysed the group's discussion and the intellectual backdrop to the *Proposals*. Also see Winkler, *League of Nations Movement*, pp. 18–20; Peter Yearwood, *Guarantee of Peace: The League of Nations in British Policy, 1914–1925* (Oxford University Press, 2009), pp. 14–15; Helen McCarthy, *The British People and the League of Nations: Democracy, Citizenship and Internationalism, c. 1918–45* (Manchester University Press, 2011); Egerton, *Britain and the Creation of the League*, pp. 7–11; Keith Robbins, *The Abolition of War: The 'Peace Movement' in Britain, 1914–1919* (University of Wales Press, 1976); Stromberg, 'Uncertainties and Obscurities about the League of Nations', pp. 139–54. For the American pro-League activities, see Bartlett, *The League to Enforce Peace*; Wertheim, 'The League of Nations', pp. 210–32; Wertheim, 'The League That Wasn't', pp. 797–836; Thomas J. Knock, *To End All Wars: Woodrow Wilson and the Quest for a New World Order* (Oxford University Press, 1993); C. Bouchard, *Le citoyen et l'ordre mondial (1914–1919): Le rêve d'une paix durable au lendemain de la Grande Guerre (France, Grande-Bretagne, États-Unis)* (Paris, 2008).

[11] Robbins, *Abolition of War*, pp. 49–50; Ceadel, *Semi-Detached Idealists*, pp. 204–5.

[12] Egerton, *Britain and the Creation of the League*, pp. 7–11; Yearwood, *Guarantee of Peace*, pp. 14–15; Winkler, *League of Nations Movement*, pp. 18–20; Dubin, 'Toward the Concept of Collective Security', p. 291.

[13] Alexander Orakhelashvili, *Collective Security* (Oxford University Press, 2011), p. 1. Also note, the phrase 'collective security' was not used during the war but only began to be widely used in the inter-war period.

[14] Richard K. Betts, 'Systems for Peace or Causes of War? Collective Security, Arms Control, and the New Europe', *International Security*, vol. 17, no. 1 (Summer 1992), p. 5; Egerton, *Britain and the Creation of the League*, p. 11.

Before investigating the Bryce Group's discussion, it is useful to revisit how labels such as 'utopianism' and 'realism' emerged.[15] The term 'utopianism' was first employed in the context of international relations by E. H. Carr in his foundational text *The Twenty Years' Crisis, 1919–1939*.[16] Although Carr's definitions of realists and utopians were not always consistent, standard accounts suggest that realists were those who concentrated on the role of power such as military force and *realpolitik* rather than ideals and morality in international politics. On the other hand, utopians have been portrayed as those who emphasised the role of morality and the force of public opinion and who, by regarding the use of force to resist power as an evil, advocated non-resistance.[17] Carr's

---

[15] While the Bryce Group members did not use the terms 'realism' and 'idealism', the terms they used, such as 'utopian' and 'practicable', closely corresponded to the conception of idealism and realism as employed in traditional IR scholars' terminology. The category was an alleged theoretical dichotomy constructed after the Great War and further elaborated during the Cold War years. I therefore apply the terms 'realistic' and 'idealistic', which are not intended to reify the binary of realism and idealism or attribute retroactively the lineaments of idealist or realist positions to earlier forms of thinking. For the Bryce Group members' use of the term 'utopian', see G. Lowes Dickinson, 'The Way Out', *War and Peace*, vol. 1, no. 12 (September 1914), pp. 345–46; Lowes Dickinson to Bryce, 20 October 1914, James Bryce Papers (hereafter JBP), MS. Bryce 58, Bodleian Library, Oxford (hereafter BLO); 'Mr. Ponsonby's Note on the Suggested Amendment to the Proposals for the Avoidance of War', Willoughby Dickinson Papers (hereafter WHP), MS. Eng. Hist. c.402, BLO; *Proposals for the Avoidance of War, with a Prefatory Note by Viscount Bryce, As Revised up to 24 February 1915* (hereafter *Proposals for the Avoidance of War*), Edwin Cannan Papers 970, BLPES. For practical and impracticable terms, see Lowes Dickinson, 'The Way Out'; 'Mr. Ponsonby's Note', WHP, MS. Eng. Hist. c.402, BLO; Lowes Dickinson to Bryce, 20 October 1914, JBP, MS. Bryce 58, 14, BLO; 'Notes on Lord Bryce's Memorandum by Richard Cross', 27 November 1914, WHP, MS. Eng. Hist. c.402, BLO; 'Mr. Lowes Dickinson's Notes', WHP, MS. Eng. Hist. c.402, BLO; Arthur Ponsonby, 'Democracy and Foreign Diplomacy', *War and Peace*, vol. 2, no. 15 (December 1914), pp. 40–41; Bryce to Ponsonby, 5 December 1914, Ponsonby Papers (hereafter PP), MS. Eng. Hist. c.661, 146–47, BLO; 'Mr. Ponsonby's Notes', 10 December 1914, WHP, MS. Eng. Hist. c.402, BLO; 'Lord Bryce's Memorandum with E. Richard Cross's Notes and the Revisions Made up to Jan. 19th, 1915 by the Group in Conference', Wallas Papers 4/5, BLPES; Lowes Dickinson to C. R. Ashbee, January 1915, The Papers of Charles Robert Ashbee, CRA3/4, King's College Archives, Cambridge; *Proposals for the Avoidance of War*, Cannan Papers 970, BLPES. Also, as for the original meaning of realism, see John Bew, *Realpolitik: A History* (Oxford University Press, 2016).

[16] E. H. Carr, *The Twenty Years' Crisis, 1919–1939: An Introduction to the Study of International Relations* (Macmillan, 2001). Before the publication of *The Twenty Years' Crisis*, 'realities' and 'ideals' were employed to analyse international affairs including the League of Nations. See Halford J. Mackinder, *Democratic Ideals and Reality: A Study in the Politics of Reconstruction* (Constable & Co., 1919).

[17] Carr, *Twenty Years' Crisis*, pp. 92–93, 102; Peter Wilson, *The International Theory of Leonard Woolf: A Study in Twentieth-Century Idealism* (Palgrave Macmillan, 2003), p. 20; John Baylis, Steve Smith and Patricia Owens (eds.), *The Globalization of World Politics: An Introduction to International Relations* (Oxford University Press, 2016), pp. 4–5,

depiction of inter-war international relations, a debate between realists and utopians, was profoundly influential and once broadly accepted by scholars in the fields of IR theory and the history of international politics.[18] Although idealism now tends to be closely associated with liberal internationalism, widely used IR textbooks still refer to these two concepts as the classical dichotomy.[19]

Upon closer inspection, however, Carr's intention of employing this dichotomy was not to attack utopianism but to maintain a delicate balance between realism and idealism, because 'any sound political thought must be based on elements of both utopia and reality'.[20] Suggesting that utopian and realistic thinking were 'inextricably blended' in any responses to political situations, Carr argued that neither of them should be ignored in politics.[21] Even though Carr's rather nuanced position once drew little attention from IR scholars, such clear-cut dichotomies of international relations theory have been called into question by recent scholarship. Some scholars such as Lucian Ashworth have examined whether a 'great debate' in fact took place between the two clearly defined schools of thought, while others such as Peter Wilson have argued that Carr's category of utopianism was a rhetorical device he used to discredit a rich variety of liberal internationalist thought that he disagreed with.[22]

These nuanced positions of revisionist IR scholars, I suggest, can provide historians with a useful point of departure to reassess the history of liberal internationalism.[23] A careful reading of the records of the intellectual founders of the League of Nations shows that its early discussion of collective security likewise defies simple categorisation. What

---

100–25; John W. Young, *International Relations Since 1945* (Oxford University Press, 2013), p. xxiv; Chris Brown and Kirsten Ainley, *Understanding International Relations* (Palgrave Macmillan, 2009), pp. 18–26; Tim Dunne, Milja Kurki and Steve Smith (eds.), *International Relations Theories: Discipline and Diversity* (Oxford University Press, 2013), chapters 3, 5, 7.

[18] For example, Hedley Bull framed IR theory based on this antithesis: realism in the Hobbesian or Machiavellian tradition that stressed material power and war versus idealism in the Kantian tradition that underlined moral unity and the shared interests of all humankind. Hedley Bull, *The Anarchical Society: A Study of Order in World Politics* (Palgrave Macmillan, 1995), pp. 23–25.

[19] Dunne, Kurki and Smith (eds.), *International Relations Theories*; Brown and Ainley, *Understanding International Relations*; Scott Burchill et al., *Theories of International Relations* (Palgrave, 2005); Steven C. Roach, Martin Griffiths and Terry O'Callaghan, *International Relations: The Key Concepts* (Routledge, 2013).

[20] Carr, *The Twenty Years' Crisis*, p. 87, also pp. 10, 14.   [21] Ibid., pp. 88, 92.

[22] See Introduction, n. 29.

[23] As Chapter 1 has discussed, liberal internationalism in this book refers to the idea of the early twentieth century that focused on the problem of war in international politics, based on the belief in the moral progress of humanity.

was traditionally categorised as a realistic view rested on what IR scholars have tended to consider an idealistic one, and an idealistic perspective rested on what they considered a realistic one, without excluding each other. While the group's war-prevention plan was moderate, practical and realistic, as historians have pointed out, a wide range of manuscript sources reveal that it also depended critically on idealistic expectations. The group's ideas about preventing future war ranged from idealistic devices such as the moral force of world public opinion against war to deter aggression to what it considered to be realistic measures, such as collective military force against an aggressor state. As Glenda Sluga has argued, in the discussion of 'the national and international', realistic and idealistic concepts were entwined as complementary ways of thinking about peace.[24]

Note that the symbiosis between 'idealistic' and 'realistic' impulses should be a point of departure, not a conclusion. For the detailed reconstruction of the group's early discussion reveals that some parts of its war-prevention plan were logically inconsistent: it aimed to be 'practical' but fundamentally depended on liberal internationalists' belief in the 'gradual progress' of the world, an international organisation and public opinion in particular. The members were conscious of the flaws and contradictions in their war-prevention plan, such as the necessity to threaten and ultimately to use force to maintain peace. Nevertheless, they never arrived at a coherent solution for striking a balance between realistic views and idealistic ones. By employing the terms 'realistic' and 'idealistic', this chapter therefore illustrates not only a mixture of these categorisations but also – more crucially – their profound ambiguities and instabilities. The innate weaknesses and the perennial dilemma of collective security that exercised the Bryce Group were never fully resolved in the foundation of the League of Nations and remain a pervasive problem to this day.

War-Prevention Measures in the League of Nations Plan

Before analysing the discussions of the Bryce Group, we need first to look at how the group came into being in 1914. It was the group members' backgrounds and varying reactions to the beginning of the war that gave rise to their war-prevention plan. The coming and outbreak of the war pressed some intellectuals in Britain to urgently form private groups

---

[24] Glenda Sluga, *Internationalism in the Age of Nationalism* (University of Pennsylvania Press, 2013), p. 150; Glenda Sluga and Patricia Clavin (eds.), *Internationalisms: A Twentieth-Century History* (Cambridge University Press, 2017).

against the war, such as the Union of Democratic Control and the British Neutrality Committee that existed for only a few days in the summer of 1914. The Bryce Group, one of such organisations, most strongly influenced public debates about a new peaceful order. The group was organised by the Cambridge classicist Goldsworthy Lowes Dickinson, who first sketched out the scheme for a league of nations a few weeks after the British entry into the war and brought together those who might be interested in it.[25] Chaired by James Bryce, the former British ambassador in Washington and a specialist in international law, the group called a meeting at the beginning of November 1914.[26] The main members, including Lowes Dickinson and Bryce, were seven liberal intellectuals, politicians and journalists. The other five were two Liberal MPs, Sir Willoughby H. Dickinson and Arthur Ponsonby; the Quaker lawyer and the business manager of the *Nation*, Richard Cross; the political philosopher Graham Wallas and the economist and critic of imperialism John A. Hobson. The Bryce Group shared personal connections, overlapping institutional ties and common intellectual influences. Some of the members not only knew one another as friends or colleagues at universities[27] but also had overlapping institutional ties and social circles such as *The Nation* and the National Liberal Club that connected them in the pre-1914 period.[28] More significantly, liberal internationalism was a distinctive feature of the Bryce Group membership and profoundly influenced its thinking about the post-war organisation.[29]

At the outbreak of the war, some members supported Britain's entry into the war; others were determinately against it. Despite their disagreement, group members still shared core values and, above all, the goal of preventing another war in the future. The initiator of the group, Lowes

---

[25] G. Lowes Dickinson, *Autobiography of G. Lowes Dickinson and Other Unpublished Writings* (Duckworth, 1973); Papers of Goldsworthy Lowes Dickinson, GLD 1/2/4, King's College Archive Centre, Cambridge.

[26] Graham Wallas to Ada Wallas, 30 October 14, Wallas Family Papers, WALLAS 1/1/24, Newnham College, Cambridge; Arthur Ponsonby's Diary (transcript), 11 November 1914.

[27] See Chapter 1; Peter Clarke, *Liberals and Social Democrats* (Cambridge University Press, 1978), p. 51.

[28] See Chapter 1.

[29] Ibid. Also, larger concerns about humanitarian interventions and humanitarianism during this period did not exercise the group to a significant degree, although the concerns and the group's war-prevention plan shared a common intellectual origin in nineteenth-century Britain. See Caroline Shaw, *Britannia's Embrace: Modern Humanitarianism and the Imperial Origins of Refugee Relief* (Oxford University Press, 2015); Bruno Cabanes, *The Great War and the Origins of Humanitarianism, 1918–1924* (Cambridge University Press, 2014).

Dickinson, and subsequently the author of *European Anarchy* (1916),[30] identified the international system based on the 'balance of power' as a principal cause of war that should be replaced by a new peaceful order.[31] Initially, he called for 'the League of Nations of Europe' –'something much more like a federation than concert' – that would unite European powers as in the United States.[32] Although James Bryce was initially undecided about the war,[33] he changed his mind. As a jurist who advocated the rule of law and the rights of small nations, the German invasion of Belgium was a sufficient cause for his commitment to the war.[34] Bryce argued that unless nations respected treaties as sacred undertakings, international order would be destroyed.[35]

The two MPs, Willoughby Dickinson and Arthur Ponsonby, were perceived in very different ways by the public. Inspired by his Anglican faith, Dickinson had already worked for progressive causes prior to the war and was widely respected as a man of principle.[36] To him, joining the Bryce Group was the continuation of his peace work.[37] Ponsonby, on the other hand, was one of the five radical MPs who decried the government's foreign policy on 3 August – the very day Foreign Secretary Edward Grey announced the British entry into the war.[38] As a leading member of the Union of Democratic Control, he was publicly attacked as 'pro-German' by jingoists.

A moving spirit of the group, Richard Cross was a very able solicitor of the Yorkshire entrepreneurial Rowntree family and 'associated with good political work behind the scenes'.[39] A careful study of the negotiations

---

[30] G. Lowes Dickinson, *The European Anarchy* (London, 1916).

[31] Lowes Dickinson, 'The Way Out'; Lowes Dickinson to Bryce, 20 October 1914, JBP, MS. Bryce 58, 14–17, BLO.

[32] Lowes Dickinson, 'The Way Out'; Ceadel, *Semi-Detached Idealists*, pp. 204–5.

[33] Keith G. Robbins, 'Lord Bryce and the First World War', *Historical Journal*, vol. 10, no. 2 (January 1967), p. 255; H. A. L. Fisher, *James Bryce*, vol. 2 (London, 1927), pp. 126–27.

[34] Robbins, 'Lord Bryce and The First World War', p. 255; Fisher, *James Bryce*, p. 127.

[35] Robbins, 'Lord Bryce and The First World War', p. 256.

[36] Daniel Gorman, 'Ecumenical Internationalism: Willoughby Dickinson, the League of Nations and the World Alliance for Promoting International Friendship through the Churches', *Journal of Contemporary History*, vol. 45, no. 1 (January 2010), pp. 52, 54.

[37] Hope Costley White, *Willoughby Hyett Dickinson, 1859–1943: A Memoir* (Gloucester, 1956), pp. 64–66.

[38] PP, MS. Eng. Hist. c.660, 74–81, 93–101, BLO; R. A. Jones, 'Ponsonby, Arthur Augustus William Harry, First Baron Ponsonby of Shulbrede (1871–1946)', *Oxford Dictionary of National Biography*, www.oxforddnb.com/view/article/35566?docPos=1; House of Commons, Parliamentary Papers, http://parlipapers.chadwyck.co.uk/hansard/fullrec.do?source=config5.cfg&area=hcpp&id=CDS5CV0065P0–0011.

[39] G. Lowes Dickinson, *The Autobiography of G. Lowes Dickinson and Other Unpublished Writings* (Duckworth, 1973), p. 190.

before the war convinced him of 'the complete bankruptcy of European statesmanship' and 'the absolute futility of the attempt to keep the peace of Europe by dividing its peoples into two groups'.[40] To tackle these problems, he specified some objectives, including the creation of a new order, for which those who worked for peace, such as the Bryce Group, ought to be 'prepared to take action as opportunity offers'.[41]

The other two members, Graham Wallas and John A. Hobson, were the founders of the British Neutrality Committee of 1914. Fearing that 'political or social progress' – principal features of liberal internationalism in those days – would be 'names without a meaning for our time' as a consequence of the war,[42] Wallas became a member of the Bryce Group; yet he was 'more concerned to press [for] international cooperation in general than [the group's] particular and definite plan for preventing war'.[43] Prior to the war, Hobson was already critical of traditional European diplomacy and considered that the balance of power should be replaced by a new international order[44] – a federation of popular governments, which would not only prevent war but also help solve economic and imperial problems.[45] Hobson joined circles such as the Bryce Group and the Union of Democratic Control to influence their course and their eventual outcome. The Bryce Group remained a loose study group throughout the war, and therefore its membership was not necessarily restricted to the regular members listed above.[46]

---

[40] E. Richard Cross, 'The Rights of the War', *The Nation*, 29 August 1914, pp. 791, 793; Marion Wilkinson, *E. Richard Cross: A Biographical Sketch with Literary Papers and Religious and Political Addresses* (J. M. Dent, 1917), pp. 39–40.

[41] Cross, 'The Rights of the War', pp. 791, 793.

[42] Clarke, *Liberals and Social Democrats*, pp. 166–67.

[43] Lowes Dickinson, *Autobiography of Lowes Dickinson*, p. 304; The Papers of Goldsworthy Lowes Dickinson, GLD 1/2/4, King's College Archive Centre, Cambridge.

[44] David Long, 'J. A. Hobson and Idealism in International Relations', *Review of International Studies*, vol. 17, no. 3 (July 1991), pp. 290, 292–93.

[45] Robbins, *The Abolition of War*, pp. 51, 53; Martin Ceadel, *Thinking about Peace and War* (Oxford University Press, 1987), p. 96; Sylvest, *British Liberal Internationalism*, pp. 213–14.

[46] The architect and social reformer Charles Robert Ashbee indicated that he was a member of the Bryce Group. See The Papers of Charles Robert Ashbee, CRA 3/4, King's College Archives, Cambridge. Further, the peace campaigner and author Norman Angell was an absentee member. Although Angell kept in touch with the group, he did not submit comments on the Bryce's drafts of the *Proposals* in the group's meetings. See Lowes Dickinson, 'Plans for a Discussion about the Establishment of an International Council', 1914?, Wallas Papers 1/55, BLPES; Ponsonby's Diary, 11 November 1914; Marvin Swartz, *The Union of Democratic Control in British Politics during the First World War* (Clarendon Press, 1971), pp. 97–98; Martin Ceadel, *Living the Great Illusion: Sir Norman Angell, 1872–1967* (Oxford University Press, 2009), pp. 171, 177, 180, 195–96.

In its meetings, building upon the members' notes about possible international schemes, the group singled out as the primary cause of the war the existing European order founded on the balance of power.[47] Behind this common ground, we can detect evidence of a profound shift in British liberal internationalism from the late nineteenth century to the inter-war years. As Chapter 1 showed, British liberal internationalism's focus gradually changed from moral arguments to institutional ones, a trend that became accelerated after the beginning of the war.[48] Placing the Bryce Group's debates in the context of this shift enables us to understand a key intellectual background that shaped the development of the war-time ideas about a peaceful organisation, including that of collective security. According to the Bryce Group's institutional approach to international reform, the old system driven by the balance-of-power politics had caused the war and had endorsed the view that 'the best way to maintain peace was to prepare war'. Such a view triggered arms races, a sharp division between alliance blocs and, in the end, large-scale wars.[49] Although the members' initial visions of the post-war order ranged from informal agreements among the powers to a world federation, they were unanimous in agreeing that 'the organization of Europe on the basis of two opposing groups [military alliances] should come to an end'.[50] Unless a new blueprint for an international order was devised by the end of the war, the balance of power would only be restored and cause great wars again.[51]

To provide an alternative to the old European system, the Bryce Group proposed four interrelated war-prevention measures that would be central to the workings of a league of nations organisation: the judicial settlement of international disputes, the formation of a so-called Council of Conciliation, a moratorium on hostilities and ultimately, collective security. Underlying these four measures was the tacit assumption, explored below, that the force of public opinion against aggression would also serve to maintain the world order. These four main measures appeared in the first version of the Bryce Group's *Proposals for the Avoidance of War*, composed for private circulation in February 1915. While it went through revisions leading up to the publication of the *Proposals* in 1917, these main points remained on their agenda

---

[47] Sylvest, *British Liberal Internationalism*, pp. 198–99, 268–70.   [48] Ibid. See Chapter 1.
[49] 'Mr. Ponsonby and the War', 7 October 1914, PP, MS. Eng. Hist. c.661, 60–66, BLO; Ponsonby to Donaldson, 10 August 1914, PP, MS. Eng. Hist. c.660, 106–12, BLO.
[50] 'Mr. Graham Wallas's Note', WHP, MS. Eng. Hist. c.402, BLO.
[51] Lowes Dickinson, 'The Way Out'; Lowes Dickinson to Bryce, 20 October 1914, JBP, MS. Bryce 58, 14–17, BLO.

throughout the war. Members of a future league would also commit themselves to all four measures.

In terms of a judicial settlement of disputes, the *Proposals* of February 1915 stated that the signatory powers would agree to submit disputes to the existing Hague Tribunal.[52] Further, the *Proposals* introduced the idea of creating a Council of Conciliation with a view to considering suggestions about the settlement of disputes, including settlement of non-justiciable disputes that could not be settled by diplomatic means.[53] The third measure, a moratorium on hostilities in the midst of a crisis on the verge of war, was called a 'cooling off period'.[54] The *Proposals* suggested that signatory states should not resort to hostilities in advance of submission of cases to arbitration or the council or within six months after the publication of the council's report.[55] Finally, the fourth measure, collective security, was stipulated in articles 18–19 of the *Proposals* of February 1915:

18. All the signatory Powers to undertake that in case any signatory Power resorts to hostilities against another signatory Power, without first having submitted its case to an arbitral tribunal, or to the Council of Conciliation, or before the expiration of the prescribed period of delay, they will support the Power so attacked by such concerted measures, diplomatic, economic or forcible, as, in the judgement of the majority of them, are most effective and appropriate to the circumstances of the case.

19. The signatory Powers to undertake that if any Power shall fail to accept and give effect to the recommendations contained in any report of the Council, they will consider, in concert, the situation which has arisen by reason of such failure, and what collective action, if any, it is practicable to take in order to make such recommendations operative.[56]

The Bryce Group's *Proposals* thus introduced collective security, a new system to maintain peace. Although it was one of the four measures to prevent war and would only be considered after exhausting the other three measures, this idea provoked vigorous debates within the group about whether collective action should include the use of force.

[52] 'Lord Bryce's Notes "When the War Comes to an End"', WHP, MS. Eng. Hist. c.402, BLO.
[53] The members of the Council of Conciliation were to be appointed by the signatory Powers for a fixed term of years. The Bryce Group's *Proposals* indicated that the function of the Council would be similar to the diplomatic representative of the powers but 'should enable its members to take a more international view'. The group also suggested that the great powers 'might be given a greater representation' since they 'would have a larger number of men qualified to be a members'. *Proposals for the Avoidance of War*, Cannan Papers, 970, BLPES.
[54] Dubin, 'Toward the Concept of Collective Security', pp. 291–92.
[55] *Proposals for the Avoidance of War*, Cannan Papers, 970, BLPES.   [56] Ibid.

'Realistic' Opinions about Forcible Action: Force As Necessity

The Quaker lawyer Richard Cross first raised the issue of collective security at a meeting of the Bryce Group in November 1914.[57] Post-war Europe, he said, should respect the Christian ideal of brotherhood and international law. Cross argued that 'the powers should bind themselves to assist each other in repelling any attack by powers not party to the [league]'.[58] Lowes Dickinson also endorsed the necessity of force, claiming that there was 'no other way of guaranteeing the reference to conciliation'; if 'there is no threat of force behind the agreement, and States retain their armaments (which I am supposing) the temptation of a State to take the law into its own hands when the situation seems favourable might be irresistible'.[59] Having agreed with Lowes Dickinson, John A. Hobson, who aspired to a world federation, argued that an effective organisation required military sanctions.[60] Insisting that international society needed a police force just as any society did, he denied a doctrine that supposed economic sanctions to be 'more moral' than military coercion.[61] He also presumed that an international organisation with a centralised force would reduce illegitimate force.[62] In varying degrees, most of the Bryce Group members agreed to adopt collective security on these terms – the use of military sanctions to prevent war.

On the assumption that the 'council has been created' and 'the principal Powers have agreed to submit to it all non-justiciable disputes which they have not been able to settle by diplomatic means', Lowes Dickinson presented three main cases in which the adoption of forcible collective security could be justified.[63] In the first case, he suggested, if some states took or threatened military action before submitting a matter to conciliation, all the other signatory states had the duty to 'intervene by the threat of force to coerce the offender'.[64] The second case he cited was when a

---

[57] 'Notes on Lord Bryce's Memorandum by Richard Cross', 27 November 1914, WHP, MS. Eng. Hist. c.402, BLO.

[58] E. Richard Cross, 'The New Year and the New Europe', 3 January 1915, in Wilkinson, *Richard Cross*, pp. 227–30; 'Notes on Lord Bryce's Memorandum by Richard Cross', 27 November 1914, WHP, MS. Eng. Hist. c.402, BLO.

[59] 'Mr. Lowes Dickinson's Notes', WHP, MS. Eng. Hist. c.402, BLO.

[60] Robbins, *The Abolition of War*, p. 131; Winkler, *League of Nations Movement*, pp. 144–45; Long, 'Hobson and Idealism', pp. 288, 294; Sylvest, 'Continuity and Change', pp. 281–82.

[61] Winkler, *League of Nations Movement*, pp. 144–45.

[62] Long, 'Hobson and Idealism', p. 295.

[63] 'Mr. Lowes Dickinson's Notes', WHP, MS. Eng. Hist. c.402, BLO.   [64] Ibid.

dispute was referred to the Council of Conciliation and its suggestion was unacceptable to some or all of the parties. If all the parties were small powers, if they refused the suggestion and if their dispute did not involve the interests of great powers, diplomatic pressure with the threat of force would be put on all parties after consultation among the powers.[65] In the same circumstance, but where the great powers were involved, the threat of force would still be posed. This threat could trigger a war but should limit it to the immediately interested parties.[66] If, as in the third case, one or more parties accepted the suggestion but the others rejected it and resorted to military action, the signatory states were obliged to protect the accepting states against aggressive action by the rejecting states.[67] Having reviewed these potential cases in the context of the actual situation at the outbreak of the Great War, Lowes Dickinson concluded that there should have been no war or that at least the war could have been confined to some powers, had their scheme been applied.[68]

From what IR scholars have traditionally called the realistic viewpoint, the Bryce Group thus promoted the use of force, or the possibility of the use of force, to maintain peace. Indeed, the group members judged that force would be necessary for a post-war league to be an effective and realistic organisation. Although in their scheme collective security should only be implemented after exhausting the other options such as a judicial settlement, it was an essential part of their war-prevention scheme, because otherwise, as Bryce put it, 'the whole thing will seem pointless and ineffective'.[69]

'Idealistic' Views about Forcible Action: The Criticism of the Use of Force

Arthur Ponsonby strongly opposed forcible action to promote peace.[70] He underlined three interrelated problems of the use of force: the impracticability of military sanctions, the danger of triggering larger wars and the potential damage to morality in international relations. Even though his objection to collective security might seem idealistic from conventional IR perspectives, what is striking about Ponsonby's objections is how grounded and pragmatic – one might say realistic – they were.

---

[65] Ibid.   [66] Ibid.   [67] Ibid.   [68] Ibid.
[69] 'Lord Bryce Memorandum on Mr. J. A. Hobson's Notes', WHP, MS. Eng. Hist. c.402, BLO.
[70] Ponsonby's Diary, 15–16 December 1914.

First, even though, according to the group's scheme, forcible action should be undertaken only after other attempts at a peaceful settlement had failed, Ponsonby highlighted that 'questions that are capable of settlement by arbitration are not the most critical or dangerous'.[71] Disputes that were incapable of settlement by arbitration would likely include not only the vital concerns of powers but also serious political differences, contributing to 'spreading and intensifying the causes of quarrel'.[72]

By presenting some examples, as Lowes Dickinson did, Ponsonby criticised the impracticability of military sanctions. He illustrated that if a dispute were so acute as to induce one of the parties involved to begin hostile preparations immediately, the obedient parties then 'would receive not obligatory, but spontaneous support from other powers'.[73] Where both parties were making immediate preparations and beginning war before a cooling-off period, non-intervention would be the only solution for the limitation of war. As we will see, this argument was a compelling one against military action to prevent another world war in the future. Further, following the claim of the eighteenth-century international lawyer Emmerich de Vattel, Ponsonby noted that both sides in a conflict would allege that they had acted rightly in the event of war:[74]

The nation responsible for the breach does not necessarily act from dishonourable and aggressive motives, but often because it believes that the national danger arising from the strict observance may out-balance the evil involved in the violation of an international agreement.[75]

Ponsonby therefore affirmed that unless the involved states' purposes or circumstances were considered on a case-by-case basis, obligatory collective sanctions might be disadvantageous to the maintenance of future peace.

Second, Ponsonby warned that compulsory forcible action could preserve the old balance of power and trigger great wars. In his view, military sanctions meant 'preserving peace by war', which would 'destroy the

---

[71] 'Mr. Ponsonby's Notes', WHP, MS. Eng. Hist. c.402, BLO.   [72] Ibid.

[73] 'Mr. Ponsonby's Note', 10 December 1914, WHP, MS. Eng. Hist. c.402, BLO.

[74] As Chapter 1 has discussed, Vattel argued that the reasoning of justifiable war would be impractical because in international society no authority could judge which side was to be blamed, and both sides would claim their own side was right. See also, Michael Howard, *The Invention of Peace: Reflections on War and International Order* (Profile Books, 2000), p. 25; Emer de Vattel, *The Law of Nations: Or, Principles of the Law of Nature, Applied to the Conduct and Affairs of Nations and Sovereigns*, Joseph Chitty (ed.) (Cambridge University Press, 2011), pp. 304–5.

[75] 'Mr. Ponsonby's Notes', WHP, MS. Eng. Hist. c.402, BLO.

possibility of impartial deliberation' about each dispute. Having indicated that the Council could not always be unanimous, he pronounced that collective force would lead to 'a break-up of the Council [of the League], a majority and minority, a grouping of powers, the formation of alliances, and all the old evils perpetuated'.[76] Compulsory military action, he concluded, would thus create 'a new method of making all wars European wars' that would forever prevent universal disarmament – a major issue on the league's action agenda.[77]

Third, Ponsonby presupposed that force was the antithesis of morality, which would undermine the moral foundations of international law.[78] He maintained that the absence of a supreme executive international authority was a prime cause of war and that the threat of collective force might inhibit the condition of anarchy from triggering wars. However, he also stressed that morality should be, and must be, the basis of international relations:

The observance of general precepts of international law as well as of particular agreements between sovereign states besides being the general rule ... has been all the stronger and more durable from the fact that it is backed by permanent moral authority and not by shifting physical force.[79]

Ponsonby asserted that forcible action would not only be a step backwards for future peace but would also mean the destruction of the moral authority of the new international order.[80] In other words, he distinguished between a negative peace enforced by the threat of force and a positive peace based on moral authority.[81] His rejection of forcible action and his plea for international morality therefore cannot be cited as substantial evidence for his idealistic standpoint, as conventionally defined by IR scholars. A closer look at Ponsonby's argument reveals that his objection instead reflected what his colleagues would have deemed realistic perspectives on the intricate relationship of politics, war and morality in the international order.

---

[76] 'Mr. Ponsonby's Notes', 10 December 1914, WHP, MS. Eng. Hist. c.402, BLO.
[77] Ibid.
[78] Ibid.; Aneurin Williams, *A New Basis of International Peace* (Watts & Co., 1915), 5, E(I) 33.
[79] 'Mr. Ponsonby's Notes', 10 December 1914, WHP, MS. Eng. Hist. c.402, BLO.
[80] Ibid.
[81] The concepts of negative and positive peace were first introduced by Johan Galtung, who defined them as 'negative peace which is the absence of violence, absence of war – and positive peace which is the integration of human society'. 'An Editorial', *Journal of Peace Research*, vol. 1, no. 1 (March 1964), pp. 1–4. See also Paul Williams, *Security Studies: An Introduction* (Taylor and Francis, 2012), pp. 83, 395.

Mutual Understanding between 'Realistic' and 'Idealistic' Views

The conflicting views within the Bryce Group about forcible action might seem irreconcilable. They were not; manuscript letters and notes of the group members reveal that both sides acknowledged the validity of the other's logic and the weakness of their own positions. As we have seen above, they shared similar intellectual backgrounds as British liberal internationalists, and their arguments were neither purely idealistic nor realistic. Hence, their disagreements arose between different priorities in their war-prevention scheme.[82]

In their meetings, Ponsonby's objection to the use of force aroused the other members' sympathy, although his view was not incorporated in their *Proposals*. After reading Ponsonby's note, for example, Bryce wrote to him that it was 'very weighty – the strongest argument I have seen against the Force plan and personally I agree with most of it, and see little or no chance that the Powers will adopt such scheme [with forcible action], and not very much chance that they could be relied on to work it if adopted'.[83] In addition, it is evident that Lowes Dickinson, like Ponsonby, also regarded morality – a fundamental principle of liberal internationalism – as one of the most critical and effective aspects that the new system should rely on, although he thought it could emerge after the creation of the league and indeed through strenuous efforts to establish it.[84] Lowes Dickinson indicated that 'if the Council of Conciliation succeeded in establishing a real moral authority its recommendations might be received in a friendly spirit and perhaps acted upon'; this would in turn lead the states to respect and be subject to the council's suggestions.[85] Even though the Bryce Group decided to include military sanctions in order to keep the scheme effective, other group members in addition to Ponsonby agreed that forcible action was potentially dangerous to the whole scheme of the league as well as to morality in international relations.

Meanwhile, despite his strong objection, Ponsonby could not altogether deny that the threat of force or forcible action might be required as a last resort. Although Ponsonby may be remembered as a pacifist and indeed 'seemed close to pacifism', as Ceadel has put it,[86] he

---

[82] Sylvest, *British Liberal Internationalism*, pp. 3–4, 11; Sylvest, 'Continuity and Change', pp. 268.

[83] Bryce to Ponsonby, 14 December 1914, PP, MS. Eng. Hist. c.661, 190–91, BLO.

[84] 'Mr. Lowes Dickinson's Notes', WHP, MS. Eng. Hist. c.402, BLO.   [85] Ibid.

[86] Raymond A. Jones, *Arthur Ponsonby: The Politics of Life* (Bromley, 1989), p. 2; Robbins, *The Abolition of War*, p. 203; Ceadel, *Semi-Detached Idealists*, pp. 268–69.

did not fully commit to pacifism until the 1920s, and neither did he unconditionally reject the use of force during the Great War.[87] What he objected to was 'compulsory' forcible action and its stipulation in the scheme:

A flagrant breach of the international regulations laid down by the [League] Council or deliberate disobedience to the decisions of the Council might very well be so provocative in character as to lead naturally to combined military action on the part of the majority of the powers which were in agreement. The fear of this possibility is deterrent enough without the definite stipulation that such force should and must be used in certain circumstances.[88]

In mentioning the case of a rule-breaking state, Ponsonby thus raised the possibility of joint military action. Like Bryce and Lowes Dickinson, he saw that the use of international force to maintain peace could and indeed should be spontaneously generated if the threat was imminent and the aggressor provocative enough.[89]

After the outbreak of the war, the emphasis of liberal internationalists gradually shifted from the force of morality to the importance of institutional frameworks for creating the conditions for peace among nations.[90] Despite its sympathies for the value of morality in international relations, the Bryce Group's *Proposals* downplayed it and highlighted collective security, thus reflecting the larger transition in liberal internationalist thinking. This trend helps to explain why even Ponsonby, who resisted war and the codification of forcible action, was never oblivious to the fact that international stability would require the threat of collective force as a potential deterrent. While the group members attached significance to morality, they, as IR scholars have traditionally done, judged it to be too utopian, too idealistic, to be incorporated in the *Proposals*. They calculated that an international organisation required what they thought of as realistic measures such as force to enforce peace, which would reveal their shared expectations of being realistic about a possible peaceful organisation.

A 'Realistic' Plan for a Peace Organisation

The Bryce Group drafted their *Proposals* for the creation of a league based on two other – what they deemed realistic – points of view in addition to

[87] Ponsonby changed his mind in the 1910s–1920s and was intellectually inconsistent. See Ccadel, *Semi-Detached Idealists*, pp. 268–69.
[88] 'Mr. Ponsonby's Notes', 10 December 1914, PP, MS. Eng. hist. c.402, BLO.
[89] Jones, *Arthur Ponsonby*, p. 2.
[90] See Chapter 1; Sylvest, *British Liberal Internationalism*, pp. 50–51, 198–99.

forcible action: they generally realised that war could not completely be abolished and that the reality of international relations would require a post-war scheme that could be implemented without stirring up significant opposition. These views were influenced by Bryce's direction that the post-war proposal must not be radical, which was probably formulated through communication with politicians and his experience as an ambassador to the United States.[91] In addition, in 1914 and 1915, anti-German riots erupted in London, and those who called for peace, including the Union of Democratic Control, became the targets of mob attacks.[92] To evade being tarnished by any hints of pacifism or an anti-war campaign, Bryce directed group members to adopt a limited plan and to deny any possibilities of promoting a world federation.

The group's aim was not so much to eradicate war as to reduce the risk of war and limit its scale. This is why one of the possible titles that the group considered for the 1915 proposal was *Proposals for Reducing the Number of Future Wars*.[93] War could not be abolished unless a world state was founded, effective control over foreign policy was achieved by a sufficiently educated public opinion and other war-prevention measures. Given their recognition that war would break out in the future despite all their proposed devices against it, the Bryce Group's post-war scheme sought to introduce a system for preventing war from spreading beyond immediately interested parties. Lowes Dickinson, after acknowledging the possibility that war might occur, proclaimed that under their proposed scheme the involved parties or area could be limited.[94] Subject to the agreement not to resort to war or to help the involved parties in the event of war, other states were not supposed to join or assist the warring states. Meanwhile, as mentioned above, limiting war to a smaller scale was also one of the reasons why Ponsonby rejected forcible action. He argued that non-intervention would 'have the effect of confining hostilities to two disputants', whereas military sanctions would involve many

---

[91] See Chapter 3.

[92] Ibid.; Ponsonby's Diary, 14 May 1915; Kate Courtney, *Extracts from a Diary during the War* (Victor Press, 1927), pp. 36–37; Charles Trevelyan to Ponsonby, 24 July 1915, PP, MS. Eng. Hist. c.662, BLO. Regarding the Union of Democratic Control, see 'Mr. Ponsonby Hustled', *The Times*, 22 July 1915, p. 6; 'More German Darlings', *The Times*, 23 July 1915, p. 9; G. Murray to Ponsonby, 22 July 1915, PP, MS. Eng. Hist. c.662, 139, BLO; Ponsonby's Diary, 23 and 28 July 1915; C. Trevelyan to Ponsonby, 24 July 1915, PP, MS. Eng. Hist. c.662, 152–55, BLO; A. Williams to Ponsonby, 24 July 1915, PP, MS. Eng. Hist. c.662, 156, BLO.

[93] *Proposals for Reducing the Number of Future Wars, with a Prefatory Note by Viscount Bryce, As Revised up to 24 February 1915*, WHP, MS. Eng. Hist. c.402, BLO.

[94] 'Mr. Lowes Dickinson's Notes', WHP, MS. Eng. Hist. c.402, BLO; *Proposals for the Avoidance of War*, Cannan Papers, 970, BLPES.

parties without immediate interests and lead to a large-scale war.[95] In either argument, the point was to disrupt the process of escalation in order to prevent another Great War.

Further, the group deemed that the implementation of its post-war plan depended on statesmen and the public recognising the value and the attainability of their proposal. If the group's plan was viewed as pragmatic, particularly from the statesmen's perspectives, it would raise the prospect of their considering it. In their debates about military action, for instance, group members were conscious of obstacles to enforcing collective sanctions on states, especially great powers. As Ponsonby suggested, the league to enforce concerted action might even fail to obtain general consent for preliminary diplomatic cooperation.[96] Whereas Lowes Dickinson also recognised the difficulty of binding powers to compulsory military sanctions, Bryce went as far as to say that any scheme involving the obligation of armed coercion would be impossible, or at least highly unlikely, for governments to adopt.[97] Although the Bryce Group agreed on the necessity of military sanctions, they were concerned that the obligation to participate in collective military action might be unacceptable to governments and therefore wreck the whole idea of a league of nations.

To tackle this problem, the group stressed that their proposed league as a whole should not deviate far from the existing international system of sovereign states even as it proposed radical reforms. The *Proposals* declared in its introduction as follows:

> It is clear that the reforms to be introduced must be drastic if they are to be effective. For, as John Stuart Mill has said: 'Small remedies for great evils do not produce small effects. They produce no effects.' On the other hand, there must be continuity; for proposals involving too violent a breach with the established order are not likely to be seriously considered. What is attempted here is to put forward a scheme which, while it involves a real and radical advance upon the present organization of international relations, yet does not break so violently with the course of historical development as to be fairly described as Utopian.[98]

To prevent another war and also for the *Proposals* to be adopted by decision-makers, small remedies were insufficient, but a degree of continuity would be crucial.

[95] 'Mr. Ponsonby's Notes', 10 December 1914, WHP, MS. Eng. Hist. c.402, BLO.
[96] Ibid.
[97] 'Mr. Lowes Dickinson's Notes' and 'Lord Bryce Memorandum on Mr. Hobson's Notes', January 1915, WHP, MS. Eng. Hist. c.402, BLO; Bryce to Ponsonby, 14 December 1914, PP, MS. Eng. Hist. c.661, BLO.
[98] *Proposals for the Avoidance of War*, Cannan Papers, 970, BLPES.

Yet, in reality, 'a real and radical advance' of the existing international order was hard to achieve unless one advocated world government or, as Lenin and his followers would do, the withering away of the state through workers' revolutions. Even though the Bryce Group underlined the difference of its plan from the old international system, its war-prevention plan was fundamentally an evolutionary – not revolutionary – improvement.[99] The group members, for example, had called for utilising the existing Hague court since November 1914 when Bryce had suggested that signatory states should refer to the Hague for the settlement of disputes.[100] They advocated strengthening the Hague court rather than inventing a new one.[101]

Indeed, the group members recognised the difficulties of pursuing an evolutionary approach to reforming international politics. They predicted that the war itself would leave a lasting legacy of antagonism between the victors and the vanquished. The divide would mirror the pre-war competitive system of great powers alliances that they identified as a cause of war. Hence, in the long run, it was crucial to unify the great powers into one group, not two, around a new system of collective security. Lowes Dickinson, for instance, in his letter to the economist Edwin Cannan of the London School of Economics, described the idea of overcoming the divide between winners and losers using a 'snow-ball' analogy:

[The snow-ball] might so easily never 'roll up', but remain two opposing snowballs, as before this war. I should think it more hopeful to make your big snowball now at once. If Germany came in (you seem to think she might) I see no difficulty about any other power.[102]

As the group's *Proposals* asserted, its planned scheme was 'not a league of some States against others, but a union of as many as possible in their common interests'.[103] If the league did not have universal membership, the danger was that international politics would evolve again into armed alliances vying for a balance of power. In the hope of overcoming post-war divisions, they anticipated that one powerful league of great powers would gradually develop into a universal organisation. Such expectations

[99] Ibid.
[100] 'Lord Bryce's Notes, "When the War Comes to an End"', WHP, MS. Eng. Hist. c.402, BLO; 'Lord Bryce's Memorandum with E. Richard Cross's Notes and the Revisions Made up to Jan. 19th, 1915 by the Group in Conference', Wallas Papers 4/5, BLPES.
[101] 'Mr. Lowes Dickinson's Notes', 'Mr. Graham Wallas's Notes' and 'Memorandum by Mr. Graham Wallas', 8 February, 1915, WHP, MS. Eng. Hist. c.402, BLO.
[102] Lowes Dickinson to E. Cannan, 26 March 1915, Cannan Papers, 970, BLPES.
[103] Ibid.

of the group, stemming from liberal internationalists' belief about the progress of international society, are discussed below.

'Idealistic' Expectations: Peaceful Public Opinion As a War-Prevention Measure

The Bryce Group's war-prevention scheme was not devised by realistic calculations alone, as historians and IR scholars have tended to suggest.[104] While the group's post-war plan depended on what scholars and group members considered realistic viewpoints, what they would label idealistic ones also inspired them. An idealistic part of their post-war vision was encapsulated by their fifth, 'unwritten' measure to prevent war: public opinion. Although *Proposals* did not specify public opinion as a war-prevention device, it played a pivotal role in the group's thinking about a peaceful international order.[105] In the tradition of Enlightenment thinkers such as Montesquieu, Rousseau and Kant, the group attributed past wars to the aggressive ambitions of the dynasties and aristocratic elites that had dominated European governments. These ruling elites had manipulated popular opinion to their own ends. If freed to determine their own choices, ordinary people would shun the dreadful costs of war and opt for peace.[106] Thus, according to the Bryce Group and liberal internationalists in general, if popular opinion could be liberated from the sway of governments and mobilised for peace, it would serve as a powerful war-prevention mechanism.[107] Hobson, especially in the pre-war years, tended to believe that the public was peaceful in nature[108] and

---

[104] See n. 7.

[105] The fact that Bryce, who agitated public opinion with the Bryce Report of May 1915, which proclaimed German war outrages during the invasion of Belgium, argued for the maintenance of peace by public opinion, might seem contradictory. See Trevor Wilson, 'Lord Bryce's Investigation into Alleged German Atrocities in Belgium, 1914–15', *Journal of Contemporary History*, vol. 14, no. 3 (July 1979), pp. 369–83; Nicoletta F. Gullace, 'Sexual Violence and Family Honor: British Propaganda and International Law during the First World War', *American Historical Review*, vol. 102, no. 3 (July 1997), pp. 714–47. However, the Bryce Group and war-time pro-League activists regarded the Allies' victory as the premise of the creation of a new peaceful order; victory, they assumed, required public support for the war. Hence, in their theory, agitating the public for supporting the war and arguing the public's role in world peace hardly contradicted each other.

[106] See Chapter 1.

[107] Michael Howard, *War and the Liberal Conscience* (Oxford University Press, 2008), pp. 13–15; Immanuel Kant, *Perpetual Peace: A Philosophical Essay, 1795* (Swan Sonnenschein, 1903), pp. 122–23. Also see Immanuel Kant, *Perpetual Peace, and Other Essays on Politics, History, and Morals*, Ted Humphrey (trans.) (Hackett Pub. Co, 1983), pp. 112–13.

[108] Long, 'Hobson and Idealism', pp. 288, 292.

that the harmonies of interest between people were 'simply waiting to surface'.[109] If popular governments were established, people would not become enemies and neither would they support war.[110] As Ponsonby put it:

The exclusive management of international relations rests in the hands of a small number of men in each country, whose perspective is restricted, whose vision is narrow, and whose sense of proportion is vitiated by the very fact that their work is screened from the public eye. The people, whose greatest interest is peace, would be able to take a broader view on main principles, and their influence, were they in a position to exercise it, would, undoubtedly, be pacific.[111]

While the Bryce Group proposed some specific measures to maintain peace, such as a judicial settlement and the Council of Conciliation, it saw public opinion as an effective remedy for future war.[112]

Yet at the same time, group members were conscious that public opinion at the time was unprepared to serve this role or even to discuss possible peace terms of the ongoing war, due to jingoism and war-time propaganda.[113] Hobson acknowledged that the progress of international morality still needed help.[114] Even Ponsonby, who called for war prevention through morality, not force, observed that 'the binding force of moral obligation may be insufficient at present owing to the comparatively low standard of international morality'.[115] The group members, therefore, regarded the education of public opinion as indispensable for future peace. Lowes Dickinson stated that their league plan relied heavily on public opinion's expected role in war prevention: 'Without pretending that public opinion is always and everywhere pacific, we believe that, when properly instructed, it is more likely to favour peace than do the secret operations of diplomacy.'[116] According to the group, the post-war order had to be founded on an educated Europe where the people were

---

[109] Robbins, *Abolition of War*, p. 24. The impact of pre-war idealist thinking on J. A. Hobson and other liberal internationalists is also discussed in Michael Freeden (ed.), *Reappraising J. A. Hobson: Humanism and Welfare* (Routledge, 2009); Colin Tyler, *Common Good Politics: British Idealism and Justice in the Contemporary World* (Palgrave Macmillan, 2017), pp. 131–71.

[110] Robbins, *Abolition of War*, p. 24.

[111] '"Parliament and Foreign Policy" by Arthur Ponsonby', Union of Democratic Control pamphlet no. 5, MOREL/F13/6, BLPES.

[112] About what the group members meant by public opinion, see Chapter 3.

[113] See Chapter 1; Lowes Dickinson to Bryce, 20 October 1914, JBP, MS. Bryce 58, 14, BLO; 'Mr. Ponsonby's Notes', WHP, MS. Eng. Hist. c.402, BLO.

[114] Howard, *War and the Liberal Conscience*, 74; Sylvest, 'Continuity and Change', pp. 281–82.

[115] 'Mr. Ponsonby's Notes', WHP, MS. Eng. Hist. c.402, BLO.

[116] *Proposals for the Avoidance of War*, Cannan Papers, 970, BLPES.

sufficiently instructed so that public opinion could prevent war.[117] In short, the group's *Proposals* rested on three assumptions about public opinion's role in preventing war: people were essentially peaceful, the public could be educated about international relations in the way and with the results that the group imagined; and, finally, if was adequately informed, instructed and mobilised, popular opinion would suffice to prevent future wars. A passage by Bryce in the *Proposals* in 1915 summarised such ideas and thus deserves a long quotation:

The only effective and permanent remedy [for future wars] would be to convince the several peoples of the world that they have far more to lose than to gain from strife, and to replace by a sentiment of mutual international goodwill the violent national antagonisms that now exist. But this, we may well fear, would be a slow process. Meantime that which may be done, and which it seems possible to do at once, is to provide [a] machinery by and through which that great body of international public opinion which favours peace may express itself, and bring its power to bear upon the governments of those nations in which there may, from time to time, exist a spirit of aggression, or a readiness to embark on war in pursuit of selfish interests or at the bidding of national pride. The public opinion of the world would surely prove to possess a greater force than it has yet [shown] if it could but find an effective organ through which to act.[118]

Bryce suggested that a league be established as a first step, which would allow time for public opinion to be sufficiently educated to express its peaceful views and thus prevent wars.

Group members hoped that public opinion would play its role during a moratorium on hostilities – the cooling-off period – after the submission of a case to the Council of Conciliation and before the implementation of collective security. The group believed that a moratorium would give decision-makers and the public time to calmly reflect on the costs versus benefits of what was at stake and the danger of the war at hand; it would also give intellectuals and opinion-makers like the group members time to influence the 'public opinion of the world in favour of peace'.[119] This assumption also implied that public opinion, as an unwritten measure of war prevention in their *Proposals*, might serve to prevent the actual implementation of collective military action. In other words, if public opinion opposed war during a cooling-off period and succeeded in stopping war, war-prevention measures would not reach the next stage of collective security, which could only be implemented after exhausting the other three measures.

---

[117] See Chapter 1; Cross, 'The New Year and the New Europe', 3 January 1915, in Wilkinson, *Richard Cross*, pp. 22, 228–29; Ponsonby, 'Parliament and Foreign Policy'.

[118] *Proposals for the Avoidance of War*, Cannan Papers, 970, BLPES.   [119] Ibid.

As mentioned above, the Bryce Group maintained that collective security would pose the potential danger of escalating war and that the great powers might disagree about military sanctions. Therefore, if war could be prevented before the implementation of collective sanctions, that would be more secure and reliable than commencing military action. In fact, such an assumption was founded upon liberal internationalists' belief about progress: public opinion would gradually develop and become a strong measure to prevent war. Although the league would initially require collective force, it would, once international morality was developed, evolve into the organisation that fundamentally relied upon the force of public opinion, thereby making the threat of collective action less and less crucial in the future war prevention mechanism. Of course, the Bryce Group understood that educating public opinion would require time and that the force of public opinion alone could not avoid war. Hence, the group included collective security in their *Proposals*, but only as a last resort. The group's discussions of public opinion thus combined what IR scholars as well as members themselves called realistic views on the contemporary international affairs with what they might say was an idealistic anticipation of the progress of international morality, which constituted a vital part of their war-prevention plan.

Yet, the Bryce Group members were disappointed by the public's jingoistic reaction to the outbreak of the war. Even prior to this, they were aware of the less pacific public reactions to the Boer War[120] and the possibility of the public becoming 'the tyranny of the majority'.[121] Why, then, did they still presume the moral progress of the public in the future? It was because the war-time liberal internationalists, including the Bryce Group members, were in the middle of the transition from moral arguments to institutional ones and maintained both perspectives. While the group members were disillusioned about the rationality of human beings, they still supposed the public, if appropriately informed, would in future be able to prevent war.[122] Perhaps, as Lowe Dickinson put it, they considered that even though public opinion was fallible, 'one does have a chance of enlightening opinion, but one has none of

---

[120] Jacqueline Beaumont Hughes, 'The Press and the Public during the Boer War, 1899–1902', *Historian*, vol. 61 (Spring 1999), pp. 10–15; Mark Hampton, 'The Press, Patriotism, and Public Discussion: C. P. Scott, the Manchester Guardian, and the Boer War, 1899–1902', *Historical Journal*, vol. 44, no. 1 (2001), pp. 177–97; Long, 'Hobson and Idealism', pp. 285–304; John A. Hobson, *The Psychology of Jingoism* (Grant Richards, 1901).

[121] John Stuart Mill, *On Liberty* (London, 1864); John Stuart Mill, *J. S. Mill: 'On Liberty' and Other Writings*, Stefan Collini (ed.) (Cambridge University Press, 1989).

[122] Sylvest, 'Continuity and Change', pp. 281–82.

enlightening foreign office officials and militarists and diplomats'.[123] Lowe Dickinson remained a believer in the moral internationalists' argument and envisaged the post-war order resting on the moral progress of humanity.[124] To the Bryce Group, the creation of an international organisation could not only solve the problem of anarchy but also offer the public the help required for moral progress.[125]

Indeed, the Bryce Group's assumption of the future evolution of an international organisation was founded on its belief in progress – moral, social and political.[126] Group members assumed that once a league was established, it would evolve over time into a better organisation, however imperfect it was at the time of its formation. Stressing institutional arguments rather than moral ones, they still considered the moral and rational progress of humanity as a core element of preventing future war. Lowes Dickinson observed that the interplay of moral and institutional elements would be able to enforce a liberal international order after the war,[127] even though the process of educating the public would be slow and gradual. Bryce Group members were conscious of obstacles to educating the public, promoting moral progress and uniting the world under an international organisation. Nevertheless, they did not, or could not, offer an antidote to these obstacles, striving to maintain a balance between their realistic calculations and their idealistic expectations. While the primary focus of the group, based on liberal internationalists' arguments, was shifting from moral elements to institutional ones, their intellectual scope remained firmly embedded within the framework of these two.

Conclusion

A closer look into the Bryce Group in 1914–1915 has shown that neither realism nor idealism alone generated its ideas about war prevention that later crystallised in the League of Nations. The rich manuscript records of the group have confirmed that IR scholars are right to question the notion that their discipline was founded in the first great debate between idealists and realists. Whereas the group's post-war proposal aimed to be moderate and realistic, as scholars have indicated, it was also firmly

---

[123] Lowes Dickinson to E. Cannan, 11 September 1914, Cannan Papers, 1022, BLPES.
[124] Stuart Wallace, *War and the Image of Germany: British Academics, 1914–1918* (Donald, 1988), p. 115.
[125] Sylvest, 'Continuity and Change', pp. 281–82.
[126] Sylvest, *British Liberal Internationalism*, pp. 3–4, 11, 26, 139, 197.
[127] Sylvest, 'Continuity and Change', p. 281.

underpinned by its idealistic views on public opinion and on the future development of the league of nations. The group's ideas about preventing future war ranged from what scholars and the group members regarded as idealistic devices, such as the force of world public opinion against war to deter aggression, to what the group considered realistic measures, such as collective military force against an aggressor state. In the group's debates, realistic ideas and idealistic ones could hardly be separated; the members – not pure realists or idealists but a mix of both – attempted to strike a balance between views.

As a war-prevention measure, the group considered collective security to be a last resort to be implemented after exhausting all other closely connected measures: a judicial settlement, the Council of Conciliation, a moratorium on hostilities and ultimately, the force of public opinion. While agreeing on this general framework, the group was sharply divided over the question of whether collective security with military sanctions should be incorporated into the future league of nations. Some, including Bryce and Lowes Dickinson, advocated the necessity of force to deter aggressive action and to make their scheme effective, while others, such as Ponsonby, criticised it for its impracticability, its danger of triggering even larger wars and the damage the use of collective force would do to international law and morality. From a realistic point of view, the group members appreciated that war could not be abolished and that their plan needed to be achievable from the diplomats' points of view. Meanwhile, from an idealistic perspective, they assumed that public opinion could eventually serve as an underlying mechanism for preventing war. Analysis of their arguments reveals that realistic and idealistic viewpoints rested on each other and that these views were not regarded as *opposing* but instead *inseparable*, illustrating how hard it was to clearly specify what was idealistic and realistic in practice.

Although the Bryce Group members understood the problems of their *Proposals*, they anticipated that the league would gradually evolve into a better organisation that would chiefly rely on the force of public opinion instead of collective action. This belief was built by the shift in liberal internationalists' position, to which the Bryce Group intellectually subscribed. The focus of British liberal internationalists' arguments was changing from moral arguments to institutional ones, and the Bryce Group was in the midst of this larger transition. From both moral and institutional perspectives, the group envisaged a new peaceful order and sought to change international norms of behaviour by a mix of measures, including the use of force at least for a time. Like those of the inter-war 'utopians', the Bryce Group's early debates about war prevention were subtle and could hardly be described by any single existing category.

The members of the Bryce Group in fact realised the deficiencies of both realistic and idealistic measures against war and the perceived ambiguities of their mixtures. Nonetheless, they merged these two without coming up with remedies for their weaknesses, attempting to maintain a balance between them – what Carr valued as 'sound political thought'.[128] The balance, however, was at best delicate and even explosively unstable. The group members agreed that collective military force was necessary notwithstanding its risk of escalating wars; they also expected public opinion to prevent wars, having admitted that it might, on the contrary, be jingoistic due to a lack of the type of liberal internationalist education they believed essential to future peace. The failure of collective security in the form of the League of Nations efforts to address the breakdown of international order in the 1930s played a major role in discrediting early liberal internationalist thought and in the dichotomy in Cold War IR theory between realist and idealist perspectives. The great irony of that outcome is that the Bryce Group's early discussion about collective security anticipated the problems that the League of Nations would face in the 1930s because it had recognised the possibilities and limitations of both idealistic and realistic thinking about international order.

---

[128] Carr, *The Twenty Years' Crisis*, pp. 10, 14, 87.

3 Strategies for Winning Public Opinion
The Success and the Loss of the League of Nations
Society, 1915–1917

Introduction

In May 1915, the League of Nations Society was founded to promote to the public the idea of a post-war organisation, on the model of the league developed in the Bryce Group's *Proposals for the Avoidance of War* in February 1915. To avoid being denounced as pacifists in the turmoil of the war, the League of Nations Society worked undercover until May 1917, when Society leaders thought the time had come to hold their first public meeting. Featuring prominent speakers such as the South African statesman General Jan Christiaan Smuts and the Archbishop of Canterbury Randall Davidson, the first meeting was a 'huge success' and widely reported in the press with favourable comments.[1] After this, the League of Nations Society publicly started promotional activities, such as hosting meetings and issuing pamphlets, for the creation of a post-war organisation.

Scholars of the league of nations movement have usually regarded May 1917 as a turning point for the movement and have tended to focus on broad support for the league thereafter.[2] As a result, not only do we know almost nothing about how the Society realised this 'successful' meeting by its non-public activities, but previous accounts have left the impression that the meeting in May 1917 was an entirely positive development for the pro-league movement.[3] In fact, regarding the May 1917 meeting as an unalloyed 'success' hinders us from analysing the war-time pro-league movement as a whole in all its complexity and sophistication.

---

[1] Henry R. Winkler, *The League of Nations Movement in Great Britain, 1914–1919* (Rutgers University Press, 1952), pp. 54–56.

[2] Ibid.; George W. Egerton, *Great Britain and the Creation of the League of Nations: Strategy, Politics, and International Organization, 1914–1919* (Scolar Press, 1978); Keith Robbins, *The Abolition of War: The 'Peace Movement' in Britain, 1914–1919* (University of Wales Press, 1976).

[3] Winkler, *The League of Nations Movement*, pp. 52–56; Egerton, *Great Britain and the Creation of the League of Nations*, pp. 49–50.

66

Hence, this chapter examines how the League of Nations Society came to organise the May 1917 meeting and thereby re-evaluates its success.

Instead of accepting the conventional logic that the Society's first public meeting was purely a success because it provided impetus to the movement, this chapter argues that the meeting contributed to the popularity of the Society but that this came with a cost – that is, the league idea lost its complexity expressed by the Bryce Group and, as a result, the Society lost control over shaping the post-war debate. The issue of the league of nations became widely known after the first public meeting; the leaders of the Society thought, at least, that they had achieved one of the most central aims of their activities of 1915–1917 – obtaining public support for the idea of a new international organisation. To fulfil this aim, the Society, as one of its principal strategies, kept the official league scheme concise for mass consumption by stressing only the creation of the league without going into the details in the public domain and allowing different ideas about the organisation of the league to be expressed even inside the Society. The first public meeting in May 1917 was the point at which its activities in the early years of the war culminated and rallied support for a league the Society craved. Yet simultaneously, the meeting was also the point that the pro-league movement lost the control of defining what the league would be. Originally, the Society's vision of the league based on the Bryce Group's *Proposals* was intricate and sophisticated; while war prevention relied on intangible devices such as morality or public opinion for influencing the behaviour of states in the international system, the threat or even the use of force was also needed to maintain peace.[4] Such in-depth and nuanced discussions about an international organisation were *lost* by May 1917.

By the first public meeting in 1917, the influence of the pro-league movement led by the League of Nations Society reached the critical mass for pushing the league as an important item on the political agenda. Indeed, from 1916 to March 1918 the number of the Society's members increased from about 400 to 2,000.[5] Yet, in order to galvanise public support, the League of Nations Society had to abandon its detailed ideas about a new international order. Having been constrained by both international and domestic contexts,[6] the Society's strategies were not solely its choice but something it had to adopt for widely publicising a post-war

---

[4] See Chapter 2.

[5] Egerton, *Great Britain and the Creation of the League of Nations*, pp. 13, 51.

[6] See Chapter 4 for the details of international situations, especially regarding the relationship between Britain and the United States.

organisation. In fact, abandoning the detailed ideas about a post-war order was a key to both the success and loss of the Society. This strategy led the Society to lose control of the discussion about a league and its own ability to determine its destiny. At the same time, the strategy precluded the Society from employing a dogmatic approach to the design of a league, thereby allowing actors outside the pro-league circle to discuss the post-war plan and to evolve it in political spheres. This flexibility opened up the way for the Society to obtain widespread support and realise its ultimate goal of creating a league, which prepared the emergence of a new international order after the war.[7] This chapter, after reviewing the early history and the aims of the League of Nations Society, inspects its activities and strategies to garner popular support. In order to unveil the Society's efforts to win popular backing, this chapter investigates the Society's strategies to this end and for holding the meeting in May 1917.[8] Since the Society's activities became public knowledge for the first time at its initial meeting, its activities from its foundation in May 1915 to the meeting in May 1917 are explored. To analyse what the May 1917 meeting represented and what it brought about will enable us to rethink the little-known history of the pro–league of nations movement and how it led to its later successes and losses at the end of the war.

The Foundation and the Aims of the League of Nations Society

Before looking into the League of Nations Society's activities and strategies, this section observes its foundation. It reveals that the Society's leadership aimed to rally public support even before they went public, based on their assumption that the creation of a league required popular backing. The Society originated at a small meeting on 5 February 1915 to discuss the Liberal MP Aneurin Williams' article titled *Proposals for a League of Peace and Mutual Protection among Nations*, published in November 1914.[9] Although the attendees had a considerable variety of opinions about the post-war peace scheme and future war prevention, after a few meetings, the League of Nations Society was formed on 3 May

---

[7] Paul W. Schroeder, *Systems, Stability, and Statecraft: Essays on the International History of Modern Europe* (Palgrave Macmillan, 2004), pp. 249, 258.

[8] The League of Nations Society's League scheme has been studied by historians such as Winkler. Winkler, *The League of Nations Movement*, pp. 6–26.

[9] Oxford, Bodleian Library, Willoughby Dickinson Papers, MS. Eng. hist. c.406, 'Note as to the Origin of the League of Nations Union 1914 and 1915'.

1915.[10] The leading members included the Liberal MP Willoughby H. Dickinson, the Cambridge classicist Goldsworthy Lowes Dickinson, the architect Raymond Unwin, the Justice of Peace Mr and Mrs Claremont, Senator La Fontaine of Belgium, the barrister and legal writer Frank. N. Keen and Aneurin Williams.[11] Society members were in general liberal intellectuals, and two of the leading members, W. H. Dickinson and G. Lowes Dickinson, also belonged to the Bryce Group.[12] Apart from the overlapping membership with the Bryce Group, in the early days of the Society, the members were mostly recruited in two ways. First, those who had published works about a post-war organisation were targets for recruitment. For example, one of the oldest members, Keen, recalled that he had been invited to join the Society's discussion about a post-war order in consequence of his publication of *The World in Alliance* in February 1915.[13] Second, as the Bryce Group had done, the League of Nations Society approached intellectuals, jurists and others who might be sympathetic to the league idea.[14] In other words, the Society remained a select group that recruited new members by referring to the current members' suggestions about potential new members or sometimes by extending personal invitations.[15]

The official and ultimate object of the League of Nations Society was to establish a peaceful post-war organisation and 'to advocate an Agreement among civilized States, which will serve as a basis of permanent peace among them, by providing for the Peaceful Settlement of Disputes, for Mutual Defence and the observance of Treaties and International Law'.[16] Adopting the Bryce Group's *Proposals*, the Society's objectives also included collective security and the peaceful settlement of disputes by the Hague Court or the Council of

---

[10] Ibid. Also see the League of Nations Society Publications, no. 3, 29 November 1915; The League of Nations Society Publication, no. 16, 'Proceedings of the first Meeting held at the Caxton Hall, incl. the Report of the Executive Committee from the Beginning of the Society to March 31, 1917', 20 July 1917.

[11] OBL, Willoughby Dickinson Papers, MS. Eng. hist. c.406, 'League of Nations Society, Notes as to its Origin by Sir W. Dickinson'.

[12] Ibid.

[13] F. N. Keen, *The World in Alliance: A Plan for Preventing Future Wars* (W. Southwood & Co., 1915).

[14] OBL, Bryce Papers, MS. Bryce 58, a Letter from G. Lowes Dickinson to Bryce, 20 Oct 1914; Cambridge, King's College, The Papers of Charles Robert Ashbee, CRA3/4; OBL, Bryce Papers, MS. Bryce 240.

[15] British Library of Economic and Political Science, Beveridge 2B/16, 11, Helen Sutherland to Beveridge, 18 October 1916.

[16] The League of Nations Publications, no. 2, 'Explanation of the Objects of the Society', March 1916.

Conciliation.[17] From the perspective of the leading members of the Society, the realisation of these post-war visions required public backing.[18] For instance, immediately after the outbreak of the war, G. Lowes Dickinson highlighted the importance of public support for the establishment of the league. In his letter to the political scientist Graham Wallas of 8 September 1914, Lowes Dickinson expounded two steps that the pro-league movement should take.[19] The first step was 'to concentrate, on a few definite principles, the new European order we want to be introduced at the peace and after it, as the mandate of this nation to its government'.[20] As the second step, by using the principles that the first step outlined, the pro-leaguers should endeavour to gain popular support for the league scheme. The first step should be taken to facilitate the effort of the second step – to convince the public that such a league ought to be created at the end of the war. It was, therefore, 'not necessary, not even desirable' to prepare the whole machinery of the league in detail and 'to meet beforehand all the difficulties and objections'.[21] Detailed discussion should take place but behind the propaganda activities; in public, the league plan should be simple so that the public could grasp it and run with it.[22] A post-war organisation, Lowes Dickinson indicated, could only be realised by securing the public's and eminent people's support for the league idea. He perhaps assumed that backing from both depended on the other for the whole process to unfold. While the endorsement of eminent people would help increase public enthusiasm, strong public opinion would lead eminent people, including statesmen and officials, to view the league issue seriously.[23] When the Bryce Group finished the first edition of its *Proposals* in February 1915, the initial step of formulating the post-war league plan was completed. Building upon the scheme that the Bryce Group had devised, the League of Nations Society moved to the second phase of its activities: winning public support.[24]

---

[17] Ibid.
[18] One of the League of Nations Society's official pamphlets stated that 'League of Nations Society has been formed to spread the knowledge of the plan', in the League of Nations Society Publication, no. 9, March 1917.
[19] BLEPS, WALLAS 1/55, a letter from G. Lowes Dickinson to Wallas, 8 September 1914.
[20] Ibid.   [21] Ibid.   [22] Ibid.   [23] Ibid.
[24] For instance, one of the leading league advocates in the United States, Theodore Marburg, described the difference between the League of Nations Society and the Bryce Group as follows: 'Dickinson's was a public group, aiming not only at maturing the plan but also at popularising it. On the other hand, Lord Bryce's was a private group seeking to formulate its own ideas and, through private correspondence, to ascertain and possibly influence the attitude of others elsewhere.' in OBL, Willoughby Dickinson Papers, MS. Eng. hist. c.406, 'For The Lord Dickinson Memorial Volume by T. Marburg'.

Public opinion was crucial for a post-war order since, as Chapter 2 illustrated, the leading members of the Society presumed its pacific character and force would serve to avert future wars.[25] Even though public opinion at that time was in need of further education for peace, leading activists assumed that public opinion would play its active role in war prevention once a league of nations was established.[26] Society leaders such as Lowes Dickinson thought that public opinion was vital not only after the foundation of the league but also for the process of creating it. As Lowes Dickinson's plan above proposed, they supposed that a broad base of popular support would enable the league to become a critical issue requiring a political response, an essential factor for establishing an international organisation. In effect, the force of public opinion would 'mandate' the league into existence, and then as the league evolved it would act as a major check on future war.

While the Society members hoped the ongoing war would teach 'a fruitful lesson' about the folly of war, public opinion was in reality jingoistic enough to hinder the Society from working in public, especially between 1914 and 1916.[27] There were anti-German riots in London in 1915 and those who advocated ideas regarding peace or the settlement of the war could easily be the targets of mob attack.[28] Indeed, the jingoistic, ultra-nationalist atmosphere was not only evident among the general

---

[25] For example, Aneurin Williams, 'Proposals for a League of Peace and Mutual Protection among Nations' (reprinted from the *Contemporary Review*, November 1914), March 1915.

[26] See Chapter 2. In addition, see OBL, Ponsonby Papers, MS. Eng. hist. c.662, a letter from Bryce to Ponsonby, 1 May 1915; The League of Nations Society Publications, no. 11, 'the League of Nations Society Report of meeting, speeches by Bryce, Smuts, the Archbishop of Canterbury, Lord Buckmaster, Lord Hugh Cecil and others', 14 May 1917.

[27] The League of Nations Society Publication, no. 7, 'An Address Delivered by the Right Honourable Lord Shaw of Dunfermline at a General Meeting of the Society', December 1916; The League of Nations Society Publications, no. 11, 'the League of Nations Society Report of meeting, speeches by Bryce, Smuts, the Archbishop of Canterbury, Lord Buckmaster, Lord Hugh Cecil and others', 14 May 1917; A letter from Bryce to Root, 21 December 1917 in Herbert Albert Laurens Fisher, *James Bryce*, vol. II (Macmillan, 1927), p. 178; BLEPS, WALLAS 1/55, a letter from G. Lowes Dickinson to Wallas, 8 September 1914; for the war-time jingoism in Britain, see I. F. Clarke, *Voices Prophesying War, 1763–1984* (Oxford University Press, 1966), pp. 131–32; Marvin Swartz, *The Union of Democratic Control in British Politics during the First World War* (Clarendon Press, 1971), pp. 36–41; Adrian Gregory, *The Last Great War: British Society and the First World War* (Cambridge University Press, 2008); André Keil, 'The National Council for Civil Liberties and the British State during the First World War, 1916–1919', *The English Historical Review*, vol. 134, no. 568 (June 2019), pp. 620–45.

[28] Arthur Ponsonby's Diary (transcript), 14 May 1915; Kate Courtney, *Extracts from a Diary during the War* (Victor Press, 1927), pp.36–37; OBL, Ponsonby Papers, MS. Eng. hist. c.662, a letter from Charles Trevelyan to Ponsonby, 24 July 1915.

public but also in intellectual circles.[29] For example, Sidney Webb of the Fabian Society, who was considered a 'generally pretty calm' left-wing figure, became 'hardened against Germany' and made his publication the *New Statesman* 'a jingo organ'.[30] Many English people even believed 'themselves to be the instruments of divine justice', while regarding Germany as 'a permanent menace' to their liberal and pacific civilisation.[31] In such circumstances, a storm of criticism including physical attacks on an anti-war lobby group, the Union of Democratic Control (the UDC) and its members, were extremely severe although predictable.[32] In fact, in addition to criticism or attacks in public, the UDC suffered from government censorship. UDC pamphlets, publications and the lists of some names of UDC members were all under strict surveillance by the British Government.[33] Whereas these attacks and censorship towards the UDC inevitably inhibited its activities, the League of Nations Society existed in another milieu. Even though individual members of the Society received some criticism as anti-war

[29] For instance, 'many of the Radical journalists who had criticized Grey now supported the war', in A. J. P. Taylor, *The Trouble Makers: Dissent over Foreign Policy, 1792–1939* (Hamish Hamilton, 1957), p. 133.

[30] Courtney, *Extracts from a Diary*, p. 37; OBL of Commonwealth & African Studies at Rhodes House, Political and Colonial Papers of Charles Roden Buxton, Box 1, folder 2, a letter from Robert Dell to Mrs Buxton, 19 July 1915; BLEPS, Passfield 2/4/G, a letter from George Barnard Shaw to Sydney Webb, 5 October 1916.

[31] British Library, Add. MS 50908, 93, a letter Scott to Hirst, 24 May 1915; OBL of Commonwealth & African Studies at Rhodes House, Political and Colonial Papers of Charles Roden Buxton, Box 1, folder 2, a letter from Robert Dell to Mrs Buxton, 19 July 1915; Gregory, *The Last Great War*, pp. 2–3, 156, 296.

[32] For instance, the UDC meeting in July 1915 ended up in a 'free fight' by the jingoistic crowd and the speaker Arthur Ponsonby 'received many blows and was severely hustled', in 'Mr. Ponsonby Hustled', *The Times*, 22 July 1915, p. 6; 'More German Darlings', *The Times*, 23 July 1915, p. 9; Arthur Ponsonby's Diary (transcript), 23 and 28 July 1915; OBL, Ponsonby Papers, MS. Eng. hist. c.662, 139, a letter from G. Murray to Ponsonby, 22 July 1915, 152–55, a letter from C. Trevelyan to Ponsonby, 24 July 1915 and 156, a letter from A. Williams to Ponsonby, 24 July 1915.

[33] For example, Ponsonby wrote in his diary that 'my U.D.C. leaflet reproduced in America quoted in the German papers was found on a prisoner and this was unscrupulously used by Ll. George in his case against the Nation by his saying I was a director of the Nation. This lying and trickery has its effect. The unfairness to the Nation is blatant but more prejudice if possible will be roused against me', in Arthur Ponsonby's Diary (transcript), 4 May 1917; Also, see the National Archives, HO/45/10742/263275, 157A, 'List of Proceedings Recommended by the Chief Constable for Prosecution Under the Defence of The Realm Regulations (No. 27) Together With The Decisions of the Military Authorities In Cases In Which They have Recommended That No Proceedings Should Be Taken', for instance, the name of Ramsay MacDonald was on the list for the offence of 'making statements at a meeting at Aberaman on the 12th November 1916'.

activists or had their work censored for that very reason,[34] the Society as a group experienced few of the difficulties the UDC encountered.[35] This was due, in part at least, to the success of the Society's strategies for winning over public support without incurring the wrath of the state or provoking jingoistic opinion, to which we will now turn.[36]

The League of Nations Society's Strategies to Win Public Opinion

In the jingoistic turmoil of the early years of the war, the League of Nations Society had been advocating the league idea quietly but carefully enough to realise its aim – mobilising public support when the time became opportune. Through writing league pamphlets and articles as well as holding private meetings, the Society worked for its purpose by pursuing five strategies: to discretely lobby influential people, to stress that prominent figures approved a post-war organisation, to emphasise existing precedents in international law for league-style conflict resolution, to appear to uphold the ongoing war and to simplify its political message for public consumption.[37] While these strategies helped garner popular support for the league, it is important to note that they were not necessarily the group's choice but often what it had to adopt in order to widely publicise a new order.

The first and very important strategy, behind the scenes lobbying, was directed by James Bryce, former British Ambassador to Washington and specialist in international law who chaired the Bryce Group.[38] Most of the notes recalling the early days of the League of Nations Society reflected that its activities from 1915 to 1917 had been kept behind locked doors.[39] Bryce deemed that the time was not yet appropriate for

---

[34] For example, Lowes Dickinson's works were attacked in the press and in 1917 were on the prohibition list of being exported to Norway where the Nobel Committee worked. See, E. M. Forster, *Goldsworthy Lowes Dickinson* (E. Arnold, 1938), p. 175–76; Cambridge, King's College, The Papers of Charles Robert Ashbee, CRA 2, 661, 'Mr. Lowes Dickinson and the War', *Westminster [Gazette]*, 4 May 1916.

[35] Stuart Wallace, *War and the Image of Germany: British Academics 1914–1918* (Donald, 1988), pp. 116–17.

[36] 'Mr. Lowes Dickinson and the War', *Westminster [Gazette]*, 4 May 1916.

[37] BL, Add. MS 50908, a letter from G. Lowes Dickinson to Scott, 10 June 1916; OBL, Willoughby Dickinson Papers, MS. Eng. hist. c.403, a letter from G. Lowes Dickinson to Willoughby Dickinson, 1917; BL, Add. MS. 60664, a letter from G. Lowes Dickinson to Lytton, 8 March, 1917.

[38] See Chapter 2.

[39] The League of Nations Society Publications, no. 8, Aneurin Williams, 'A League of Nations: How to Begin It', January 1917; The League of Nations Society publication, no. 14, 'W. H. Dickinson, A League of Nations and its Critics', July 1917.

public agitation for a peaceful organisation. Any attempts to put forward proposals for the post-war settlement, he judged, would gain nothing or even do some harm to its proposals as well as the settlement of the war.[40] Bryce's fundamental policy – to wait 'till the end of the war appears in sight' – was probably formulated through communication with the press or politicians such as Edward Grey who were favourable to the idea of a league but contemplated that it could only be raised once the war was over.[41] Bryce's prudence, however, frustrated other pro-leaguers who presumed he was reluctant to take any direct public action to promote the league. Lowes Dickinson, for example, described Bryce as 'nervous' and wanting 'courage'; even those outside the Society noted that Bryce would not be 'ready' to move until the war's end.[42] Nonetheless, Bryce's attitude was not precisely reluctant. Rather, it was scrupulous as he sincerely advised how publications regarding a post-war order could generate publicity.[43] His cautiousness probably protected the Society from harsh criticism and censorship. He wrote to the US President Woodrow Wilson in November 1916 about the president's declaration in favour of a post-war organisation: 'the lead you have given ... is invaluable, and we are most grateful. Here we cannot yet start a public movement in that direction, for the conduct in this war absorbs all thoughts, but we are walking quietly in the direction you indicate'.[44]

The second strategy of the League of Nations Society was to emphasise that influential statesmen had already upheld the league idea regardless of such statesmen's actual opinions about it. In the Society's official pamphlets, members frequently quoted parts of the speeches of celebrated political figures that sympathised with a broadly defined post-war league-type organisation. These excerpts were predominantly from the speeches of US President Wilson, the former British Prime Minister

---

[40] CKC, The Papers of Charles Robert Ashbee, CRA 3/4, chapter Ten, 266, a letter from Bryce to C. R. Ashbee, 13 September 1915; Fisher, *James Bryce*, vol. II, p. 140.

[41] During the year 1916, for example, the League of Nations Society was 'described in "The Times" as "inopportune"', in OBL, Willoughby Dickinson Papers, MS. Eng. hist. c.406, 'Note as to the Origin of the League of Nations Union 1914 and 1915'; CKC, The Papers of Charles Robert Ashbee, CRA 3/4, 153, 12 February 1915; OBL of Commonwealth & African Studies at Rhodes House, Political and Colonial Papers of Charles Roden Buxton, Box 1, folder 4, 68, a letter from E. Grey to C. R. Buxton, 4 May 1916.

[42] Bryce was not ready for Willoughby Dickinson's suggestion to make the Society a public group in February 1916. See, OBL, Willoughby Dickinson Papers, MS. Eng. hist. c.406, 'For the Lord Dickinson Memorial Volume by T. Marburg'; CKC, The Papers of Charles Robert Ashbee, chapter Ten, 266, a letter from Bryce to C. R. Ashbee, 13 September 1915; Courtney, *Extracts from a Diary*, p. 80.

[43] OBL, Papers of Gilbert Murray 125, a letter from Bryce to Murray, 11 November 1916.

[44] A letter from Bryce to Wilson, 16 November 1916 in Fisher, *James Bryce*, vol. II, p. 157.

William Gladstone, Prime Minister Herbert Asquith, the Foreign Secretary Edward Grey and his successor Arthur James Balfour. For instance, Asquith's Dublin speech in September 1914, which referred to Gladstone's advocacy of a peaceful Europe, was frequently cited in the Society's pamphlets.[45] Grey's and Balfour's oblique statements about a peaceful settlement that hinted at some sort of new post-war order were quoted as solid evidence that the foreign secretaries advocated a post-war organisation.[46] The Society's letter for recruiting new members in June 1916, for example, proclaimed the purpose of establishing a league by extracting from Grey's and Balfour's speeches to affirm an international organisation.[47] In this letter, the Society pointed out, Grey declared that 'what we want to achieve by the war is "a settled peace throughout Europe and throughout the world which will be a guarantee against aggressive war"'; 'the same idea' was presented by Balfour.[48] By referring to these famous politicians' speeches, the League of Nations Society endeavoured to make the issue of the league appear as if it was already well supported. This was, in short, a strategy of endorsement by association. Eminent people's advocacy of the post-war organisation, even if they were hardly earnest about it, was utilised to impress the public about the legitimacy, wisdom and indeed even the popularity of the idea about the league of nations.

Related to the second strategy, the third strategy, to underscore precedents in international law for league-style conflict resolution mechanisms, sought to impress upon people the practicality of the league ideal. In the League of Nations Society's official pamphlets, for instance, the Bryan Treaties between Britain and America in 1913–1914 were frequently mentioned as a precedent for a peaceful settlement procedure that provided a model for a post-war organisation and that was 'recommended by the League of Nations Society'.[49] The treaties stipulated that disputes shall be referred to the Court of Arbitration and that the contracting parties shall not begin hostilities during investigation and before the report was submitted. This set precedents for the conciliation process and a permanent commission for peaceful settlements. As another

---

[45] The League of Nation Publications, no. 2, 'Explanation of the Objects of the Society', March 1916.
[46] Ibid. In addition, the League of Nations Society Publication, no. 6, 'Speeches of American Statesmen in Favour of a League of Nations to Keep the Peace', November 1916.
[47] Parliamentary Archives, DAV/325, 'the League of Nations Society', June 1916.
[48] Ibid.
[49] The League of Nations Society Publication, no. 4, 'Treaty between the United Kingdom and the United States of America with regard to the Establishment of a Peace Commission', November 1916.

example of the treaty adopting the same approach as the Bryan Treaties to more than two states, the Treaty of Arbitration between Argentina, Brazil and Chile in May 1915 was also featured in one of the Society's official pamphlets with the same comment 'recommended by the League of Nations Society'.[50] In 1916, one pamphlet even discussed the Swiss federation as a model international organisation that would not threaten national sovereignty. The Swiss federation, the pamphlet explained, was similar 'to the proposals of the League of Nations Society, [in that] it does not set up a new "super-State," but establishes a working agreement between existing States'.[51] These examples underlined the similarities between the proposed league with precedents in order to impress upon readers that the vision of the league did not in fact represent a radical or utopian break with the past.

Further, as the fourth strategy, the League of Nations Society sought to make itself appear to be a supporter of the ongoing war. In one of its pamphlets, the Society emphasised that working for the war and envisaging the post-war order were mutually compatible:

At the present time the best energies and thoughts of every patriot are directed to supporting our country. Anything which tended to diminish those energies ... would be reprobated. But besides bringing the war to a successful end, there is another task incumbent upon every patriot who can give thought to it ... we must think out some better relation of the nation, some basis upon which a permanent peace may be built up.[52]

Having implied that the future peace after the ongoing war was the ultimate object, the group declared that 'we shall fight and work the better' by envisioning a league along with fighting the war for victory.[53] Fearing marginalisation, the Society strove to evade any hint of being a pacifist, defeatist or anti-war organisation.[54] In 1914–1916, as Bryce wrote to the editor of the *Manchester Guardian* C. P. Scott, 'whoever

---

[50] The League of Nations Society Publication, no. 5, 'The Treaty between the Argentine Republic, the United States of Brazil, and Chile', April 1917.

[51] The League of Nations Society Publication, no. 3, 'The First Perpetual League between the Swiss Cantons of URI, Schwytz and Unterwaldes', November 1916.

[52] The League of Nation Publications, no. 2, 'Explanation of the Objects of the Society', March 1916.

[53] Ibid.

[54] Lord Shaw of Dunfermline declared that 'pacifism, as hitherto planned, has failed', in the League of Nations Society Publication, no. 7, 'An Address Delivered by the Right Honourable Lord Shaw of Dunfermline at a General Meeting of the Society', December 1916; In addition, G. Lowes Dickinson began his pamphlet by stating that 'this pamphlet is not a "stop the war" pamphlet', in Goldsworthy Lowes Dickinson, *The War and the Way Out* (Chancery Lane Press, 1917), p. 7.

talked about peace' would not only risk being denounced as a pacifist but also draw no attention to what they had to say.[55]

Of course, the Society members were no pacifists and did not 'pretend' to be war supporters. Even the vice-president of the League of Nations Society Willoughby Dickinson, who was a devout Anglican and believed the war to be 'the inevitable result of the failure of mankind to rise to the level which God had intended', very much cared whether the British were 'doing well' on the battlefield.[56] Along with his passion for peace work, Willoughby Dickinson also deemed that people should do their duty and fight.[57] The desire for an Allied victory and working for that end were shared by the Society members as well as those who worked for peace in general.[58] Victory over Germany and devising a post-war peace organisation were mutually reconcilable in their minds. Indeed, an Allied victory was a premise of the creation of a league. As League of Nations Society member Aneurin Williams put in his pamphlet, Society members assumed that 'we and our Allies are eventually victorious' and that the league was what they expected to follow the victory.[59] Even to Society leaders such as Bryce, Germany embodied a militarism that would jeopardise the maintenance of future peace, therefore the Allies had to win and initiate a new order.[60] Hence, their strategy to show the public the Society's support of the war was hardly in conflict with their real attitude to the relationship of the ongoing war and the idea about the post-war organisation.

Finally, as the fifth strategy, the League of Nations Society simplified its message for public consumption without describing the intricacies as well as challenges that an international organisation would entail. More precisely, it was not quite its chosen strategy but what it had to do in order to appeal to a mass audience. From the foundation of the Society, simplicity in its political message – to only highlight the creation of the league without conveying a lot of details about how it would work – was

[55] OBL, Bryce Papers, MS. Bryce 158, 213, a letter from Bryce to Scott, 25 October 1916.

[56] Hope Costley White, *Willoughby Hyett Dickinson, 1859–1943: A Memoir, etc.* (Privately printed, 1957), p. 139.

[57] White, *Willoughby Hyett Dickinson, 1859–1943*, p. 141.

[58] For example, an active member of the Union of Democratic Control, Charles Trevelyan, mentioned that, 'this government had to make peace as well as war', in OBL, Ponsonby Papers, MS. Eng. hist. c.662, a letter from Charles Trevelyan to Ponsonby, 27 May 1915; Further, the political scientist in the Bryce Group, Graham Wallas, wrote in his letter, 'I'm not doing "my bit" in the world crisis', in OBL, Papers of Gilbert Murray 27, a letter from Wallas to Murray, 22 June 1915; For the other examples, please see Arthur Ponsonby's Diary (transcript), 7 May 1915; Courtney, *Extracts from a Diary*, pp. 62, 102.

[59] For instance, Williams, 'Proposals for a League of Peace and Mutual Protection among Nations'; BLEPS, WALLAS4/5, 'Mr. Graham Wallas's Notes', March 1915.

[60] OBL, Bryce Papers, MS. Bryce U.S.A. 23, 6, a letter from Bryce to Butler, 1 Oct 1915.

essential for mobilising popular backing. The league scheme had to be general enough for the public to understand it and to fire up war-weary imaginations about a future peace.[61] The scheme was, as Bryce explained, not to provide the details about the ultimately adopted machinery but to 'shew that the idea is capable of being put into a practical shape ... so that there may be profitable discussions of these difficulties'.[62]

In addition, the Society had to keep the league plan simple not only because of its necessity for public consumption but also because of a lack of agreement inside the Society about the mechanism of a post-war organisation would work. In the official Society pamphlets that were authored by several individual members, their visions and emphases varied. In a letter to Theodore Marburg, one of the leading figures of the American pro-league group, Willoughby Dickinson admitted that there were differences of opinion inside the group: 'The fact is ... I cannot say that there is any real agreement with reference to the detailed machinery which should be inaugurated in order to carry the principles of our societies into effect.'[63] He continued as follows:

My personal feeling is that it is not wise to attempt too much in this direction at the present moment [towards the elaborating details of machinery]. Our main object should be to bring the nations together so that they may set up the Tribunal of Arbitration and the Council of Conciliation as permanent institutions. If that alone is done we shall have made a great advance and the rest of the machinery will follow later on.[64]

Thus, Willoughby Dickinson defended the Society's lack of a single concrete plan as a calculated strategy, even though it was also due to various opinions inside the Society. Despite the absence of an agreed post-war plan, Society members including Dickinson anticipated that the league would spontaneously develop along the lines they foresaw once it was created.[65]

Hence, the League of Nations Society had to keep its message simple in public. It stressed the single idea that a new international machinery would be required after the current war, simultaneously permitting its

[61] BLEPS, WALLAS1/55, a letter from G. Lowes Dickinson to Wallas, 8 September 1914.
[62] A letter from Bryce to Lowell, 8 April 1917 in Fisher, *James Bryce*, vol. II, pp. 160–62.
[63] OBL, Willoughby Dickinson Papers, MS. Eng. hist. c.403, a letter from Willoughby Dickinson to T. Marburg, 17 May 1917.
[64] Ibid.
[65] Similarly, Lowes Dickinson mentioned that '[the League scheme] would be a germ which might develop by degrees into an international polity', in BLEPS, CANNAN 970, *Proposals for the Avoidance of War, with a Prefatory Note by Viscount Bryce, As Revised up to 24 February 1915*, pp. 7–8.

individual members to express their own opinions about how the league would operate in practice. Many of the official pamphlets published by the Society had notes to maintain that 'the Society is not committed to the views of this or any other publication bearing the name of the author. They are issued to form a basis for the considerations and discussion of questions connected with the proposals of the Society'.[66] The Society allowed its members to enjoy considerable latitude for disagreeing or criticising its official post-war scheme, which indicated to the public its flexibility and capability to accept criticism and debate. The President of the Society, Lord Shaw of Dunfermline, for instance, criticised some parts of the Society's plan in one of its official pamphlets in 1916. He proclaimed that he 'would not wish this Society to be committed for a moment to the proposition that its programme merely means that there is to be a preservation of the status quo'.[67] Dunfermline's argument was that 'nations rise or fall' and if the league reinforced the status quo and created a system to maintain it, it might cause injustice and even problems when the power balance between states changed.[68] He was concerned that 'there may be circumstances in which the preservation of the status quo would not be right, when the preservation of the status quo may be a wrong in itself, and a steadily increasing wrong'.[69] His principal suggestion was, therefore, to include an elastic scheme that would enable the league to readjust the power balance when necessary,[70] which the Society's later pamphlet in August 1917 reflected upon and analysed.[71] Propagating a simple message – to create a league without committing itself to a particular vision and to downplay the complexities of the organisation – certainly made the Society appear to be open to its critics' opinions. Yet, at the same time, the Society was beginning to lose its ability to control the agenda and shape the post-war debate. This particularly became a crucial factor in 1917.

---

[66] The League of Nations Society Publication, no. 8, Aneurin Williams, 'A League of Nations: How to Begin It', January 1917; The League of Nations Society Publication, no. 27, George Paish, 'The Economic Interdependence of Nations', March 1918; The League of Nations Society Publication, no. 28, Willoughby H. Dickinson, 'Disarmament and A League of Nation', March 1918; Also see the League of Nations Society Publication, no. 18, Aneurin Williams, 'Schemes of International Organisation, no. I. The Minimum of Machinery', November 1917; The League of Nations Society Publication, no. 19, Raymond Unwin, 'Schemes of international Organisation, no. II, "Functions of a League of Nations"', November 1917.

[67] The League of Nations Society Publication, no. 7, 'An Address Delivered by the Right Honourable Lord Shaw of Dunfermline at a General Meeting of the Society', December 1916.

[68] Ibid.   [69] Ibid.   [70] Ibid.

[71] The League of Nations Society Publications, no. 15, 'The Project of a League of Nations', August 1917.

Speeches for Popular Support: The First Public Meeting in May 1917

The year 1917 was a 'turning point' for the League of Nations Society with the great success of its first public meeting in May. However, the success in gaining growing popularity came at the cost of losing the grip on the agenda and the debate. The first public meeting was held at this time because both external and domestic factors finally sufficed to convince the ever-cautious Bryce to conclude that the opportunity to go public had arisen. External factors were the American entry into the war and the Russian Revolution; internal factors were war-weariness and the increase of the league's public profile. As an external – indeed the most crucial – element, the American entry into the war was notable to Society members because, for them, its participation was indispensable for forming the league.[72] The American entry entailed President Wilson's endorsement of a post-war organisation in his Fourteen Points and a commitment that the United States would be part of it.[73] Hence, it resolved the Society leadership's concern that the league without the United States would simply be another Concert of Europe based on the balance of power that they identified as the primary cause of war.[74] Wilson's call for a 'League of Peace' played a decisive role in pushing the post-war idea forward as a critical political issue, not simply a utopian fantasy.[75] It helped the pro-league groups appear legitimate and practical, concurrently arousing the considerable interests of many actors to discuss a league for their own purposes.[76] Along with Wilson's address, Bolshevik leader Lenin's call for new diplomacy led the war to acquire a stronger ideological character of democracy versus autocracy.[77] This

---

[72] Mark Mazower, *Governing the World: The History of an Idea* (Penguin Books, 2012), p. 118; Jay Winter (ed.), *The Cambridge History of the First World War*, vol. 2 (Cambridge University Press, 2013), pp. 597–98.

[73] The League of Nations Society Publications, no. 11, 'the League of Nations Society Report of meeting, speeches by Bryce, Smuts, the Archbishop of Canterbury, Lord Buckmaster, Lord Hugh Cecil and others', 14 May 1917.

[74] See Chapter 4.

[75] Egerton, *Great Britain and the Creation of the League of Nations*, pp. 52, 216, 221; Peter Jackson, *Beyond the Balance of Power: France and the Politics of National Security in the Era of the First World War* (Cambridge University Press, 2013), pp. 6, 521.

[76] William Mulligan, *The Great War for Peace* (Yale University Press, 2014), p. 218; Winter (ed.), *The Cambridge History of the First World War*, vol. 2, pp. 597–98; Jackson, *Beyond the Balance of Power*, p. 6.

[77] See Chapter 5; Alan Sharp, 'The New Diplomacy and the New Europe, 1916–1922', in Nicholas Doumanis (ed.), *The Oxford Handbook of European History, 1914–1945* (Oxford University Press, 2016); Robert W. Tucker, 'Woodrow Wilson's "New Diplomacy"', *World Policy Journal*, vol. 21, no. 2 (Summer, 2004), pp. 92–107.

development also urged the Allied governments to tackle the issue of a new peace organisation as a war aim that could justify fighting the war.[78] Meanwhile, the significance of the Russian Revolution to the pro-league activities was insufficiently spelt out by Society members.[79] Yet some were worried that the revolution might even affect Britain;[80] others assumed that the revolution might be good for the league since, despite the fact that there was little news from Russia, they anticipated that the revolution was led by 'a peace party' committed to a new order.[81]

On the other hand, domestic factors such as war-weariness and the league's obtaining a relatively high profile among intellectuals, senior officials and even the public were also necessary conditions for the League of Nations Society to start its mass public activities. In 1917, the war had already been grinding on for three years and had produced 'a distinct tendency to weariness which only the realisation of high and inspiring ideas could effectively counteract'.[82] Further, by May 1917 the name 'league of nations' was becoming widely known by the general public due to the Society's careful strategies.[83] As one leading member of the Society, Aneurin Williams, stated in a pamphlet in early 1917, the phrase a league of nations 'was unknown two years ago and is in everybody's mouth'.[84] Both of these external and domestic factors, on the table in 1917, enabled the League of Nations Society to launch its activities in public.

The Society leaders supposed the outcome of the first public meeting would hinge on the question of who to choose as speakers. They still feared being tarnished by any hints of pacifism, defeatism or worse, utopianism.[85] Bryce and Willoughby Dickinson, who selected most of

---

[78] See Chapter 5; David Stevenson, *Cataclysm: The First World War As Political Tragedy* (Basic Books, 2004), p. 375; Egerton, *Great Britain and the Creation of the League of Nations*, p. 45.

[79] The League of Nations Society Publications, no. 11, 'the League of Nations Society Report of meeting, speeches by Bryce, Smuts, the Archbishop of Canterbury, Lord Buckmaster, Lord Hugh Cecil and others', 14 May 1917.

[80] Stuart, *War and the Image of Germany*, p. 108.

[81] Arthur Ponsonby's Diary (transcript), 5 and 21 April 1917; Courtney, *Extracts from a Diary*, pp. 116–18; A letter from Bryce to Root, 15 September 1917 in Fisher, *James Bryce*, vol. II, pp. 173–74.

[82] OBL, Papers of Gilbert Murray 34, 12, a letter from Smuts to Murray, 5 April 1917; Arthur Ponsonby's Diary (transcript), 21 April 1917.

[83] 'In the year 1917 the idea of a League of Nations began to appeal to the public imagination and the Society was able to organise meetings in its favour', in OBL, Willoughby Dickinson Papers, MS. Eng. hist. c.406, 'Note as to the Origin of the League of Nations Union 1914 and 1915'.

[84] The League of Nations Society Publications, no. 8, Aneurin Williams, 'A League of Nations: How to Begin It', January 1917.

[85] A letter from Bryce to Lowell, 20 July 1917 in Fisher, *James Bryce*, vol. II, pp. 166–67.

the speakers, desired to 'avoid Utopian cranks who talk about a "world state" and the immediate and final abolition of all war' in order not to 'spoil the meeting'.[86] Further, speakers should be eminent enough to influence public opinion profoundly. One of the most important candidates for a speaker was the South African statesman General Jan Christiaan Smuts, who had just landed in Britain in March 1917 to attend the first Imperial Conference.[87] The league advocates and Smuts exchanged the opinions regarding the post-war order and were impressed with each other.[88] At the same time, both recognised differences of opinion. The British activists were under the impression that Smuts had a different attitude towards war and a post-war peace. Smuts, on the other hand, thought that the whole scheme of the league was not completely convincing, yet he was attracted to the idea of establishing a sort of post-war organisation.[89] When Bryce, urged by Willoughby Dickinson, wrote a letter to invite Smuts to the meeting as a speaker, the leaders of the League of Nations Society, including Bryce and Dickinson, must have known about the difference in perspectives between them and Smuts. The difference, nonetheless, was not an obstacle to cooperation because the first public meeting's purpose was 'a discussion of the general idea of a League of Nations' without going into details of its machinery.[90] If the Society could invite influential speakers, different viewpoints hardly mattered as long as they agreed with the creation of an international organisation. After all, its strategy remained consistent – to propagate the simple idea that a league was the solution to future war, while playing down all the challenges founding such an organisation would pose. Hence, when Smuts conveyed that he was 'not quite in agreement with the programme' of the league but agreed to speak at the meeting on the condition of reserving 'a certain freedom of speech', Bryce and Dickinson willingly accepted his condi-

---

[86] PA, DAV/325, a letter from Bryce to Willoughby Dickinson, 21 April 1917.

[87] Jan C. Smuts, *Jan Christian Smuts* (Cassell, 1952), p. 179; Mark Mazower, *No Enchanted Palace: The End of Empire and the Ideological Origins of the United Nations* (Princeton University Press, 2009), chapter 1.

[88] Courtney, *Extracts from a Diary*, pp. 113–14; A letter from Smuts to J. A. Hobson, 21 April 1917 in Jan Christiaan Smuts, W. K. Hancock and Jean van der Poel (eds.), *Selections from the Smuts Papers Vol. 3, June 1910–November 1918* (Cambridge University Press, 1966), p. 476; Arthur Ponsonby's Diary (transcript), 4 May 1917.

[89] See n. 88.

[90] OBL, Bryce Papers, MS. Bryce 58, 42–43, a letter from Willoughby Dickinson to Bryce, 20 April 1917; PA, DAV/325, a letter from Bryce to Willoughby Dickinson, 21 April 1917.

tion and fixed the date of the meeting.[91] Another important speaker was the Archbishop of Canterbury Randall Davidson who had been sympathetic to the league idea and peace groups in general but had not been actively involved in such works before. It seemed that the Archbishop of Canterbury agreed to speak at the meeting after reflection and then recommended some other potential speakers such as the Conservative MP Hugh Cecil.[92] Having followed the Archbishop's recommendations, Bryce and Willoughby Dickinson eventually decided on the following list of speakers: Bryce, the Archbishop of Canterbury, Hugh Cecil and the ex-Lord Chancellor Stanley Owen Buckmaster.[93] Some other invited speakers such as Robert Borden, Prime Minister of Canada, could not attend but expressed sympathies for the event and the Society's aims, which was enough for the Society to underline 'an assurance ... that the Great Dominions are heartily with us in any good work we can do for Peace' to the audience at the meeting.[94]

On 14 May 1917, the first public meeting of the League of Nations Society was held at the Central Hall, Westminster in London with a large attendance.[95] Speakers only had less than one month to prepare and admitted their lack of preparedness.[96] In his speech, Bryce made it clear to the audience that they would 'not be asked to-day to discuss the various plans that have been framed with this object, but only to consider the general aim in view'. The organisers of the meeting wanted people to simply understand the general aim of establishing a league without getting bogged down or side-tracked about details.[97] After reflecting on

[91] A letter from Smuts to John A. Hobson, 21 April 1917, in Smuts, *Selections from the Smuts Papers Vol. 3*, p. 476; OBL, Bryce Papers, MS. Bryce 243, 74, a letter from Smuts to Bryce, 29? April 1917.

[92] PA, DAV/325, a letter from Bryce to Willoughby Dickinson, 1917.

[93] A Liberal MP Viscount Lewis Vernon Harcourt also spoke at the request of Bryce on the day.

[94] The League of Nations Society Publications, no. 11, 'League of Nations Society report of meeting, speeches by Bryce, Smuts, the Archbishop of Canterbury, Lord Buckmaster, Lord Hugh Cecil and others', 14 May 1917; PA, DAV/325, a letter from Bryce to Willoughby Dickinson, 21 April 1917, a letter from R. L. Borden to Bryce, 28 April 1917 and a letter from W. K. Massey to Willoughby Dickinson, 30 April 1917.

[95] Egerton, *Great Britain and the Creation of the League of Nations*, p. 49.

[96] At the meeting, the Chief Rabbi said that 'I regret this Resolution has been placed in my hands only a few minutes ago', in The League of Nations Society Publications, no. 11, 'League of Nations Society report of meeting, speeches by Bryce, Smuts, the Archbishop of Canterbury, Lord Buckmaster, Lord Hugh Cecil and others', 14 May 1917; Also, Smuts mentioned that 'my speech which unfortunately had to be delivered from some short jottings and was therefore very formless', a letter from Smuts to Willoughby Dickinson, 18 May 1917, in Smuts, *Selections from the Smuts Papers Vol. 3*, p. 518.

[97] The League of Nations Society Publications, no. 11, 'League of Nations Society report of meeting, speeches by Bryce, Smuts, the Archbishop of Canterbury, Lord Buckmaster, Lord Hugh Cecil and others', 14 May 1917, p. 3.

the horrors of the war, Bryce proposed two ways to escape such future calamities: a widespread emotional transformation and the establishment of a new international organisation.[98] First of all, expressing his concern about 'too much nationalism and too little of international mind', Bryce appealed to the audience for 'a change of heart in the peoples of the world, a disappearance of those passions of national pride and vanity which prompt aggression, and the replacing of those passions by a respect for the rights of others and for international good faith'.[99] What was necessary for future war prevention was to advance towards the goals that Christianity set before human beings – the peace and growth of the sentiment of human brotherhood. Usually Bryce spoke little about Christianity or the forces of good and evil in the post-war debates, but he perhaps employed such terms and the metaphor of light and darkness to describe what should be done to establish lasting peace for his audience in an accessible fashion. 'The reawakened spirit of Christianity', Bryce addressed the crowd, would be a very slow but the best remedy for human 'evils' – namely, wars.[100]

In addition, Bryce explained that future war prevention required the creation of a league of nations, with a brief description of its machinery:

only one other way ... is to turn to account among all the nations that desire peace, and have a due sense of the value of peace – to turn to account the longing for peace by forming a combination of States each of which will pledge itself to employ its material and its economic forces in order to protect each and every one of its members from aggression, while at the same time finding a pacific means of settling disputes by arbitration and conciliation.[101]

Following the Society's strategies, Bryce also underscored that the idea about a league of nations had already received the endorsement of prominent statesmen such as the American President Wilson, Grey, Balfour and Lloyd George.[102] This well-supported idea, Bryce added, had only two aims: the resettlement of rules to define the right especially of non-combatants and collective security with a process to resolve disputes peacefully. As the first aim of the league, Bryce suggested that a body of rules to govern international rights and behaviour should be defined along with the means of enforcing them. He mentioned the cases of the massacre of civilians in Belgium and Armenia as examples of behaviour to be banned as well as subject to enforcement.[103] The second aim, collective security, was one of the most critical and central points in the league scheme about which Bryce held opinions.[104] Touching upon

---

[98] Ibid., p. 1.   [99] Ibid.   [100] Ibid., p. 2.   [101] Ibid.   [102] Ibid., pp. 2–3.
[103] Ibid., p. 4.   [104] See Chapter 2.

obstacles involved in setting up a system of collective security, Bryce argued that the threat of force as sanctions would enhance the effectiveness of the league. Nevertheless, in the meeting he refrained from entering 'into any of those schemes' or discussing the challenges of the system in detail.[105] Bryce's comments were limited to the aims of a postwar organisation: to combine peace-loving States to settle disputes by peaceful methods and to 'support any member which was attacked by a Power that had refused to employ those methods before commencing hostilities'.[106] Bryce's speech hardly represented his views on the postwar organisation, cautiously evading the illustration of the tremendous difficulties in enforcing international peace.

Smuts' speech after Bryce's was the highlight of the meeting, attracting the most attention.[107] Even though Smuts was unconvinced by the existing plans for a league, he underlined a transformation of the public's mindset and the establishment of the league as Bryce did. Following Bryce's line, Smuts pointed out that a change of people's hearts would be the most crucial guarantee against another world war since war was 'not the work of some superhuman agency'[108] but man-made. Repeatedly, he indicated that 'a strong, healthy, sound public opinion ... will be the best guarantee of peace, which will see that governments are kept in order and that diplomats are kept in order'.[109] Any treaties or machinery after the war required the support of public opinion because otherwise the world would again be divided into two hostile camps with mutual hatred and trigger another war.[110] The formation of a league of nations based on the force of public opinion, Smuts stressed, was a necessary condition for peace, while he prudently added that he was neither certain of what particular scheme should be adopted nor in a position to dogmatise about it.[111] Despite such statements, Smuts openly voiced his disagreement with the scheme of the League of Nations Society as follows:

I must honestly confess that all the schemes that I have heard of so far have failed to carry conviction to my mind that they are practical and that they will achieve

[105] The League of Nations Society Publications, no. 11, 'League of Nations Society report of meeting, speeches by Bryce, Smuts, the Archbishop of Canterbury, Lord Buckmaster, Lord Hugh Cecil and others', 14 May 1917, pp. 4–5.
[106] Ibid.
[107] 'The Will to Peace: Striking Speech by Gen. Smuts Conditions of a "Good Treaty"'. *The Manchester Guardian*, 15 May 1917, p. 3; 'The League of Nations', *The Manchester Guardian*, 16 May 1917, p. 4; 'Security from War. The Leaguing of Free Nations. General Smuts's Support', *The Times*, 15 May 1917, p. 10.
[108] The League of Nations Society Publications, no. 11, 'League of Nations Society report of meeting, speeches by Bryce, Smuts, the Archbishop of Canterbury, Lord Buckmaster, Lord Hugh Cecil and others', 14 May 1917, pp. 6–7.
[109] Ibid., pp. 6–12.   [110] Ibid.   [111] Ibid.

the objects we have in view. I would favour something more elastic, something more flexible, something which will be capable of adapting itself to the very complex circumstances which arise from time to time in our complex European relations.[112]

He further continued his suggestions to the league plan, such as the establishment of an Anglo-American committee to discuss the scheme, the league's flexibility to adapt to changes in the power balance and the necessity of military sanctions and disarmament. At the end of his speech, his resolution simply stated that 'some machinery should be set up after the present war for the purpose of maintaining international right and general peace' and that the meeting welcomed President Wilson's proposals as well as the British people's deliberations.[113]

The rest of the speakers underlined the various points of the broadly defined post-war peace. As Smuts did, the Archbishop of Canterbury also pronounced that the detail of the machinery should be devised not by himself but 'those who are best qualified on these matters' such as the Society members.[114] By calling war an act of devils and peace the will of God, the Archbishop spoke of the league of nations as an idea in the realm of Christian theology. An endeavour to create a post-war international organisation was considered the fulfilment of God's will. Similarly, Hugh Cecil appealed for going back to Christianity, having diagnosed boundless devotion to their own country as a cause of the war. Cecil asserted that Christianity provides a higher doctrine – the brotherhood of man – than nationalism to unite people regardless of nationality. This, he supposed, would not only deter national hatred and avert war but also eliminate the evil of war. Although Cecil referred to public opinion as an ultimate sanction in a league, his focus was a worldwide return to Christianity that could replace nationalism. While the Chief Rabbi, from another religious point of view, argued that religion would emerge from the ongoing war stronger than ever before, Buckmaster announced that the league would fail unless Germany was included in it. The speakers barely agreed that a post-war organisation should be established after the war, yet the thrust of their speeches was varied and rather general.

The meeting was reported in the press as a large gathering for a league of nations with favourable comments probably due to the eminence of the speakers, especially Smuts.[115] Smuts' 'remarkable' speech most

---

[112] Ibid., p. 10.   [113] Ibid., p. 13.   [114] Ibid., p. 14.
[115] 'The Will to Peace: Striking Speech by Gen. Smuts Conditions of a "Good Treaty"', *The Manchester Guardian*, 15 May 1917, p. 3; 'The League of Nations', *The Manchester Guardian*, 16 May 1917, p. 4; 'Security from War. The Leaguing of Free Nations. General Smuts's Support', *The Times*, 15 May 1917, p. 10.

attracted the attention of newspapers as 'extraordinarily close and power-ful in its reasoning, and touched with an entirely unforced eloquence', despite the fact that his speech was occasionally repetitive and vague.[116] In addition to the increase of the Society's membership,[117] whether the Society, compared with the situation in 1915, obtained popular endorse-ments for the league by 1917 can be examined by asking three questions. The first question is whether newspapers wrote positively about the issue of a post-war organisation or the pro-league activists. In 1915, many activities for peace or the settlement of the war received critical or even antagonistic comments from newspapers as the 'stab-my-country-in-the-back' campaign.[118] Yet in 1917, as we saw above, the first public meeting of the Society was in general reported approvingly and welcomed by the press. The second question is whether well-known public figures publicly upheld the idea about the league. Although some statesmen, such as the Foreign Secretary Edward Grey, were sympathetic to a post-war organ-isation in the early years of the war as 1915, even he had avoided openly advocating the creation of a league until 1917.[119] On the other hand, the public meeting in May 1917 itself succeeded in inviting some famous figures as speakers such as Smuts and the Archbishop of Canterbury.[120] The third question is whether the league-related meetings were dis-rupted. Whereas any early meetings to discuss the post-war settlement were interrupted and its speakers were occasionally attacked by jingoistic mobs, the Society's first meeting smoothly proceeded with a large and receptive audience. Looking at these three conditions, one could argue that the League of Nations Society did not have public support for the league in 1915–1916 but gained it by the first public meeting in May 1917.

The meeting satisfied its main organisers, Bryce and Willoughby Dickinson, who proudly depicted it as 'an unexpected success'.[121] Concluding that their principal aim to capture public attention was

---

[116] 'The Will to Peace', *The Manchester Guardian*, 15 May 1917, p. 3; 'Our London Correspondence: Commander Briggs's Escape', *The Manchester Guardian*, 15 May 1917, p. 4.

[117] Egerton, *Great Britain and the Creation of the League of Nations*, pp. 13, 51.

[118] For example, 'Secret Peace Societies. Cranks Who Clamour for Openness in Diplomacy', *Daily Express*, London, 9 August 1915.

[119] Grey favoured the League of Nations idea but did not openly support it until 1917.

[120] The League of Nations Society Publications, no. 11, 'League of Nations Society report of meeting, speeches by Bryce, Smuts, the Archbishop of Canterbury, Lord Buckmaster, Lord Hugh Cecil and others', 14 May 1917.

[121] OBL, Willoughby Dickinson Papers, MS. Eng. hist. c.403, 74, a letter from Willoughby Dickinson to R. Cecil, 20 May 1917; A letter from Bryce to Lowell, 20 July 1917, in Fisher, *James Bryce*, vol. II, p. 166–67.

fulfilled by the first public meeting, they now decided to go one step further – to create an inter-governmental committee to consider the league, especially between Britain and America as Smuts suggested in the meeting.[122] Accordingly, the first public meeting in May 1917 led not only to the public awareness and popularity of the League of Nations Society's work but also established the league as a key issue in public and official discussions about war aims and peacemaking.[123]

The speeches at the meeting, however, barely shared agreement that a post-war organisation was needed and were much more general than what the league advocates such as the Bryce Group members had been discussing. This generalisation of the debate about the league was caused by the Society's work and strategies to garner public support, such as showing prominent figures' approval for the league and simplifying its message for public consumption. Goldsworthy Lowes Dickinson's comments about the meeting, mixed with his bleak outlook for the future, adequately captured what the Society had gained and lost by May 1917:

> The League of Nations Society has got the following to speak at its annual meeting .... So we seem at last to have become respectable. But at what price I wonder? I get so cynical about all public persons. Governments appear to me to exist for the simple purpose of destroying mankind, which however shows every willingness to be destroyed. The only people [I] admire and respect are the Russian workmen's committees. They have more sense and humanity in their least word than the rest of the governments have in the whole of their incapable noddles and perverted hearts and souls! There! I feel better ....[124]

Conclusion

The first public meeting of the League of Nations Society in May 1917 was indeed the Society's turning point in making its activity public. Yet it was not purely a positive development as scholars have previously considered. Although the Society succeeded in achieving its central aim of mobilising public support with a big rally, it simultaneously sacrificed control over discussions about the league and downplayed much of the sophisticated reasoning and nuances that had marked the Bryce Group's *Proposals*. From the outset, the Society's aim was to win popular support

---

[122] See Chapter 4.

[123] The issue of a league of nations began to be discussed by a wide range of actors including politicians from 1917. See Peter J. Yearwood, *Guarantee of Peace: The League of Nations in British Policy, 1914–1925* (Oxford University Press, 2009), chapters 2–3; Egerton, *Great Britain and the Creation of the League of Nations*.

[124] CKC, The Papers of Charles Robert Ashbee, CRA 3/5, a letter from G. Lowes Dickinson to J. E. Ashbee, May 1917, p. 36.

for a post-war organisation that Society leaders such as Lowes Dickinson presumed would be able to promote the league as a major issue for the settlement. Seeking to garner public backing, the Society adopted five main strategies that culminated in its first public meeting: to discretely lobby influential people, to stress that influential figures advocated the league, to underscore existing precedents in international law for league-style conflict resolution, to uphold the ongoing war and to simplify its political message for public consumption. These strategies were not always what the Society consciously chose but what it had to adopt for appealing to a wide audience. Its strategies to attract public support led to the successful meeting in May 1917 that, however, concluded with only a broad agreement about the necessity of a post-war organisation.

By the meeting, the influence of the pro–league of nations movement hit the crucial point of putting the issue of the league on the political agenda. The Society's strategies served to successfully realise the most important goals of the pro-league movement: to develop the league project for the creation of a post-war organisation and for the emergence of a new international order. Yet, at the same time, the meeting marked the beginning of activists' losing control of framing the post-war debate and defining what the league would be – the loss of the pro-league movement in the long term. The League of Nations Society was bound to lose the grip on its own destiny, facing the challenge of galvanising social support in the international and domestic contexts in which it was embedded. It led the Society to simplify its message and abandon in-depth discussions as well as nuances about an international organisation, which only accelerated afterwards.

Even though the Society leaders such as Lowes Dickinson were obsessive about what they called public opinion, they did not define what it exactly meant. Yet, from what they said and wrote during the war, public opinion in their view was probably an amorphous combination of 'elite opinion' as expressed in newspapers and other public venues as well as a more general expression of the wishes of the various people. Often they seemed to assume that the first more or less reflected the second. As the Bryce Group discussed, the Society's leading members such as Willoughby Dickinson anticipated that a post-war organisation would spontaneously evolve after its creation through the 'mandate' of public opinion upon the government. Not only would public opinion help turn their activities into popular and politically important ones, but it could also play a role in averting wars in the future. Despite their recognition that the public needed to be educated for future war prevention,[125] they

---

[125] See Chapter 2.

did not attempt to do so during the war, even after the year 1917 when they found that the public favoured the idea of the league in general. It was partly because pro-league activists presumed that the public could only be educated gradually but also because they came to think, in the end, that not informing the public of details would work better for their goal of creating a league of nations.

4   A Transnational Movement?

The British and American Pro–League of Nations
Groups, 1914–1918

Introduction

The ideas of the Bryce Group did not remain within Britain; they crossed the Atlantic. The group's *Proposals for the Avoidance of War* influenced not just the League of Nations Society but also its counterpart in the United States, the League to Enforce Peace.[1] The majority of scholars have considered the US President Woodrow Wilson's war-time diplomacy – rather than these private pro-league groups – as the overriding factor in creating the League and have thoroughly analysed Wilson's policy as well as ideas about a new world order.[2] Meanwhile, even studies on the pro-league movement have predominantly investigated the two groups in the English-speaking world separately in the context of each country's domestic politics, by examining national archival sources alone.[3] Although some scholars such as Warren Kuehl have touched upon the relationship between the two groups, it is still largely unknown whether and how they interacted with each other.[4] What has been critically missing in the previous research is how the Bryce Group's ideas about the league were received beyond Britain and how they inspired not only cooperation but also disagreements across the Atlantic. This chapter explores these issues by examining American and British records for the first time extensively together.

The pro–league of nations groups in Britain and the United States, working towards the same goal of reforming the global order, can be

---

[1] In the United States, not only the League to Enforce Peace but some other individuals and groups such as a social reformer Jane Addams and the Socialist Party of America also advocated a new international order for peace. Yet, this chapter focuses on the League to Enforce Peace as the counterpart of the British League of Nations Society as well as the leading American group for the creation of a league of nations. See Thomas J. Knock, *To End All Wars: Woodrow Wilson and the Quest for a New World Order* (Oxford University Press, 1992), pp. 49–55.

[2] See Introduction, n. 3.   [3] See Introduction, nn. 3 and 26; Chapter 2, n. 4.

[4] Warren Kuehl, *Seeking World Order: The United States and International Organization to 1920* (Vanderbilt University Press, 1969).

recognised as a transnational *network*. Yet, this does not mean that they constituted a monolithic, transnational *movement*. As Patricia Clavin has indicated, a transnational community could be interpreted 'not as an enmeshed or bound network, but rather as a honeycomb, a structure which sustains and gives shapes to the identities of nation-states, institutions and particular social and geographic space'.[5] Whereas this observation of a transnational *community* is particularly true of the pro–league of nations groups, their *movement* was less than transnational. As Holger Nehring has argued in his analysis of communication between British and West German protesters against nuclear weapons in the 1950s to 1960s, the two pro-league groups also 'campaigned primarily within the context of their respective nation-states'.[6] In particular, both groups were more concerned about gaining political backing for their own post-war schemes and regarded their counterparts as mere mediums for approaching politicians in each other's country. While communicating with each other and promoting the same ideal of an international organisation for peace, they were still 'embedded firmly in their respective political systems and their national political traditions'.[7] As we will see, both the League of Nations Society and the League to Enforce Peace sprang from the liberal internationalist tradition and began their work with the Bryce Group's *Proposals*.[8] Both attempted to cooperate with each other in the face of the same problem of how to exert influence on politicians and other key decision-making elites. Nonetheless, such similarities did not necessarily enable them to foster constructive collaboration. They were, as Nehring has described it, 'national internationalists'. Not only did they work in their respective domestic contexts, but the British and American liberal internationalist traditions also differed significantly.[9] British pro-leaguers were more cautious about the use of force and believed that progress towards a new world order should be gradual, not radical. On the other hand, American pro-leaguers supposed world progress required force and sought to create a new order at the war's end.

---

[5] Patricia Clavin, 'Defining Transnationalism', *Contemporary European History*, vol. 14, no. 4 (November 2005), pp 438–39.

[6] Holger Nehring, 'National Internationalists: British and West German Protests against Nuclear Weapons, the Politics of Transnational Communications and the Social History of the Cold War, 1957–1964', *Contemporary European History*, vol. 14, no. 4 (November 2005), p. 581.

[7] Ibid., p. 560.

[8] Casper Sylvest, *British Liberal Internationalism, 1880–1930: Making Progress?* (Manchester University Press 2009); Kuehl, *Seeking World Order*; Ronald E. Powaski, *Toward an Entangling Alliance: American Isolationism, Internationalism, and Europe, 1901–1950* (Greenwood Press, 1991).

[9] Nehring, 'National Internationalists'.

Framed by domestic contexts, their different ideas and their prioritisation of lobbying politicians prevented them from forming a foundation of mutual trust as well as close cooperation. The war-time cooperation and disagreement between the US and British pro-leaguers illustrates the mobilising power of the Bryce Group's original set of ideas about an international organisation and the limits of those ideas as unifying force in a transnational context.

The *Proposals* of the Bryce Group not only helped to develop the pro-league movements and plans in Britain and the United States but also shaped some of the fundamental thinking of the Covenant of the League of Nations in 1919, such as the peaceful settlement of disputes by a judicial settlement. The *Proposals*' original set of ideas, however, did not remain intact during the war. Faced with the political challenge of galvanising widespread support, both groups had to simplify their ideas for mass consumption. They promoted the ideal of the creation of a post-war organisation without dwelling on the details of their sophisticated programmes, such as those for war prevention contained in the Bryce's Group's *Proposals*. These elaborate plans were 'the leagues that weren't', to use Stephen Wertheim's striking phrase.[10] It is true that the imagined leagues of these private groups had little if any chance of displacing the post-war plans adopted by politicians at the Paris Peace Conference of 1919. Their ideas, however, did not simply lose the political battle. In the process of developing the wider movement, they opened the way for various alternative league plans, including the one that finally triumphed at Paris in 1919. In consequence, their ideas were able to evolve in a way that could achieve their goal of establishing a post-war organisation. Such flexibility regarding pro-league activities was crucial for promoting the league as an international issue, even though it severely limited their influence on its ultimate design.

The Same Goal and the Different Strands of Liberal Internationalism, 1914–1916

The two pro-league groups had a lot in common from the outset. In 1915, liberal internationalists both in Britain and the United States were inspired by the Bryce Group's *Proposals for the Avoidance of War* and organised pro-league popular movements. In Britain, the League of

---

[10] Stephen Wertheim, 'The League That Wasn't: American Designs for a Legalist-Sanctionist League of Nations and the Intellectual Origins of International Organization, 1914–1920', *Diplomatic History*, vol. 35, no. 5 (November 2011), pp 797–836.

Nations Society was founded in May 1915 to promote the idea of the post-war league to the public. Following the Bryce Group's *Proposals*, they advocated the peaceful settlement of disputes by a judicial settlement, the Council of Conciliation and collective security.[11] The leading members of the League of Nations Society included two Bryce Group members, the Liberal MP Willoughby H. Dickinson and the Cambridge classicist Goldsworthy Lowes Dickinson.[12] Although the chair of the Bryce Group, former British ambassador to Washington James Bryce, was not formally a member of the Society, he guided it and acted as the Society's go-between in communication with the American group.

Concurrently in the United States, the League to Enforce Peace was organised in June 1915.[13] After the outbreak of the war in 1914, Hamilton Holt, the editor of the liberal weekly New York magazine *Independent* who had already been active in peace work before the war, published his plan for a new order.[14] It attracted public attention and stimulated the activities of some internationalists – the majority of them had been connected with pre-war peace activities.[15] From January 1915, they held a series of dinners to discuss the creation of a post-war organisation, out of which the League to Enforce Peace emerged.[16] The Bryce Group of Britain, after completing the first version in February 1915, sent copies of their *Proposals* directly to the founders of the American groups including the former ambassador to Belgium, Theodore Marburg.[17] American internationalists therefore reviewed the Bryce Group's post-war plan in their dinner meetings in advance of the formation of the League to Enforce Peace.[18] At its first public convention in June 1916, the League to Enforce Peace adopted their first official

---

[11] See Chapter 3; BLEPS, FBP/B/26, The League of Nations Publications, no. 2, 'Explanation of the Objects of the Society', March 1916.

[12] Other leading members included the architect Raymond Unwin, the Justices of the Peace Mr and Mrs Claremont, Senator La Fontaine of Belgium, the barrister and legal writer Frank. N. Keen and the Liberal MP Aneurin Williams. OBL, Willoughby Dickinson Papers, MS. Eng. hist. c.406, 'League of Nations Society, Notes as to its Origin by Sir W. Dickinson'.

[13] Harvard University, Houghton Library, League to Enforce Peace Records (Int 6722.8.25*), Box 4, Minutes, 1915 January–April 9, 25 January 1915 and 30 March 1915; Peter J. Yearwood, *Guarantee of Peace: The League of Nations in British Policy, 1914–1925* (Oxford University Press, 2009), p. 10.

[14] Kuehl, *Seeking World Order*, pp. 181–84; Ruhl J. Bartlett, *The League to Enforce Peace* (University of North Carolina Press, 1944), pp. 29–32.

[15] Bartlett, *The League to Enforce Peace*, p. 25.

[16] Kuehl, *Seeking World Order*, p. 184; Bartlett, *The League to Enforce Peace*, p. 34.

[17] Kuehl, *Seeking World Order*, p. 179; Bartlett, *The League to Enforce Peace*, p. 35.

[18] Kuehl *Seeking World Order*, pp. 186–87, 189; Bartlett, *The League to Enforce Peace*, p. 35; HUHL, LEPR (Int 6722.8.25*), Box 4, Minutes, 1915 January–April 9, 30 March

platform to advocate the formation of a post-war organisation.[19] As the British League of Nations Society had done, the American group also advocated the justiciable settlement of disputes, the Council of Conciliation, collective security and conferences to codify international law. Their platform and activities were coordinated by the group leaders such as the former Republican President William H. Taft, Abbot Lawrence Lowell, the President of Harvard University, in addition to Theodore Marburg and Hamilton Holt.

The leading members of both the American and British movements were highly educated intellectuals who worked as university professors, journalists, politicians and lawyers.[20] As liberal internationalists, they tended to believe in human nature and progress and sought to provide a counter-argument to features of the old international system such as the balance of power and international anarchy.[21] The fact that both groups began with the Bryce Group's *Proposals* meant that they shared many basic ideas and core values of future war prevention:[22] all justiciable questions should be submitted to judicial tribunals, non-justiciable disputes should be referred to the Council of Conciliation and signatory states should unite in any action necessary in the event of a state refusing to submit cases to the above and committing acts of hostility etc.[23] They even agreed on the fundamental point that the league could not abolish all wars but could only lessen the possibilities for the outbreak of war and limit its expansion.[24]

1915, 30 March 1915; Cambridge, King's College, The Papers of Goldsworthy Lowes Dickinson, GLD 1/2/4, 303–6.

[19] Bartlett, *The League to Enforce Peace*, pp. 35–40.

[20] Gary B. Ostrower, 'Historical Studies in American Internationalism', *International Organization*, vol. 25, no. 4 (September 1971), p. 903.

[21] See Chapter 2; Sylvest, *British Liberal Internationalism*, pp. 3, 198; Sandi E. Cooper, 'Liberal Internationalists before World War I', *Peace & Change*, vol. 1, no. 2 (April 1973), p. 12.

[22] One of the American leaders, A. Lowell, admitted that the League to Enforce Peace's plan was, just as the British group was, founded upon the Bryce Group's *Proposals*. See BLEPS, WALLAS 4/5, a letter from Lowell to G. Lowes Dickinson, 17 August 1915; Kuehl, *Seeking World Order*, pp. 186–89.

[23] For the British plan, see BLEPS, FBP/B/26, The League of Nations Publications, no. 2, 'Explanation of the Objects of the Society', March 1916; The American plan can be found at, HUHL, ALLPP (*2005-481), Box 10, 882, 'League to Enforce Peace American Branch, Formed at a Conference in Independence Hall, on Bunker Hill Day', 17 June 1915.

[24] As for the American view, see HUHL, ALLPP (*2005-481), Box 11, League to Enforce Peace Publication, no. 25, A. Lawrence Lowell, 'A Platform on Which the Whole World Can Stand', 26 May 1916; ibid., Box 7, '"The Price of Peace", A. Lawrence Lowell in Advocate of Peace', October 1916, vol. LXXVIII, p. 9; HUHL, LEPR (Int 6722.8.25*), Box 4, Minutes, 1915 January–April 9, 9 April 1915. As for the British view, see Chapter 2; Another possible title of the Bryce Group's 1915 Proposal was *Proposals for*

Moreover, both groups deemed American participation essential for the establishment of the league. In Britain, pro-leaguers were aware that the Monroe Doctrine, the American foreign policy of mutual non-intervention between America and Europe, might present potential diffi-culties for the United States in joining a league.[25] Still, American participation was vital because, as James Bryce put it, 'without America, there would be small hope of progress; with America, much might be done' to prevent future wars.[26] Their post-war plan required the United States to participate in replacing a European alliance system with an international organisation for peace.[27] The new organisation, they thought, could only be achieved by the inclusion of as many states as possible but at least all of the liberal great powers such as Britain, France and the United States as the league's core members;[28] the most crucial state among them was the United States. British pro-leaguers feared that the league without the United States would simply perpetuate the pre-war European alliance blocs that they had identified as a major cause of war.

Meanwhile, the League to Enforce Peace agreed that the creation of the league was impossible without American membership, yet on differ-ent grounds. From the beginning of its activities, the American group emphasised that it was 'desirable for the United States to join a league of nations'.[29] Merely joining it, in fact, was unsatisfactory. As Irving Fisher, a member of the American group and an economist at Yale University stated, the 'initiative for the formation of a League of Peace ought to be taken by the United States'.[30] They did not record any reasons why the United States should take the initiative. Practically, American activists perhaps found it useful to counter isolationists' opposition to their post-war project. To take 'a prominent part in its formation' could improve

---

    Reducing the Number of Future Wars not abolishing wars in OBL, Willoughby Dickinson Papers, MS. Eng. hist. c.402, *Proposals for Reducing the Number of Future Wars, with a Prefatory Note by Viscount Bryce, As Revised Up to 24 February 1915.*

[25] Aneurin Williams, 'Proposals for a League of Peace and Mutual Protection among Nations', Reprinted from the *Contemporary Review*, November 1914 (Garden City-Press Limited Letchworth-Herts), p. 8.

[26] OBL, James Bryce Papers, MS. Bryce U.S.A. 23, 55, Bryce to House, 26 August 1916.

[27] BLEPS, FBP/B/26, The League of Nations Publications, no. 2, 'Explanation of the Objects of the Society', March 1916.

[28] For example, see Society member Aneurin Williams' article, BLEPS, E(I)33, Aneurin Williams, 'A New Basis of International Peace' (London, 1915), pp. 8–9.

[29] HUHL, ALLPP (*2005-481), Box 10, 882, 'League to Enforce Peace American Branch, Formed at a Conference in Independence Hall, on Bunker Hill Day', 17 June 1915.

[30] HUHL, LEPR (Int 6722.8.25*), Box 4, Minutes, 1915, January–April 9, 30 March 1915.

the chances of persuading the Americans to unite behind a moral crusade to bring peace from the new world to the old world.[31]

More importantly, American activists' belief in an American initiative originated in the American strand of liberal internationalism that was framed by their linear perspective of history – unidirectional progress from barbarism to civilisation.[32] In their understanding of progressive history, manifest destiny in nineteenth century America would extend overseas, disseminating central concepts such as liberty and democracy.[33] In addition to America's God-given leadership in civilising the world,[34] progressive history embraced the social gospel for reform at home and abroad and to redeem the old world from its outmoded alliance system and balance of power.[35] Such perspectives led American activists to view contemporary America as the model of a peaceful league as well as the source of hope for future international relations.[36] As American pro-leaguers such as Fisher indicated, war – a major world problem – was a European disease that was 'hard for us Americans ... to understand'.[37] A remedy to this disease, in American activists' theory, was to create a league of peace that would unite Europe in a federation similar to the United States of America. Thus, they supposed American institutions could serve as analogues of a league, for instance, the US Supreme Court as a model for a post-war international court. Further, American pro-leaguers drew a strong parallel between the current war and the American Civil War.[38] Fisher, for example, remarked that the original thirteen colonies in America had

[31] HUHL, ALLPP (*2005-481), Box 11, League to Enforce Peace Publication, no. 25, A. Lawrence Lowell, 'A Platform on Which the Whole World Can Stand', 26 May 1916, p. 5.

[32] Lloyd E. Ambrosius, *Wilsonian Statecraft: Theory and Practice of Liberal Internationalism during World War I* (Scholarly Resources Books, 1991), p. 7; Lloyd E. Ambrosius, *Woodrow Wilson and American Internationalism* (Cambridge University Press, 2017), pp. 2–3, 236.

[33] Ambrosius, *Wilsonian Statecraft*, pp. 3, 21.

[34] Adam Tooze, *The Deluge: The Great War and the Remaking of Global Order, 1916–1931* (Allen Lane, 2014), pp. 27–29; Ambrosius, *Wilsonian Statecraft*, p. 3.

[35] Ambrosius, *Wilsonian Statecraft*, pp. 3, 10–13.

[36] C. Roland Marchand, *The American Peace Movement and Social Reform, 1898–1918* (Princeton University Press, 1972), p. 327; Lloyd E. Ambrosius, *Woodrow Wilson and the American Diplomatic Tradition: The Treaty Fight in Perspective* (Cambridge University Press, 1988), pp. 3–6; D. Cameron Watt, *Succeeding John Bull: America in Britain's Place 1900–1975: A Study of the Anglo-American Relationship and World Politics in the Context of British and American Foreign-Policy-Making in the Twentieth Century* (Cambridge University Press, 1984), chapter 2.

[37] HUHL, ALLPP (*2005-481), Box 10, Irving Fisher, 'After the War, What? A Plea for A League of Peace', pp. 6–7.

[38] OBL, Willoughby Dickinson Papers, MS. Eng. hist. c.402, a letter from Marburg to R. Cross, 28 Sept 1915; see also, Max M. Edling, 'Peace Pact and Nation: An

distrusted each other as the contemporary European states did, yet such hostility disappeared when they were formed into the United States of America.[39] Fisher continued, 'for world peace we must follow the same course', since European peace could not be attained until a federation of the European states was formed after this 'civil war of Europe'.[40] Even one of the group's leading members and the former ambassador to Belgium, Theodore Marburg, recommended that the British Foreign Secretary Edward Grey should publicly announce British support for a league 'just as Lincoln, in the middle of our Civil War, won the sympathy of the world for the Northern cause by his Emancipation Proclamation'.[41] As the United States had already set a precedent for the formation of a peaceful league in the aftermath of the US Civil War, so, American activists deemed, they should be in an appropriate position to initiate the formation of a post-war organisation for peace.

Indeed, the parallel between the Civil War and the ongoing war reflected the influence of Social Darwinism on American peace activists.[42] The Darwinian theory of evolution profoundly affected many disciplines including history, ethics and politics in Western Europe and America from the late nineteenth century to the early twentieth century.[43] It undergirded not only progressive history in parallel with the biological analogy[44] but also a view that 'military power and war as [were] powerful vectors of progressive state construction'.[45] In Social Darwinism, state formation, evolution and progress required violence

---

International Interpretation of the Constitution of the United States', *Past & Present*, vol. 240, no. 1 (August 2018), pp. 267–303.

[39] HUHL, ALLPP (*2005-481), Box 10, Irving Fisher, 'After the War, What? A Plea for A League of Peace', pp. 14–15.

[40] Ibid., p. 15.

[41] OBL, James Bryce Papers, MS. Bryce U.S.A. 8, 233–35, a letter from Marburg to Taft, 13 May 1916; HUHL, LEPR (Int 6722.8.25*), Box 2, 2 Foreign Peace Organizations, a letter from Marburg to E. Grey 28 Aug 1916, a letter from Marburg to White, 20 June 1917 and a letter from Marburg to Short, 11 September 1916.

[42] Tooze, *The Deluge*, pp. 28–29.

[43] H. W. Koch, 'Social Darwinism As a Factor in the "New Imperialism"', in H. W. Koch (ed.), *The Origins of the First World War: Great Power Rivalry and German War Aims* (Macmillan, 1984), pp. 319–42; Charles E. Merriam, *American Political Ideas: Studies in the Development of American Political Thought, 1865–1917* (Macmillan, 1920), p, 371. In Britain, at the turn of the century, liberal intellectuals such as Norman Angell and G. Lowes Dickinson attacked the Darwinist notion of struggle that claimed war was inevitable and instead argued that war was 'not only morally wrong but also irrational'. See Casper Sylvest, 'Continuity and Change in British Liberal Internationalism, c. 1900 1930', *Review of International Studies*, vol. 31, no. 2 (2005), pp. 272–73.

[44] Ambrosius, *Wilsonian Statecraft*, p. 9.

[45] Tooze, *The Deluge*, p. 28. See also Akira Iriye, *War and Peace in the Twentieth Century* (Tokyo University Press, 1986) [in Japanese], pp. 24–27; Ambrosius, *Woodrow Wilson and American Internationalism*, p. 87.

since it constituted a process of selection in the human species.[46] American activists expected, as the United States became united as a nation after the Civil War, that the world would evolve after the current war with the spur of force. American liberal internationalism recognised the positive role of force in the development of history and the world, which had an impact on American ideas about the post-war world order and with which their British counterparts would disagree.

Disagreements Based on Different Contexts and Ideas

While the two pro-league groups had much in common, their different national milieus and ideas created disagreements about the league. As for their different national circumstances in 1914–1916, Britain was a belligerent from the summer of 1914 and the United States neutral until April 1917. In Britain, the League of Nations Society needed to work undercover to protect itself from attacks by the jingoistic public.[47] While their quiet pro-league campaign attracted 400 members in 1916, they could not hold a public meeting until May 1917.[48] Whoever talked about peace might be denounced as a pacifist in the early years of the war, thus James Bryce, who directed the behind-the-scenes lobbying of the group, presumed that any attempts to put forward the league project might stir up opposition to it and dash their hopes.[49] In his letters to the League to Enforce Peace leaders, Lowell and Marburg, Bryce elucidated why the League of Nations Society could not go public and why any post-war plans including the American one could not openly be discussed in Britain. First, because the British public was wholly preoccupied with 'the winning of the war'; second, because 'everything said about peace'

---

[46] George Nasmyth, *Social Progress and the Darwinian Theory: A Study of Force As a Factor in Human Relations* (G. P. Putnam's Sons, 1916), pp. 7, 17, 140; Koch, 'Social Darwinism As a Factor in the "New Imperialism"', p. 336; Paul Crook, *Darwinism, War, and History: The Debate over the Biology of War from the "Origin of Species" to the First World War* (Cambridge University Press, 1994), pp. 130, 136–37.

[47] As Chapter 3 mentioned, there were anti-German riots in London in 1915; see Arthur Ponsonby's Diary (transcript), 14 May 1915; Kate Courtney, *Extracts from a Diary during the War* (Victor Press, 1927), pp. 36–37; OBL, Ponsonby Papers, MS. Eng. hist. c.662, a letter from Charles Trevelyan to Ponsonby, 24 July 1915. Also, jingoism was evident in intellectual circles as well; see A. J. P. Taylor, *The Trouble Makers: Dissent over Foreign Policy, 1792–1939* (Hamish Hamilton, 1957), p. 133.

[48] George W. Egerton, *Great Britain and the Creation of the League of Nations: Strategy, Politics, and International Organization, 1914–1919* (Scolar Press, 1978), p. 13.

[49] CKC, The Papers of Charles Robert Ashbee, CRA 3/4, chapter 10, 266, a letter from Bryce to C. R. Ashbee, 13 September 1915; Herbert Albert Laurens Fisher, *James Bryce*, vol. II (Macmillan, 1927), p. 140; OBL, James Bryce Papers, MS. Bryce 158, 213, a letter from Bryce to Scott, 25 October 1916.

was misrepresented as a demand for an immediate peace with Germany.[50] Hence, discussion of any league projects had no place in Britain before American entry into the war. As Bryce noted, even the feelings of some British pro-leaguers, 'not of Jingoes, but of peace lovers', were against negotiation or mediation but determined 'to fight on'.[51]

In contrast with the British, the League to Enforce Peace already worked in public and enjoyed growing popularity. The American group had branches to raise its own funds and control its own area in most states by the end of 1916.[52] On 28 November 1916, for instance, fifty speakers held meetings at various places at Worcester, Massachusetts, where the regional branch organised 132 local meetings during that year.[53] In meetings at Washington in May 1916, of the ninety-nine newspaper editorials that were read out, ninety-one favoured the idea of a league.[54] In the summer of that year, the American group argued that it was time to begin propaganda activities in foreign countries, exploiting President Wilson's advocacy of the league.[55] Their targets were mainly the foreign ministers, ambassadors and the foreign offices of the Allied countries: Britain, France, Russia, Belgium, Holland, Spain, Japan, Denmark, Sweden, Switzerland, Argentina and Chile.[56] The League to Enforce Peace sent its scheme to key foreign officials throughout the war, underlying the value of each country's assistance to create the league.[57]

In addition to operating in strikingly different national and international circumstances, the two pro-league groups disagreed about the architecture of a post-war organisation. Indeed, both groups argued that the other's ideas did 'not go as far as' their own side with respect to

---

[50] OBL, James Bryce Papers, MS. Bryce U.S.A.23, 52–53, a letter from Bryce to Lowell, 25 July 1916; HUHL, LEPR (Int 6722.8.25*), Box 1, a letter from Bryce to Marburg, 7 December 1916; Columbia University, Carnegie Endowment for International Peace Records, 1910–1954, Box 241, 8 The League to Enforce Peace 1917–1919, a letter from Bryce to Marburg, 6 February 1917.

[51] OBL, James Bryce Papers, MS. Bryce U.S.A.23, 38, Bryce to House, 26 November 1915 and 67–68, a letter from Bryce to House, 27 December 1916; also see David Stevenson, *1914–1918: The History of the First World War* (Penguin, 2005), pp. 36–37, 41, 271.

[52] Wertheim, 'The League of Nations'; Bartlett, *The League to Enforce Peace*, pp. 61–62.

[53] Bartlett, *The League to Enforce Peace*, pp. 62–63.   [54] Ibid., p. 64.

[55] OBL, James Bryce Papers, MS. Bryce U.S.A. 8, 233–35, a letter from Marburg to Taft, 13 May 1916.

[56] HUHL, LEPR (Int 6722.8.25*), Box 2, 2 Foreign Peace Organizations, letters from foreign statesmen to Theodore Marburg.

[57] The League to Enforce Peace exchanged many letters with foreign politicians; see the file of HUHL, LEPR (Int 6722.8.25*), Box 2, 2 Foreign Peace Organizations.

collective security – sanctions and security against attack.[58] The American plan defined collective security as follows:

The signatory powers shall jointly use forthwith both their economic and military forces against any one of their number that goes to war, or commits acts of hostility, against another of the signatories before any question arising shall be submitted as provided in the foregoing.[59]

Meanwhile, the British pro-leaguers defined it as follows:

3. That the States which are members of the League shall unite in any action necessary for ensuring that every member shall abide by the terms of the Treaty.

4. That the States which are members of the League shall make provision for Mutual Defence, diplomatic, economic, or military, in the event of any of them being attacked by a State, not a member of the League, which refuses to submit the case to an appropriate Tribunal or Council.[60]

First, whereas the British League of Nations Society proposed economic *or* military sanction *after* reviewing each case at the Court or the Council of Conciliation, the American League to Enforce Peace insisted upon *automatic* sanctions of economic *and* military force. Having read the British plan, one of the American leaders, Theodore Marburg, criticised it for 'not bind[ing] the League to certain and immediate action' in a time of crisis.[61] The British plan of punishing rule-breaking states, he said, involved 'too great an element of uncertainty as to what measures will be finally employed, and uncertainty in fact as to whether any effective measures will be employed'.[62] Such uncertainties seemed counterproductive to the Americans, since sanctions against violation of the rules of international law and peace had to be 'swift and sure' with both economic *and* military forces for successfully preventing wars.[63] The American plan, Marburg argued, was superior because 'the League had no option' but being 'obliged to unite in making war forthwith on any one of its members which makes war on another member without first having a hearing of the dispute'.[64]

---

[58] Ibid., Box 5, Committees, etc., various papers, a letter from Bryce to Marburg, 9 June 1915; OBL, James Bryce Papers, MS. Bryce 94, a letter from Lowell to Bryce, 16 July 1915.

[59] HUHL, ALLPP (*2005-481), Box 10, 882, 'League to Enforce Peace American Branch, Formed at a Conference in Independence Hall, on Bunker Hill Day', 17 June 1915.

[60] BLEPS, FBP/B/26, The League of Nations Publications, no. 2, 'Explanation of the Objects of the Society', March 1916, p. 4.

[61] OBL, Willoughby Dickinson Papers, MS. Eng. hist. c.402, a letter from Marburg to R. Cross, 28 September 1915.

[62] Ibid.   [63] Ibid.   [64] Ibid.

Why, then, did the League to Enforce Peace prefer automatic sanction with both economic and military forces?[65] Exploring this question underscores the differences in outlook between the American and British strands of liberal internationalism. The British activists were cautious about radical international reform and aware of the dangers and contradictions inherent in the use of force to uphold the peace. They seemed more alert to the negative effect of military sanctions, such as escalating small wars into bigger ones. On the other hand, the Americans, under the influence of Social Darwinism and unidirectional history, presumed that the progress towards a peaceful order naturally entailed the use of force. In practice, many leading members of the League to Enforce Peace including Taft, Lowell and Marburg were lawyers and their premise was that the international society was one legal community based on what the international relations theorist Hidemi Suganami has called the domestic analogy: the world order is analogous to domestic order.[66] As Lowell professed, 'a breach of the world's peace, like a breach of domestic peace, is an offense against public order which the public ought to have some right to prevent'.[67] Since the 'right' included the use of force, if any state resorted to war and broke world peace, then 'the world has at least a right to insist on knowing the reason for the war' and on *compelling* states to go to arbitration.[68]

In order to enforce peace, American activists assumed that the league needed automatic sanction as the 'certain, and sufficient' method.[69] Their judicial mindset expected the world to have a sort of police force for the maintenance of peace. Relating the role of a domestic police force to that of international sanctions, the Americans presupposed that only automatic sanctions would be able to convince states of the prohibitive

---

[65] HUHL, ALLPP (*2005-481), Box 10, 882, 'League to Enforce Peace American Branch, Formed at a Conference in Independence Hall, on Bunker Hill Day', 17 June 1915. Also see Kuehl, *Seeking World Order*, pp. 189–92.

[66] Hidemi Suganami, *The Domestic Analogy and World Order Proposals* (Cambridge University Press, 1989). According to Sylvest, in the debates of British internationalists, 'there was no direct correlation between arguments employed in the domestic and in the international sphere'. See Sylvest, 'Continuity and Change in British Liberal Internationalism', pp. 273–74. Also see Benjamin Allen Coates, *Legalist Empire: International Law and American Foreign Relations in the Early Twentieth Century* (Oxford University Press, 2016), chapter 7.

[67] HUHL, ALLPP (*2005-481), Box 11, League to Enforce Peace Publication, no. 25, A. Lawrence Lowell, 'A Platform on Which the Whole World Can Stand', 26 May 1916.

[68] Ibid.

[69] Ibid; also see, Mark Mazower, *Governing the World: The History of an Idea* (Penguin Books, 2012), pp. 120–21.

cost of committing armed aggression.[70] In a crisis of impending or actual war, diplomats' conclaves would be unlikely to reach agreements or achieve anything.[71] The only effective way was to persuade states that if they initiated war before submitting their case to arbitration, they would be in a state of war with all the states.[72] Once states recognised the danger of commencing hostilities, the Americans supposed, they would 'never commit such acts of hostility, and hence that such a universal war will never be needed'.[73] In other words, automatic sanctions were a police force–like deterrent against aggression,[74] ultimately required more for psychological pressure than hopefully for actual use. Even though the American activists admitted that automatic sanctions might not always deter states from going to war, it would, if adopted, make war at least extremely improbable.[75] As Lowell argued, American activists considered that 'nothing less will be effective, and such a doom [of fighting war with all the states] no nation would dare to face'.[76] In a letter to the British group, Lowell maintained this strong position and urged it to adopt automatic sanctions:

Mind you, it is very well to say, as people do, 'Why not try arms if other things fail?'; but by the time other things have failed – that is, when war has broken out – it is too late to prevent it. War must be prevented before it begins, or not at all; and wars of the present day break out so quickly that there is no time for the

---

[70] BLEPS, WALLAS 4/5, a letter from Lowell to G. Lowes Dickinson, 17 August 1915; HUHL, ALLPP (*2005-481), Box 7, '"The Price of Peace" A. Lawrence Lowell in Advocate of Peace', October 1916, vol. LXXVIII, no. 9; ibid., Box 12, International Conciliation pamphlet, no. 106, 'The Proposal for a League to Enforce Peace: Affirmative-Taft, Negative-W. J. Bryan', September 1916; Also see Coates, *Legalist Empire*, chapter 7.

[71] BLEPS, WALLAS 4/5, a letter from Lowell to G. Lowes Dickinson, 17 August 1915.

[72] HUHL, ALLPP (*2005-481), Box 7, '"The Price of Peace" A. Lawrence Lowell in Advocate of Peace', October 1916, vol. LXXVIII, no. 9; ibid., Box 10, 882, 'League to Enforce Peace American Branch, Formed at a Conference in Independence Hall, on Bunker Hill Day', 17 June 1915.

[73] BLEPS, WALLAS 4/5, a letter from Lowell to G. Lowes Dickinson, 17 August 1915; HUHL, ALLPP (*2005-481), Box 7, '"The Price of Peace" A. Lawrence Lowell in Advocate of Peace', October 1916, vol. LXXVIII, no. 9.

[74] HUHL, ALLPP (*2005-481), Box 7, '"The Price of Peace" A. Lawrence Lowell in Advocate of Peace', October 1916, vol. LXXVIII, no. 9; ibid., Box 11, League to Enforce Peace Publication, no. 25, A. Lawrence Lowell, 'A Platform on Which the Whole World Can Stand', 26 May 1916; OBL, James Bryce Papers, MS. Bryce U.S.A. 8, a letter from Lowell to Bryce, 4 February 1915; HUHL, LEPR (Int 6722.8.25*), Box 5, Committees, etc., various papers, a letter from Lowell to Short, 23 November 1915.

[75] Ibid., Box 10, 882, 'League to Enforce Peace American Branch, Formed at a Conference in Independence Hall, on Bunker Hill Day', 17 June 1915.

[76] Ibid., Box 11, League to Enforce Peace Publication, no. 25, A. Lawrence Lowell, 'A Platform on Which the Whole World Can Stand', 26 May 1916.

nations to come together in conference. Is it possible that your friends would be ready to go a step farther than they have done hitherto, and accept the plan of a league to enforce peace by threat of war?[77]

In contrast, the pessimistic and perhaps more realistic views of the British pro-leaguers about international politics did not allow them to believe that the post-war world would be organised more or less into one legal community. They, therefore, did not associate sanctions with a domestic police force and cautiously took account of the possibility that military sanctions might trigger larger wars. For the British, in the end, as Donald Watt has put it, the United States was not a state conforming to 'the same standards as those of the major European powers' due in part to their image of America as 'a quasi-Dominion, linked to Britain by a common culture and purpose'.[78] The British pro-leaguers expected that they had a better grasp of the realities of international politics than the Americans. Although the British group agreed that military sanctions were vital for the league scheme, from their standpoint, sanctions were incorporated into the league plan along with the other war prevention measures.[79] The British thought that disputes should first be submitted to the Court or the Council of Conciliation even in crisis. Sanctions – economic, diplomatic or military pressure depending on individual cases – should be executed only after and if the other war prevention measures failed, as a last resort.[80] In reaction to American optimism about automatic military sanctions, the architect and a leading member of the British group Raymond Unwin offered the sources of their reservations about it. First of all, the League of Nations Society preferred the use of force to uphold the decisions of the Court and to enforce the submission of a case. If commencing hostilities immediately led to military sanctions, a league would not have a chance to ask a rule-breaker to submit the case to the Court. It meant that the use of force would come before the Court and therefore automatic sanction would not be able to endorse the judicial decisions.[81]

Yet, that was their official explanation; the British group probably attempted to convince their American counterparts by highlighting the legal complexities and conundrums of automatic military sanctions. Ultimately, however, British opposition to automatic sanctions was

---

[77] BLEPS, WALLAS 4/5, a letter from Lowell to G. Lowes Dickinson, 17 August 1915.
[78] Watt, *Succeeding John Bull*, pp. 27–32.   [79] See Chapter 2.
[80] BLEPS, FRP/B/26, The League of Nations Publications, no. 2, 'Explanation of the Objects of the Society', March 1916, pp. 4, 18–19.
[81] HUHL, LEPR (Int 6722.8.25*), Box 5, Committees, etc., various papers, 'Exhibit 1 A', a letter from Raymond Unwin, 14 November 1915 and a letter from Bryce to Marburg, 9 June 1915.

driven by their cautiousness regarding the use of force. Members of the League of Nations Society doubted if swift armed action would always be the best way of preventing wars.[82] The British group discussed internally the question of military sanctions and was fully aware that in many disputes it was abstruse to determine which state commenced hostilities and which state was to be blamed.[83] Because of the difficulty in identifying the aggressor, they presumed that the automatic implementation of sanctions could be problematic to say the least. Additionally, they recognised the danger that military sanctions, if attempted, would escalate rapidly into a worldwide war, whereas non-military sanctions might be able to limit the scale of war or contain it.[84] Having investigated such possibilities, the British activists proposed a post-war plan that would examine each situation on its merits and judge what would be the best way to handle it. As one of the Society leaders, Goldsworthy Lowes Dickinson, wrote during his lecture tour on the league in the United States, British activists recognised irreconcilable differences between their ideas and those of the Americans: 'Americans are like all others – readier to arm than to consider the why and wherefore of arming.'[85]

Further, differing British and American outlooks produced another point of dispute: security against outside attack. British activists sought the gradual progress of international relations to a more peaceful and just order and never predicted the dramatic change of the world system. Yet the American pro-leaguers, who longed to lead the world to something new, pursued their ideal of creating a perfect organisation with universal or near universal membership. While the British scheme 'provided for protection against attack by an outside power', the American group omitted it from their plan. Such a response from their counterpart surprised British activists who did not believe a league of *all* states to be easily created. In the British view, the league would evolve over time, and in the meantime there would be potential rule-breakers. Thus, as Unwin argued, 'if protection is to be given against an inside state only, the state that may want to attack has an inducement to stay outside the League or to leave the League'.[86] The League to Enforce Peace's answer to this criticism underlined the different approaches of the two groups to the post-war world. Seeing themselves as the leaders of the world, or at least

---

[82] Ibid., Box 5, Committees, etc., various papers, 'Exhibit 1 A', a letter from Raymond Unwin, 14 November 1915.

[83] See Chapter 2.   [84] Ibid.

[85] CKC, The Papers of Charles Robert Ashbee, CRA 3/4, a letter from G. Lowes Dickinson to C. R. Ashbee, 8 February 1916.

[86] HUHL, LEPR (Int 6722.8.25*), Box 5, Committees, etc., various papers, 'Exhibit 1 A', a letter from Raymond Unwin, 14 November 1915.

on a mission to save Europe from future wars, the Americans preferred pursuing large-scale projects and setting very high standards – the creation of the peace league as perfect as possible from the beginning. To American activists who drew a parallel between the European war and the American Civil War, Europe should be peacefully organised after the current war as the United States had been after the Civil War. The American activists' legalistic thinking and analogical view of domestic and international society also enabled them to suppose that the post-war league should be a universal organisation and therefore required the membership of *all* or *almost all* the states.[87] Otherwise, Marburg argued on behalf of the group, the enforcement of peace by threatening aggressors with a war against all states would not work. He proclaimed that a league of a limited number of nations itself might make a rule-breaker withdraw from the league and form an alliance outside of it.[88]

In 1914–1916, their national circumstances and different outlooks hindered cooperation between the two groups. The cautious British group presupposed that progress in international society should be gradual. They did not assume that the post-war world could easily be united into a universal league and that military sanctions could function as an absolute deterrent. Believing in progressive history and radical development after the war, the Americans called for a dramatic change in international relations. The league should be organised as a single community, including every state and applying law as well as a police force in the form of collective force. Of course, both groups were somewhat naive: the League of Nations Society knew that its conception of the league was very conservative and minimalistic, and it might be insufficient to prevent war. Still, its members hoped that such a league would someday develop into a more perfect international organisation. On the other hand, the League to Enforce Peace, driven by its belief in unidirectional progress, legalistic thinking and its conviction about leading the world, aimed to change the international order radically and swiftly. Occasionally, its high standards and a reliance on the domestic analogy diverted them from political realities. In terms of practicability, the British conception of the league had a better prospect of being implemented and perhaps maturing; yet for war prevention, the American idea probably had a better chance of working *if* it could be implemented. These differences of opinion were not reconciled until, in 1917–1918, they realised that they shared a common problem.

[87] OBL, Willoughby Dickinson Papers, MS. Eng. hist. c.402, a letter from Marburg to R. Cross, 28 September 1915.
[88] Ibid.

The Changing Situation and the Same Problem, 1917

Despite their differences, the two pro-league groups in Britain and the United States shared one common concern: how to persuade politicians to support the foundation of a league of nations. Both groups agreed that the league could only be established through political and diplomatic efforts. Hence, they were concerned about the attitudes of Congress and important American political figures, such as President Wilson, former President Theodore Roosevelt, former Secretary of State Elihu Root and Senator Henry Cabot Lodge, towards the league plan.[89] Similarly, both sought the backing of eminent British public persons including the Foreign Secretary Edward Grey and his successor James Balfour as well as the Prime Minister Herbert Henry Asquith and his successor David Lloyd George.[90] Each group contacted politicians in both countries and lobbied for a league separately. For example, some leaders of the League of Nations Society were interviewed by Edward Grey and had already discussed their activities in 1915;[91] Theodore Marburg, a leading member of the League to Enforce Peace, also talked about an international organisation with Grey when Marburg visited London in March 1916.[92] These direct appeals to politicians such as Grey led to his public endorsement for the creation of a postwar international organisation.[93] Equally, both groups' leaders urged President Wilson to endorse the formation of a league of nations.[94] The American group invited the US President to its meeting in May 1916 and elicited his support for the idea of an international organisation.[95]

---

[89] HUHL, LEPR (Int 6722.8.25*), Box 2, 2 Foreign Peace Organizations, a letter from Marburg to Bryce, 21 July 1916 and a letter from Marburg to E. Grey, 28 August 1916; OBL, James Bryce Papers, MS. Bryce U.S.A. 8, a letter from Lowell to Bryce, 13 March 1917.

[90] OBL, James Bryce Papers, MS. Bryce U.S.A. 8, 233–35, a letter from Marburg to Taft, 13 May 1916 and 73–76, a letter from Lowell to Bryce, 13 March 1917; ibid., MS. Bryce U.S.A. 10, 183, a letter from Taft to Bryce, 21 October 1916; ibid., MS. Bryce U.S.A. 23, 62–63, a letter from Bryce to Lowell, 22 November 1916; HUHL, LEPR (Int 6722.8.25*), Box 2, 2 Foreign Peace Organizations, a letter from Marburg to E. Grey, 28 August 1916 and a letter from Marburg to Bryce, 3 March 1917.

[91] CKC, The Papers of Charles Robert Ashbee, CRA 3/3, 'Ashbee Memoir', July 1914, p. 337 and CRA3/4, 153–56, 12 February 1915.

[92] HUHL, LEPR (Int 6722.8.25*), Box 2, 2 Foreign Peace Organizations, 'England', by Marburg, 11 September 1916; OBL, James Bryce Papers, MS. Bryce U.S.A. 8, 222–23, a letter from Marburg to Bryce, 4 March 1916.

[93] OBL, Willoughby Dickinson Papers, MS. Eng. hist. c.404, 86, 'A League of Nations: Viscount Grey's Speech' (1917).

[94] BLEPS, WALLAS 1/55, a letter from A. L. Lowell to Wallas, 9 September 1914; OBL, James Bryce Papers, MS. Bryce U.S.A.8, 220–22, a letter from Marburg to Bryce, 27 February 1916.

[95] Bartlett, The League to Enforce Peace, p. 53; OBL, James Bryce Papers, MS. Bryce U.S.A. 15, 175–76, a letter from House to Bryce, 29 May 1916 and MS. Bryce U.S.A. USA 8, 66–67, a letter from Lowell to Bryce, 5 July 1916.

In 1917, the international circumstances changed and the political winds seemed to become favourable to pro-leaguers and their efforts to gain decisive political approval. As Chapter 5 will show, after the Russian Revolution and American entry into the war, the war became not simply for the liberation of Belgium or to crush Germany but for the promotion of democracy against autocracy.[96] In what was increasingly becoming a war framed as an ideological struggle against militarism and authoritarianism, politicians in Britain and the United States began to advocate a new post-war organisation to preserve future peace as a war aim to sustain their national war efforts.[97] The ideal of a league for peace offered a striking contrast to the aggressive goals of Germany and its allies,[98] and it also proved to be an effective banner under which the public could mobilise. Along with the commitment to the abolition of German militarism,[99] Lloyd George began to advocate the creation of a league,[100] which he expected to be useful for involving the United States in European affairs and maintaining peace after the war.[101] The Prime Minister had been advised to endorse ideas about a post-war organisation by his entourages and by Philip Kerr in particular.[102] As a leader of the Round Table, a group that advocated the federation of the British Commonwealth, Kerr aspired to a world state ruled by law, strengthening the unity of the British Empire as well as promoting Anglo-American harmony.[103] Especially, he presumed American participation in the league would prevent a resurgence of the European balance of power and facilitate the establishment of a new world order.[104] When

---

[96] See Chapter 5. The National Records of Scotland, Private and Political Papers of Philip Kerr, 11th Marquess of Lothian, GD40/17/866, 'Memorandum (with Amendments) on Need for New Declaration of Policy Following the Russian Revolution and Entry of the U.S. into the War, Which Have Transformed the Diplomatic Situation as Registered in the Allied Reply of [10] Jan. 1917 to [Proposals to the Warring Powers, 18 Dec. 1916 by] President Wilson', April 1917.

[97] Yearwood, *Guarantee of Peace*, pp. 38–39, 46–47.

[98] Ibid., p. 50; Peter Jackson, *Beyond the Balance of Power: France and the Politics of National Security in the Era of the First World War* (Cambridge University Press 2013), p. 96; David Stevenson, 'The First World War and European Integration', *The International History Review*, vol. 34, no. 4 (2012), pp. 841–63.

[99] David French, *The Strategy of the Lloyd George Coalition, 1916–1918* (Clarendon, 1995), pp. 35–36, 200–201.

[100] Peter Yearwood, '"On the Safe and Right Lines": The Lloyd George Government and the Origins of the League of Nations, 1916–1918', *The Historical Journal*, vol. 32, no. 1 (March 1989), p. 133.

[101] Yearwood, 'On the Safe and Right Lines', pp. 2–4; Ambrosius, *Woodrow Wilson and the American Diplomatic Tradition*, p. 4; Watt, *Succeeding John Bull*, pp. 27, 30–32; Powaski, *Toward an Entangling Alliance*, p. 14.

[102] Yearwood, *Guarantee of Peace*, pp. 41–49, 61.   [103] Ibid., p. 41.

[104] Ibid., pp. 42–43.

the Russian Revolution and Lansdowne's letter to call for a negotiated peace in 1917 forced the British government to reconsider their war aims, Lloyd George followed Kerr's advice and stressed that Britain was fighting to secure democracy and to prevent future war.[105] On 5 January 1918, the Prime Minister publicly called for a post-war league of nations, 'some international organization to limit the burden of armaments and diminish the probability of war', officially as a war aim.[106]

Across the Atlantic, advocating a league as a radical departure from Europe's perpetual wars helped the US President to justify America's abandonment of neutrality.[107] Wilson's goal was to end the European balance of power politics – including the alliance blocs, arms races and coercive diplomacy – a system that would never produce stable peace and would only have negative consequences for America's security.[108] In 1914–1916, Wilson was concerned that whichever side won, its result would threaten America's security. While a German victory would accelerate the spread of authoritarian militarism, so he presupposed, an Entente victory might lead to a continuation of balance-of-power politics in Europe and thus lay the grounds for another great war. Wilson concluded that 'his best chance of attaining peace terms conducive to international reform was in a policy of limited, informal cooperation with the Allied war efforts'.[109] He therefore strove to keep the United States out of the war and to act as a mediator, a role he adopted in order to prevent a German victory as well as the total victory of the Allies.[110] Yet in late 1916, he found his policy of mediation ineffective; neither Britain nor France were interested in a negotiated peace and they refused Wilson's mediation.[111] Having learnt that British liberals, such as pro-league activists, would welcome his peace appeal,[112] President Wilson now claimed in his 'peace without victory' speech in January 1917 that the powers of the international community must be organised into a 'League for Peace'.[113] Wilson's endorsement proved to be decisive and the issue of an international organisation became more and more popular throughout 1917.[114] These developments, to pro-leaguers on both sides of the Atlantic, appeared to be paving the way for the foundation of a league of nations more or less in accordance with their visions of that organisation.

---

[105] Ibid., pp. 45–46, 48–49, 145.   [106] Ibid., p. 59–61. See also Chapter 5.
[107] Ambrosius, *Woodrow Wilson and the American Diplomatic Tradition*, pp. 32–34.
[108] Ross Kennedy, *The Will to Believe: Woodrow Wilson, World War I, and America's Strategy for Peace and Security* (Kent State University Press, 2009), pp. xiii, 64. Prior to 1917, Wilson already favoured a concept of the league to prevent war; see Knock, *To End All Wars*, p. ix; Powaski, *Toward an Entangling Alliance*, p. 14.
[109] Kennedy, *The Will to Believe*, p. 65.   [110] Ibid.   [111] Ibid., pp. 89, 96.   [112] Ibid.
[113] Egerton, *Great Britain and the Creation of the League of Nations*, p. 52.
[114] See Chapter 3, n. 5.

In Britain, the League of Nations Society warmly welcomed the American entry into the war as 'a great step forward ... to prevent the recurrence of wars'.[115] To the Society, it was notable not only because the United States would contribute its soldiers and dollars to victory but also because the United States had entered the war on a platform of peace and justice. By identifying the formation of a league as a *just* war aim and not the utopian fantasy of pacifists, the American President helped make the case of the pro-leaguers in Britain legitimate in 1917–1918.[116] Most significantly, American entry into the war finally prompted the British group to confirm the time to go public had come. The Bryce Group's *Proposals for the Avoidance of War*, first privately circulated in February 1915 and providing since then the fundamental benchmark for pro-leaguers in Britain and the United States, was at last published in Britain in March 1917.[117] In May of that year, the British group held its first public meeting with great success and began to openly propagate its goal and activities.[118] From March 1917 to March 1918, the group organised over 170 meetings in Britain with a huge increase in membership.[119]

Even though 1917 was the year that the League of Nations Society made great strides in making its case popular and legitimate, that year also marked the time when the movement began to lose its control of defining what the league would be. In order to gain popularity as well as political backing, the League of Nations Society simplified its ideas to communicate to the general public. By doing so, its sophisticated discussions of such issues as how future war could be prevented and what sorts of fundamental problems a post-war order might have could not be reduced to slogans.[120] New converts to the idea of the league, of course, had their own conceptions of what it should be and by what political process it should come into being. For example, when it held its first public meeting, the Society recruited the South African statesman General Jan Christiaan Smuts – who later became a leading advocate of the league inside the government – as one of the speakers. After Smuts landed in Britain in March 1917, he was invited to meetings with leading British figures including league advocates and exchanged ideas about a

---

[115] OBL, James Bryce Papers, MS. Bryce U.S.A. 23, a letter from Bryce to Lowell, 8 April 1917.

[116] Marion Wilkinson, *E. Richard Cross: A Biographical Sketch, with Literary Papers and Religious and Political Addresses* (J. M. Dent & Sons, 1917), pp. 39–40; OBL, James Bryce Papers, MS. Bryce U.S.A. 23, a letter from Bryce to Butler, 25 March 1917.

[117] OBL, James Bryce Papers, MS. Bryce U.S.A. 23, a letter from Bryce to Lowell, 8 April 1917.

[118] See Chapter 3.

[119] Egerton, *Great Britain and the Creation of the League of Nations*, pp. 216, 221.

[120] See Chapter 3.

post-war settlement.[121] In April 1917, Bryce asked Smuts to speak at their first meeting, and Smuts agreed to do so on the condition that he reserved a certain freedom to speak as he wished. Pro-league leaders willingly accepted his condition by supposing, if he simply advocated the creation of the league, it sufficed for their purpose.[122]

In the meeting, Smuts proposed setting up an official Anglo-American committee to study a post-war organisation that, British activists assumed, would be able to influence politicians.[123] The British Society immediately began to prepare for the submission of a memorandum, which was to lobby for a joint study committee, to the government. For this purpose, British activists approached prominent figures in Britain to collect their signatures. For instance, Willoughby Dickinson, Chairman of the League of Nations Society, put pressure upon public figures such as the Conservative MP Hugh Cecil, who was also one of the speakers at the first public meeting. Dickinson maintained that if the British government would not take any steps in the direction of creating a league, he was 'pretty certain that either Russia or America will set the ball rolling'.[124]

In fact, such efforts of the British group were secretly encouraged by a Conservative politician, Robert Cecil, who has been remembered as the most ardent defender of the League of Nations. The outbreak of the war and his work for the Red Cross in France in 1914 shocked Cecil, and aroused his interest in the problem of war.[125] Considering that 'war squandered national resources and was morally reprehensible',[126] he favoured the idea of a new peaceful post-war order.[127] Although he first

---

[121] Courtney, *Extracts from a Diary during the War*, pp. 113–14, 119; A letter from Smuts to John A. Hobson, 21 April 1917, in Jan Christiaan Smuts, W. K. Hancock and Jean van der Poel (eds.), *Selections from the Smuts Papers Vol. 3, June 1910–November 1918* (Cambridge University Press, 1966), p. 476; Arthur Ponsonby's Diary (transcript), 4 and 15 May 1917.

[122] See Chapter 3. Also see a letter from Smuts to J. A. Hobson, 21 April 1917, in Smuts, Hancock and van der Poel (eds.), *Selections from the Smuts Papers Vol. 3*, p. 476; OBL, Bryce Papers, MS. Bryce 243, 74, a letter from Smuts to Bryce, 29? April 1917.

[123] The League of Nations Society Publications, no. 11, 'the League of Nations Society Report of meeting, speeches by Bryce, Smuts, the Archbishop of Canterbury, Lord Buckmaster, Lord Hugh Cecil and others', 14 May 1917, pp. 6–7; OBL, Willoughby Dickinson Papers, MS. Eng. hist. c.403, a letter from W. H. Dickinson to Smuts, 18 July 1917.

[124] OBL, Willoughby Dickinson Papers, MS. Eng. hist. c.403, a letter from W. H. Dickinson to Cecil, 18 July 1917; Also, in a letter to Smuts, W. H. Dickinson wrote that 'I feel pretty sure that unless we start something of the kind soon we shall find that either America or Russia will take the initiative' in ibid., W. H. Dickinson to Smuts, 18 July 1917.

[125] Gaynor Johnson, *Lord Robert Cecil: Politician and Internationalist* (Ashgate Publishing Limited, 2013), pp. 2–3, 76.

[126] Johnson, *Lord Robert Cecil*, p. 75.   [127] Ibid., p. 78–79, 87–88.

expressed his endorsement for the league in public in 1916, he did not stress it in his speeches until the middle of 1917.[128] Until then, he remained detached and even aloof from pro-league activists. As one of the original pro-leaguers, the architect Charles R. Ashbee, recalled in his memoir, Cecil said in September 1915, 'go ahead with your League, it can't do any harm … it can't possibly succeed'.[129] Nevertheless, after the successful public meeting of the Society in May 1917, Cecil seemed to be assured that the issue of the league could be utilised to advance his political career. As Gaynor Johnson has illustrated, Cecil, a politician somewhere in-between a civic monk and a Machiavellian plotter,[130] devoted himself to league activities driven not only by his Christian faith and hatred of the war but also by his political ambitions.[131] Anxious about how history would judge him, he hoped that his work for the league would have a positive impact on his legacy.[132] Smuts' speech at the Society's first public meeting coincided with Cecil's view, such as the formation of an Anglo-American committee to study the league as well as the leading roles of Britain and the United States in shaping a new order.[133] Cecil now turned to pro-leaguers and alluded to his possible efforts to promote the league inside the government if the Society produced a letter with the names of a few well-known people to demand government action to create a post-war organisation.[134] Believing his words, from May to August 1917, British activists gathered the signatures of eminent figures such as the Archbishop of Canterbury, the Archbishop of York, the Bishop of Winchester and the ex–Lord Chancellor Stanley O. Buckmaster.[135]

In November 1917, President Wilson expressed reluctance to form an Anglo-American committee to study the ideas about a post-war organisation. As we will see below, he wanted to maintain his control over the peacemaking process and was concerned that detailed discussion of the league might prompt opposition to it.[136] Cecil, who now went public as a

---

[128] Ibid., pp. 76–79, 82.
[129] CKC, The Papers of Charles Robert Ashbee, CRA 3/4, 254.
[130] Johnson, *Lord Robert Cecil*, p. 6.   [131] Ibid., p. 9–10.   [132] Ibid., p. 6.
[133] Ibid., p. 88–89.
[134] OBL, Willoughby Dickinson Papers, MS. Eng. hist. c.403, a letter to Bryce, 16 May 1917.
[135] The Chairman of the League of Nations Society, Willoughby Dickinson, wrote letters to those who were influential enough to sign the memorandum. For example, see OBL, Willoughby Dickinson Papers, MS. Eng. hist. c.403, 76, a letter from W. H. Dickinson to the Archbishop of Canterbury, 30 May 1917, a letter from W. H. Dickinson to S. O. Buckmaster, 6 June 1917 and a letter from W. H. Dickinson to Phillimore, 25 July 1917.
[136] Kuehl, *Seeking World Order*, p. 255; Ambrosius, *Woodrow Wilson and the American Diplomatic Tradition*, pp. 37–41; Bartlett, *The League to Enforce Peace*, pp. 56, 91.

strong adherent of the league, was determined to lobby for it inside the British government and urged the Foreign Secretary James Balfour to set up a committee.[137] With Balfour's lukewarm endorsement, the Phillimore Committee, an official yet still secret study body of the Foreign Office, was created at the end of 1917.[138] Thus, there was some progress on the league issue inside the British government, but it was insufficient for pro-league activists. Indeed, the Society's leaders found that many influential figures were still quite reluctant to publicly approve a league or get involved with its activities, although most of them expressed some sympathy with the group's ideals.[139] Some declined to sign the memorandum,[140] others refused to join the Society on the grounds that they already had much work on hand or had a few differences of opinion about the purpose of a league.[141] Through its activities during 1917, the leadership of the League of Nations Society came to realise how hard it was to influence politicians to implement its vision.

In 1917, the American pro-league group also had to adapt to new circumstances. In the United States, American entry into the war perplexed pro-leaguers at first, as Taft confessed in a letter to Bryce:

So many things have happened ... that it is hard to know what to discuss. We are on the brink of a war with Germany, it seems to me, and that forces us into an alliance with you and with your allies. We become, for the time being, a League to enforce a just peace.[142]

Inside the group, some members thought that pro-league activities were now inappropriate, fearing that the public would be absorbed in winning

[137] Yearwood, *Guarantee of Peace*, pp. 74–75.
[138] Ibid, pp. 74–75; For the committee's reports, see TNA: CAB29/1, The Committee on the League of Nations, Interim Report, 20 March 1918 and Final Report, 3 July 1918.
[139] See Chapter 5.
[140] OBL, Willoughby Dickinson Papers, MS. Eng. hist. c.403, letters from Hugh Cecil to W. H. Dickinson, 8 June and 25 July 1917, a letter from W. Phillimore to W. H. Dickinson, 1 August 1917?
[141] As for their reasons for not supporting the pro-league group in public, see Chapter 5. OBL, Willoughby Dickinson Papers, MS. Eng. hist. c.403, 218, a letter from E. Drummond to Marburg, 21 May 1917, letters from H. Cecil to W. H. Dickinson, 8 June 1917 and 25 July 1917, a letter from Lansdowne to W. H. Dickinson, 17 June 1917, a letter from Aiubero Pell to W. H. Dickinson 25 June 1917, a letter from Bourne to W. H. Dickinson, 19 April 1918, a letter from Seurne to W. H. Dickinson, 23 June 1917, 193, a letter from Bryce to W. H. Dickinson, 24 July 1917, 97, a letter from W. Phillimore to W. H. Dickinson, 1 August 1917; Ralph Williams, 'A League of Nations', *The Times*, 22 July 1918, p. 4; W. H. D. Rouse, 'A League of Nations: To the Editor of the Times', *The Times*, 9 Augusts 1918, p. 8; OBL, James Bryce Papers, MS. Bryce 138, 6, 27 October and 26 November 1917, a letter from Smuts to Bryce.
[142] OBL, James Bryce Papers, MS. Bryce U.S.A. 10, 188–91, a letter from Taft to Bryce, 8 February 1917.

the war and that the nature of the peace would be for later debate.[143] Against such opinions, Taft and Lowell stressed the value of continuing their work. American entry into the war, Taft asserted, would emphasise that peace was in the interest of the United States as well as of the entire world.[144] Equally, Lowell underlined the promising prospect of the League to Enforce Peace by arguing that entry into the war would mean that the policy of isolation was a failure. Hence, this was a chance to convince the American people of the need to depart from isolation and to cooperate with the rest of the world.[145]

At the same time, in order to protect and develop its movement in the changing situation, the League to Enforce Peace made its propaganda easy to understand for mass consumption, just as the British did. In 1917, American pro-leaguers thought that they had to be careful not to be labelled an anti-war campaign.[146] In a letter to Bryce, Lowell confessed that 'we shall not conduct [our campaign] quite so vociferously, because when war comes, the word peace will be thought here, as it has been in England, to mean the stopping of the war'.[147] To avoid being called pacifists, the public propaganda of the League to Enforce Peace framed the formation of the league as a democratic and just war aim and underscored the idea of victory and the ideal of patriotism, while not dwelling on the details about the league or the complexities of remaking the post-war order.[148] The slogan 'Win the War' appeared in pamphlets and was declared frequently at the group's meetings and conventions.[149]

Modifying their league propaganda in the same way as their British counterpart, the American activists also encountered the same problem as the British: how to influence key politicians at a time when the idea of a league was being adopted at the highest level of policy-making. They repeatedly urged President Wilson to organise an international committee to study the league, officially or unofficially. Wilson, however,

---

[143] Ibid.   [144] Ibid.

[145] OBL, James Bryce Papers, MS. Bryce U.S.A. 8, 73–76, a letter from Lowell to Bryce, 13 March 1917 and a letter from Lowell to Bryce, 10 July 1917.

[146] Bartlett, *The League to Enforce Peace*, pp. 80–82.

[147] OBL, James Bryce Papers, MS. Bryce U.S.A. 8, 73–76, a letter from Lowell to Bryce, 13 March 1917.

[148] HUHL, ALLPP (*2005-481), Box 10, 'League Bulletin, no. 69', 11 January 1918; League of Nations Society, Monthly Report for Members, no. 7, July 1918, pp. 6–7; 'The League to Enforce Peace does NOT seek to end the present war' in ibid., Box 11, League to Enforce Peace Publication, no. 25, A. Lawrence Lowell, 'A Platform on Which the Whole World Can Stand', 26 May 1916.

[149] HUHL, ALLPP (*2005-481), Box 10, The League to Enforce Peace Bulletin, no. 78, 15 March 1918, '"Win the War for Permanent Peace" Convention', Philadelphia on 16–18 May and 833, 'Platform Adopted by the League to Enforce Peace at the "Win the War for Permanent Peace" Convention', Philadelphia on 17 May 1918.

rejected the proposal and affirmed somewhat disingenuously that, in the middle of the fighting, it was not time to talk about a post-war plan for peace.[150] The pro-league groups in Britain and the United States showed some sympathy for such attitudes of Wilson's and refrained from criticising him in 1914–1916,[151] although they had been slightly doubtful about how sincerely Wilson tackled the issue.[152] Their concern, however, grew after 1917 when Wilson rejected the formation of a joint international committee. He ordered the League to Enforce Peace 'not to bring out definitely a draft treaty for the League' – a request that the group obeyed.[153] As Lowell explained to Bryce, Wilson had 'not wanted to have any plan put out by our League or any other body, or to have us enter into correspondences for the purposes with societies across the Atlantic'.[154] Furthermore, Wilson directly requested the American group to take its 'hands off' league plans. Having referred to its suggestion to appoint a private international committee, Wilson argued:

The only committees in the countries with whom we are associated of which I have heard were committees appointed by the governments. I should consider it very embarrassing to have a private organization like the League to Enforce Peace take this matter up, since the immediate establishment of a league of nations is a question of government policy not only, but constitutes part of the intricate web of counsel now being woven between the associated governments. I am having this matter studied myself and hope very sincerely that if the League to Enforce Peace undertakes its study, it will not in addition undertake to establish international connections with committees of a different origin abroad.[155]

[150] HUHL, LEPR (Int 6722.8.25*), Box 1, a letter from Wilson to Marburg, 8 March 1918; OBL, James Bryce Papers, MS. Bryce U.S.A. 8, 320, a letter from Wilson to Marburg, 6 May 1918. Also see Kuehl, *Seeking World Order*, p. 255; Ambrosius, *Woodrow Wilson and the American Diplomatic Tradition*, pp. 37–41.

[151] HUHL, LEPR (Int 6722.8.25*), Box 1, a letter from Bryce to Marburg, n.d., Received on 1 May 1918 and a letter from W. H. Dickinson to Marburg, 6 May 1918. Meanwhile in America, Taft mentioned, 'it is evident to us that your suggestion that we have some informal conference, with the approval of the President, is not at present possible. He changes his mind often on important matters', in OBL, James Bryce Papers, MS. Bryce U.S.A. 10, 203–5, a letter from Taft to Bryce, 24 March 1918; ibid., MS. Bryce U.S.A. 8, 318–19, a letter from Marburg to Bryce, 7 May 1918; HUHL, LEPR (Int 6722.8.25*), Box 1, a letter from Marburg to Short, 25 May 1918.

[152] OBL, James Bryce Papers, MS. Bryce U.S.A. 23, a letter from Bryce to Lowell, 23 January 1917; ibid., MS. Bryce U.S.A. 8, 66–67, a letter from Lowell to Bryce, 5 July 1916; ibid., MS. Bryce U.S.A. 10, 194–95, a letter from Taft to Bryce, 20 November 1917.

[153] Ibid., MS. Bryce U.S.A. 8, 91–94, a letter from Lowell to Bryce, 9 July 1918. Also see Ambrosius, *Woodrow Wilson and the American Diplomatic Tradition*, pp. 37–41; Mazower, *Governing the World*, p. 121.

[154] OBL, James Bryce Papers, MS. Bryce U.S.A. 8, 102–4, a letter from Lowell to Bryce, 25 October 1918.

[155] HUHL, LEPR (Int 6722.8.25*), Box 1, a letter from Wilson to Lowell, 11 July 1918.

This attitude bewildered the League to Enforce Peace leadership and Lowell found it 'very much of [a] snub'.[156] When Bryce confessed that he scarcely understood Wilson's views except his anxiety not to be committed, Lowell and Taft, who had inclined towards reserving negative comments on Wilson in their letters to British activists, now criticised him.[157] Lowell replied to Bryce by attesting that Wilson had changed his mind from time to time and made the others confused; Taft, after the armistice, even professed that 'Mr. Wilson is a very unsatisfactory man to deal with in a matter like the League of Nations to Enforce Peace'.[158]

Wilson refused the formation of an Anglo-American committee and discouraged the League to Enforce Peace from discussing details about the league in public because ambiguity worked to his advantage.[159] The more ambiguous details about the league were, the easier it was to rally support without stirring up opposition to it.[160] Going into detail about the post-war order risked conflict at home and abroad, which would interfere with his goal of international reform: to eliminate power politics, abolish German militarism and reform the policies of the Allies.[161] To achieve this goal, Wilson took advantage of the fact that Allied countries such as Britain needed American financial help in the war effort and wanted American participation in the post-war league.[162] The US President presented himself as uncommitted to the Allies as well as the details of a post-war organisation and thereby attempted to elicit the Allies' cooperation in building a new order as he wished. Wilson insisted, for example, that the United States was not a formal ally but an 'associate power' and implied that the United States might make separate peace

---

[156] Ibid., Box 1, a letter from Lowell to Short, 15 July 1918, a letter from Secretary to Lowell, 23 July 1918 and a letter from Lowell to Short, 24 July 1918.

[157] Bryce wrote, 'Frankly, I do not understand the President's position, except that he is anxious not to be committed' in OBL, James Bryce Papers, MS. Bryce U.S.A. 23, 118–19, a letter from Bryce to Lowell, 5 September 1918.

[158] Lowell and Taft's critical comments on Wilson are seen in OBL, James Bryce Papers, MS. Bryce U.S.A. 8, 98–101, a letter from Lowell to Bryce, 11 October 1918; ibid., MS. Bryce U.S.A. 10, 207–15, a letter from Taft to Bryce, 5 December 1918.

[159] Kennedy, *The Will to Believe*, pp. 130–31. Further, as Bartlett has pointed out, the majority of the American group's founders were Republicans and the post-war scheme was originally more Republican than Democratic, which also led Wilson to be careful about the league project. Bartlett, *The League to Enforce Peace*, pp. 55–6, 80–81.

[160] Ibid.

[161] David Reynolds, *America, Empire of Liberty: A New History* (Allen Lane, 2009), p. 309; Kennedy, *The Will to Believe*, pp. 130–31, 143.

[162] French, *The Strategy of the Lloyd George Coalition*, p. 37; Reynolds, *America, Empire of Liberty*, pp, 315–16; David Reynolds, *Britannia Overruled* (Longman, 2000), p. 93; Kennedy, *The Will to Believe*, pp. 89, 141–43.

with Germany with or without the Allies' consent.[163] In fact, Wilson's actual opinion about the schemes of the organisations of a new order remained obscure.[164] The President avoided articulating his post-war plan also because he deemed that the program of the league should be reached through democratic processes and that it would develop by itself after its establishment.[165] According to him, the league of nations was a matter of moral persuasion and good will rather than juridical organisation; it would work and be upheld once nations understood that their common interest lay in world peace.[166]

In the end, a joint committee might not have achieved very much beyond producing a report that statesmen and their advisors could have ignored anyway. It is highly likely, moreover, that such a committee would have excluded pro-leaguers and become an inter-allied conference on war aims broadly conceived. With or without a joint committee, the pro-league activists exercised very little direct, practical influence on policy-making elites in the crucial years of the League's formation. Yet, through their efforts to set up a committee, both groups recognised that they confronted the same, difficult problem of exerting pressure on politicians. As we shall see, it finally made the two groups turn to each other for cooperation.

The Common Scheme, Cooperation and Distrust, 1918

In 1918, the League of Nations Society and the League to Enforce Peace strove to adopt a single set of ideas about a future league. Prior to that, both groups had expressed their intention to discuss the league eye to eye and to agree on a common project.[167] To this end, they gradually attempted to modify their own ideas 'into a form as similar as possible to' their counterparts' ideas, expecting that the more they identified their own programme with the other's programme the better the chances for

---

[163] Reynolds, *America, Empire of Liberty*, p. 309; Reynolds, *Britannia Overruled*, p. 93; Kennedy, *The Will to Believe*, pp. 141–42; Ambrosius, *Woodrow Wilson and American Internationalism*, pp. 96–97.
[164] Kennedy, *The Will to Believe*, pp. 130–31.
[165] Knock, *To End All Wars*, pp. ix–x; Ambrosius, *Woodrow Wilson and the American Diplomatic Tradition*, pp. 37–39; Kuehl, *Seeking World Order*, chapter 11; Kennedy, *The Will to Believe*, p. 90, 131. Also see Egerton, *Great Britain and the Creation of the League of Nations*, p. 201; Mazower, *Governing the World*, pp. 121–22.
[166] Kennedy, *The Will to Believe*, p. 131.
[167] HUHL, LEPR (Int 6722.8.25*), Box 5, Committees, etc., various papers, 'Exhibit 1 A', a letter from Raymond Unwin, 14 November 1915 and a letter from Lowell to Short, 26 November 1915; OBL, Willoughby Dickinson Papers, MS. Eng. hist. c.403, a letter from W. H. Dickinson to Marburg, 17 May 1917; OBL, James Bryce Papers, MS. Bryce U.S.A.8, 77–78, a letter from Lowell to Bryce, 10 July 1917.

the creation of a league.[168] If the Anglo-American 'cooperation on one definite scheme' failed, they were concerned that they might be unable to assure other states such as France and Italy of the value of a future league of nations.[169]

In April and May 1918, two of the American group's leading members, Hamilton Holt, the editor of *Independent*, and Judge William Wadhams, a New York justice, visited league advocates in London and Paris, which allowed the Anglo-American activists to discuss and amend the details of their league plans for the first time in person.[170] Through meetings and dinners that the League of Nations Society organised for the two American representatives, they met not only the group's leaders, such as Lord Shaw, Bryce, Willoughby Dickinson and Aneurin Williams, but also a number of influential figures including James Balfour, Robert Cecil, Lord Haldane, Leonard Woolf, H. G. Wells and the Bishop of Winchester; the list goes on and on.[171]

As a result of these pleasant meetings and the opportunity to discuss their schemes point by point, the two leaders' visit to London led to two outcomes.[172] First, it produced a common scheme for the creation of a

---

[168] OBL, Willoughby Dickinson Papers, MS. Eng. hist. c.403, a letter from W. H. Dickinson to Unwin, 6 June 1917; HUHL, LEPR (Int 6722.8.25*), Box 1, a letter from W. H. Dickinson to Marburg, 27 Augusts 1917; HUHL, ALLPP (*2005-481), Box 11, League to Enforce Peace Publication, no. 25, A. Lawrence Lowell, 'A Platform on Which the Whole World Can Stand', 26 May 1916, p. 5.

[169] OBL, Willoughby Dickinson Papers, MS. Eng. hist. c.403, 129, a letter from W. H. Dickinson to Judge Wadhams, 1918.

[170] This chapter focuses only on pro-leaguers in Britain and America because, as Kuehl has pointed out, 'the English showed much more interest in an international organization than did advocates elsewhere in Europe, and their ideas must be compared with those in the US', Kuehl, *Seeking World Order*, p. 236. Moreover, the French intensified discussion about the league only after American entry into the war, and their league work was led by the government, not by private groups as in Britain and the United States. The French pro-league committee was appointed in June 1917, although Léon Bourgeois, the chairman of this committee, had already been thinking about a possible international organisation after the war. See Michael Clinton, '"The New World Will Create the New Europe": Paul-Henri d'Estournelles de Constant, the United States, and International Peace', *Proceedings of the Western Society for French History*, vol. 40 (Michigan Publishing, 2012); Jackson, *Beyond the Balance of Power*, pp. 178–82; Kuehl, *Seeking World Order*, pp. 234–36.

[171] Parliamentary Archives, Davidson 409, 132, a letter from W. H. Dickinson to the Archbishop, 8 April 1918; HUHL, LEPR (Int 6722.8.25*), Box 1, a letter from Holt to Short, 27 April 1918.

[172] League of Nations Society, Monthly Report for Members, no. 5, May 1918, p. 3; HUHL, LEPR (Int 6722.8.25*), Box 1, a letter from Holt to Short, 27 April 1918. Holt seemed to have enjoyed the visit to Europe and wrote to the League to Enforce Peace's secretary Short as follows: 'This is the most wonderful experience of a life time and you must come over after the Philadelphia meeting', in ibid., a letter from Holt to Short, 8 May 1918.

league for the League of Nations Society and the League to Enforce Peace; second, a formal, although incomplete, association was at last established between the two groups. Their joint meetings in London resulted in a memorandum in May 1918, whereas the debate and the process of designing the common scheme continued until 1919.[173] For the common scheme, each side conceded some points to the other's vision of a league. The memorandum proclaimed that the League to Enforce Peace should consider adopting the following:

The proposals contained in the basis of the League of Nations Society, under which the League would undertake to enforce the decision of the Judicial Tribunal in matters arising under treaties and International Law and would also protect any member of the League against attack by an outside state which refuses to submit the case to an appropriate tribunal or Council.[174]

Thus, the American group accepted the British view of the enforcement of law and security against outside attack.[175] By adopting the enforcement of the court's decision, the Americans agreed to respect the judicial settlement of disputes in the first instance even in crisis, thereby dropping automatic sanction from their plan. In exchange, the British side adopted sanctions with both economic *and* military forces as the Americans had insisted. Making such amendments, of course, was slow and gradual. The process had already begun by the exchange of letters before Holt and Wadhams' visit and continued by correspondence after that.[176] Still, by the time of their visit in April and May 1918, most of the major differences in the two groups were adjusted and their similar league schemes finally became 'much like' each other even in their eyes.[177]

---

[173] For example, Bryce still criticised and questioned some articles prepared by the League to Enforce Peace even after the joint meeting in London. See, ibid., Box 1, a letter from Bryce to Marburg, 20 June 1918.

[174] HUHL, LEPR (Int 6722.8.25*), Box 5, Committees, etc., various papers, L.O.N. Society – L.E.P. Conference 1918, 'Conference between Representatives of the League of Nations Society and the League to Enforce Peace, April & May 1918, Memorandum Setting out the Results of the Conference' (Approved on 16 May 1918).

[175] Ibid.

[176] As for some modifications before their visit, see HUHL, ALLPP (*2005-481), Box 7, '"The Price of Peace", A. Lawrence Lowell in Advocate of Peace', October 1916, vol. LXXVIII., p. 9; OBL, James Bryce Papers, MS. Bryce U.S.A. 8, a letter from Lowell to Bryce, 10 July 1917; about discussion around and after their visit, see ibid., 'Tentative Draft of a Treaty for a LN: Approved by the Executive Committee of the League to Enforce Peace, NY, April 11, 1918', and 82–86, a letter from Lowell to Bryce, 13 April 1918; HUHL, LEPR (Int 6722.8.25*), Box 1, a letter from W. H. Dickinson to Marburg, 6 May 1918 and 17 June 1918.

[177] HUHL, LEPR (Int 6722.8.25*), Box 10, 'The League Bulletin, no. 84', 27 April 1918.

Another result of the visit by Holt and Wadhams was a 'formal association' between the League of Nations Society and the League to Enforce Peace. Following their agreement to work together at meetings in London, the British group proposed to put the phrase 'Associated with the American League to Enforce Peace' after their title and to make their association formal. This was approved by the League to Enforce Peace's Executive Committee in July 1918 and thereafter that phrase began to be printed at the head of the League of Nations Society papers.[178] This was welcomed by both groups and reported in each group's newsletters.[179]

Their cooperation, however, was not entirely smooth. The British pro-league leaders were glad to clinch their formal association with the American group, expecting their American friends to 'take similar action'.[180] Yet, the American side was more circumspect and ultimately seemed to have chosen not to do so. Having noted the British anticipation of the Americans taking the same action, a Secretary of the League to Enforce Peace, William H. Short, remarked in a letter to Lowell: 'My understanding is that our Executive Committee did not think it quite discreet for us to do this [same action]'.[181] Also, touching upon information about the British Society's 'split', which will be seen below, he suggested, 'shall we, for the present, refrain from putting anything on our stationery that will publicly connect us with the League of Nations Society?'[182] This reservation continued and Marburg, in a postscript to a letter to Bryce, merely mentioned that 'we have styled our organization "League to Enforce Peace, American Branch", in the hope of its being extended to other countries who will use a similar designation'.[183] In other words, they would not put 'Associated with

[178] HUHL, LEPR (Int 6722.8.25*), Box 5, Committees, etc., various papers, L.O.N. Society – L.E.P. Conference 1918, 'Conference between Representatives of the League of Nations Society and the League to Enforce Peace, April & May 1918, Memorandum Setting out the Results of the Conference (Approved May 16th 1918)'; ibid., Box 3, Letters from Foreign Peace Organizations, England, a letter from Secretary to the League of Nations Society, 3 July 1918 and a letter from Garrett Jones to the League to Enforce Peace, 31 July 1918; ibid., Box 1, a letter from W. H. Dickinson to Marburg, 17 June 1918; HUHL, ALLPP (*2005-481), Box 10, 'The League Bulletin, no. 94', 6 July 1918.

[179] HUHL, LEPR (Int 6722.8.25*), Box 3, Letters from Foreign Peace Organizations, England, W. H. Dickinson to Secretary, 13? July 1918; HUHL, ALLPP (*2005-481), Box 10, 'The League Bulletin, no. 101', 24 August 1918; League of Nations Society, Monthly Report for Members, no. 9, September 1918.

[180] HUHL, LEPR (Int 6722.8.25*), Box 1, a letter from W. H. Dickinson to Marburg, 17 June 1918.

[181] Ibid., a letter from Secretary to Lowell, 1 Aug 1918.

[182] Ibid; HUHL, LEPR (Int 6722.8.25*), Box 3, Letters from Foreign Peace Organizations, England, a letter from W. H. Dickinson to Secretary, 13? July 1918.

[183] OBL, James Bryce Papers, MS. Bryce U.S.A. 8, 213–15, Marburg to Bryce, 16 July 1918.

the British League of Nations Society' after their title. The two groups now wanted to cooperate with each other for their common purpose and finally achieved the common scheme of the league, yet they still could not fully cooperate with each other.

What, then, hindered them from doing so? It is very difficult to specify a single overriding reason, but in order to understand the thrust of it we need to return to their fundamental disagreements based on respective national contexts and differing liberal international perspectives. Despite the same goal and the same set of political problems, their underlying differences – the cause of disagreement in 1915–1916 – prevented them from establishing mutual trust. The British had the image of America as 'a quasi-Dominion', which did not conform to European standards,[184] and presupposed that they understood the realities of international politics better than the Americans. On the other hand, the Americans believed that they should lead the world and initiate the rapid creation of a new international order. Under the influence of progressive history where manifest destiny would extend overseas, it was also crucial to seek reform at home and abroad and to redeem the old world from a balance of power.[185] For example, at the end of 1918, after the two groups agreed to have both economic *and* military sanctions in their plans, one leading member of the American group, Marburg, still underscored their difference with the British and the supremacy of the American view:

The various English plans for a league of nations call for the use of economic or military forces, whereas the plan of the American League to Enforce Peace provides for the immediate employment of economic and military forces. This is an important difference. The former provision would imply an attempt to subdue the recalcitrant by economic pressure before military force is used. The American group, on the other hand, feel that war once begun is difficult to stop and they plan to use military force forthwith in conjunction with economic force, i.e., that the League shall at once make war on the nation which goes to war without previous resort to inquiry.[186]

In addition, at almost the end of the war in 1918, their distrust could clearly be seen in their reaction when they received uncertain information about their counterparts. In Britain, the League of Nations Society split and another similar body, the League of Free Nations Association, was organised in July 1918.[187] Led by David Davies, the Liberal politician,

[184] Watt, *Succeeding John Bull*, pp. 27–32.
[185] Ambrosius, *Wilsonian Statecraft*, p. 3, 7, 10–13, 21.
[186] HUHL, LEPR (Int 6722.8.25*), Box 1, a letter from Marburg to Viscount K. Kaneko, 31 December 1918.
[187] See Chapter 5.

this new association's membership overlapped with the anti-German, right wing of the League of Nations Society.[188] The Association called for the immediate formation of the league *without* Germany, which the core leaders of the Society opposed. Defining free nations as democratic states,[189] the new group claimed that a militaristic and autocratic Germany was unqualified to be admitted into a league of free nations.[190] Since it seemed unlikely that the war would soon end with Germany's repentance,[191] the group aimed to consolidate the present alliance into a league of free nations at once for the purpose of enforcing peace.[192] By proclaiming itself to be 'a society of men and women of all parties and creeds, who accept the principles laid down by President Wilson', the Association approached the American group to establish a close relationship.[193]

The formation of the new pro-league group confused the American League to Enforce Peace. Since at first the League of Nations Society did not explain why and how the Association was formed,[194] the American group struggled to gather information about the new pro-league group through its British counterpart. They received puzzling and sometimes unreliable information that the Association was formed with the goodwill of prominent politicians such as Asquith, Grey, Cecil and even Bryce.[195]

---

[188] Ibid.; CKC, The Papers of Goldsworthy Lowes Dickinson, GLD 1/2/4; Egerton, *Great Britain and the Creation of the League of Nations*, p. 72.

[189] PA, LG/F/82/8/2, 'the League of Free Nations Association', July 1918; David Davies, et al., 'League of Free Nations Association: to the Editor of the Times', *The Times*, 18 September 1918, p. 10.

[190] 'The League of Nations: Interview with Prof Gilbert Murray, the Needs and the Difficulties Germany Must be Included', *The Observer*, 11 August 1918, p. 2; David Davies, et al., 'League of Free Nations Association: To the Editor of the Times', *The Times*, 18 September 1918, p. 10.

[191] The National Library of Wales, Lord Davies of Llandinam Papers, B3/3, 149, 'War Aims and a League of Nations', n.d.; ibid., B4/1, Box 5, 1917–18, 'Proposal Letter to Manchester Guardian', 8 October 1918.

[192] David Davies, et al., 'League of Free Nations Association: to the Editor of the Times', *The Times*, 18 September 1918, p. 10.

[193] HUHL, LEPR (Int 6722.8.25*), Box 3, Letters from Foreign Peace Organizations, England, 'the League of Free Nations Association', July 1918 and a letter from Davies to the League to Enforce Peace, 13 September 1918; ibid., Box 2, England, a letter from Davies to Taft, 15 September 1918, a letter from Secretary to Henry Canby, 19 September 1918 and 'The "League of Free Nations" Association, A British Organisation to Promote an Active Propaganda for the Formation of a World League of Free Nations as the Necessary Basis of a Permanent Peace (Excerpts from official pamphlet)'.

[194] HUHL, LEPR (Int 6722.8.25*), Box 3, Letters from Foreign Peace Organizations, England, a letter from W. H. Dickinson to Secretary, 13? July 1918.

[195] HUHL, LEPR (Int 6722.8.25*), Box 2, 2 England, Secretary to Canby, 6 September 1918, Henry S. Canby to Short, 13 September 1918, 20 September 1918, and a letter from Short, 26 September 1918; ibid., Box 1, A. L. Smith to Marburg, 5 July 1918.

Finally, in September 1918, Aneurin Williams of the League of Nations Society offered their American friends more details, stating that the new group was practically a rival society with a similar project as well as overlapping memberships. By then, the Society was able to inform the American group of the 'good probability of a reunion of the two societies' as a result of negotiations between them.[196] Even after receiving this information, attitudes towards the new British body were undecided inside the League to Enforce Peace. Whereas the American group's Secretary Short was uncertain whether the Association already superseded the League of Nations Society, Taft predicted that the new body would not be successful with its ambitious program in any case.[197] On 10 October 1918, as Williams indicated, the two British groups were united into the League of Nations Union and held the first mass meeting in London.[198] Nevertheless, this British split and reunification caused the American counterpart to hesitate about how they should respond to them and whether they could really collaborate.

Equally, the American side made the British wonder if the League to Enforce Peace had decent support in the United States. In August 1918, Bryce received information that some influential figures in the United States who had favoured the league now opposed it.[199] Immediately, he inquired of Lowell and Marburg what the objections – of the international lawyer, James Brown Scott, the former Secretary of State Elihu Root and Judge Gray of the American group – were.[200] Lowell and Marburg respectively replied to Bryce that Root and Gray had been with them from the outset, although Scott had always been against the league probably because Root had

[196] Ibid., Box 2, 2 England, a letter from A. Williams to Marburg, 6 September 1918.

[197] Ibid., a letter from Short, 26 September 1918 and a letter from Taft to Short, 30 September 1918.

[198] Egerton, *Great Britain and the Creation of the League of Nations*, p. 90; HUHL, ALLPP (*2005-481), Box 10, 'The League Bulletin, no. 110', 26 October 1918; HUHL, LEPR (Int 6722.8.25*), Box 1, a letter from Davies to Short, 31 October 1918.

[199] HUHL, ALLPP (*2005-481), Box 12, International Conciliation Pamphlet, no. 106, 'The Proposal for a League to Enforce Peace: Affirmative–Taft, Negative–W. J. Bryan', September 1916; OBL, James Bryce Papers, MS. Bryce U.S.A. 8, 322, W. Elliott to Marburg, 6 May 1918; HUHL, LEPR (Int 6722.8.25*), Box 1, a letter from Charles Eliot to Taft, 23 April 1918, a letter from Charles Eliot to Percy M. Gordon, 21 September 1918 and a letter from Charles Eliot to Stephen P. Duggan, 8 November 1918.

[200] OBL, James Bryce Papers, MS. Bryce U.S.A. 23, a letter from Bryce to Lowell, 31 August 1918 and 118–19, a letter from Bryce to Lowell, 5 September 1918; HUHL, LEPR (Int 6722.8.25*), Box 1, a letter from Bryce to Marburg, 31 August 1918. For more details about Root's and Scott's opposition, see, Hatsue Shinohara, *US International Lawyers in the Interwar Years: A Forgotten Crusade* (Cambridge University Press, 2012), pp. 21–25.

sympathy with it.[201] Such small concerns on the British side might have been amplified by Wilson's aloof attitudes to the post-war project.

Furthermore, friction between British and American pro-leaguers also occurred because each group prioritised lobbying politicians over negotiating the two groups' common position and speaking with a single voice. Indeed, the pro-league groups assumed that obtaining direct political backing and influencing top officials were much more important and effective ways to establish the league than cooperating. In seeking political approval for their own league schemes, each regarded their counterpart groups as mere mediums for approaching eminent figures in each other's country. Both groups asked the other if they could 'secure some expression' of advocating the league from politicians so that the league would 'be taken more seriously by the people and governments abroad'.[202] Lowell's account in January 1919 accurately summarised such a situation:

The people interested in a League of Nations in each country seem to look to the statesmen on the other side of the ocean to carry it through. President Wilson talks much about such a league; but whether he will push for a really serious league, with a substantial agreement and force behind it that will make it effective, does not seem clear. We have been thinking that the English statesmen had not only pledged themselves to a real league, but meant it.[203]

Although limited communication and mobility in war time was a source of some of the distrust between the US and British pro-leaguers, ultimately their disagreements about the league stemmed from conflicting ideas rooted in different national contexts. While a common goal and the need to gain direct political influence compelled them to try to cooperate, crucial differences in outlook remained. It was liberal internationalism that stimulated the idea of a new peaceful organisation to preserve peace, the exchange of ideas across the Atlantic and the various movements to create a post-war league. Yet, it was also liberal internationalism – as it developed differently in each country – that hampered the development of cooperation and trust between the British and American pro-league groups.

---

[201] HUHL, LEPR (Int 6722.8.25*), Box 1, a letter from Marburg to Bryce, 2 October 1918; OBL, James Bryce Papers, MS. Bryce U.S.A. 8, 98–101, a letter from Lowell to Bryce, 11 October 1918.

[202] Ibid., Box 2, 2 Foreign Peace Organizations, a letter from Marburg to E. Grey, 28 August 1916; ibid., Box 1, a letter from Bryce to Marburg, 8 February 1918; OBL, James Bryce Papers, MS. Bryce U.S.A. 10, 183, a letter from Taft to Bryce, 21 October 1916; ibid., MS. Bryce U.S.A. 8, 233–35, a letter from Marburg to Taft, 13 May 1916; ibid., MS. Bryce U.S.A. 23, 101–2, a letter from Bryce to Lowell, 8 February 1918.

[203] OBL, Gilbert Murray Papers, Murray 38, 149, a letter from Lowell to Murray, 24 January 1919.

Conclusion

The two pro–league of nations groups in Britain and the United States, the League of Nations Society and the League to Enforce Peace, had a lot in common. They shared the same goal of creating a post-war organisation and emerged from the liberal internationalism tradition, which might suggest that they would have cooperated with each other in the creation of a league. In reality, however, they critically disagreed with each other and could not constitute a transnational movement. This was because both groups, by seeking political support for their own league schemes, regarded their counterparts as mere mediums for approaching statesmen in each other's country. Not only were they 'national internationalists' who worked in respective domestic contexts,[204] but the British and American liberal internationalist traditions also differed in significant ways.[205] In British liberal internationalism, progress towards a new order should be gradual. Fearing that the use of force might escalate larger wars, the British pro-leaguers were more cautious about military sanctions. On the other hand, the Americans attempted to create an international organisation at the war's end, believing in progressive history in which their role was to redeem and reform the old world. Inspired by the idea of Social Darwinism that progress required violence to constitute a process of selection, American pro-leaguers supposed that world progress as well as a new order needed force. Their different ideas as well as their prioritisation of lobbying politicians over cooperation hampered the two groups from building mutual trust and a common lobbying strategy.

Although this chapter did not discuss it,[206] the post-war vision of the League to Enforce Peace was similar to that of French internationalists.[207] The French conception of a league was an international legal regime with emphasis on automatic sanctions and a machinery of enforcement.[208] Already at the two Hague Peace Conferences of 1899 and 1907, the French internationalists had campaigned to establish a system of compulsory international arbitration backed by collective force.[209] In their league plan, member states must

---

[204] Nehring, 'National Internationalist'.   [205] Ibid.   [206] See n. 170.
[207] Jackson, *Beyond the Balance of Power*, p. 516.
[208] Ibid., pp. 6, 516. See also Conclusion.
[209] Ibid., pp. 187–88; Glenda Sluga, *Internationalism in the Age of Nationalism* (University of Pennsylvania Press, 2013), pp. 35–37; Clinton, 'The New World Will Create the New Europe'; Michael Clinton, 'Wilsonians before Wilson: The French Peace Movement & the Société des Nations', Western Society for French History Conference, Lafayette, LA (October 2010).

have mutual legal obligations and a powerful international force should be created with a permanent general staff.[210] Equipping a league with sanctions was 'an absolute necessity' to provide a security guarantee and practical value for an organisation,[211] which implied potential 'restrictions on the sovereignty of member states'.[212] In fact, the French proposal was a product of its legalist political culture and should be distinguished from the liberal strain of internationalism in Britain and the United States.[213] Yet, as Peter Jackson has pointed out, their similarity was an example that political ideas travelled across the regions in the later nineteenth and early twentieth centuries.[214]

As this chapter has illustrated, the war-time relationship of the two pro-league groups in Britain and the United States highlighted the challenge of constituting a transnational movement. The ideas and ideals of the post-war order not only provided inspiration but also caused friction beyond borders. Regardless of how much common ground the groups in more than one country share, they are still embedded in their own domestic circumstances and national traditions. Whereas the two groups succeeded in putting the idea of a league on the political agenda, neither could control how the league was formed or what shape it would take. That power lay in the hands of politicians. In the end, both the British and the American groups' post-war ideas were certainly 'the leagues that weren't'.[215] To develop the wider movement, both groups had to abandon many details about the new organisation such as how the league would work or what sort of problems might emerge. Yet simultaneously, the pro-league groups inspired various post-war plans and, at the end of the war, achieved their primary goal – the creation of the League of Nations. This flexibility of the pro-league activists, while limiting their impact on its design, eventually enabled them to promote and establish the first international organisation for peace in international society.

---

[210] Jackson, *Beyond the Balance of Power*, pp. 182, 185–89, 273. See also Conclusion.
[211] Jackson, *Beyond the Balance of Power*, pp. 180–81, 184.   [212] Ibid., pp. 188–89, 273.
[213] Ibid., p. 6.   [214] Ibid., p. 516.   [215] Wertheim, 'The League That Wasn't'.

5   No Peace without Victory
The League of Victorious Allies, 1917–1918

Introduction

In 1917–1918, the final years of the war, the idea of a league of nations gained widespread support as well as political backing, which served to place it on the agenda of the Paris Peace Conference in 1919. Where, then, did the final big push to create the League come from? Many historians have pointed out that, after a long, grinding and exhausting total war, the public had suffered the reality of modern total war, were tired of it and now sought lasting peace.[1] In addition, historians have usually pointed to the advocacy of the idea by US President Woodrow Wilson and other politicians, which facilitated the creation of the League of Nations.[2] While war-weariness and top-level political support certainly helped to make the League's foundation possible, there remains the question whether the pro–league of nations movement contributed to it and in what way. Examining the years 1917–1918 through the lens of the pro-league movement reveals a different, less straightforward yet significant story behind the establishment of the League of Nations. As I shall argue in this chapter, the idea of a league of nations became popular not because it promised lasting peace but because it promised a more effective continuation and outcome of the ongoing war. As John Horne has argued, the campaign to sustain civil morale in 1917–1918 was not simply conducted by the government[3] but involved the

---

[1] See Introduction, n. 3. See also David Monger, *Patriotism and Propaganda in First World War Britain: The National War Aims Committee and Civilian Morale* (Liverpool University Press, 2012); Adrian Gregory, *The Last Great War: British Society and the First World War* (Cambridge University Press, 2008); William Mulligan, *The Great War for Peace* (Yale University Press, 2014), chapter 6.

[2] Henry R. Winkler, *The League of Nations Movement in Great Britain, 1914–1919* (Rutgers University Press, 1952); George Egerton, *Great Britain and the Creation of the League of Nations: Strategy, Politics, and International Organization, 1914–1919* (Scolar Press, 1978); Peter Yearwood, *Guarantee of Peace: The League of Nations in British Policy, 1914–1925* (Oxford University Press, 2009).

[3] John Horne (ed.), *State, Society and Mobilization in Europe during the First World War* (Cambridge University Press, 1997), pp. 198, 209.

'self-mobilisation' of civil society,[4] which bolstered the argument to fight until victory was achieved from the bottom up.[5] Indeed, most advocates of the league, including the public, politicians, the churches and even pro–league of nations movement leadership, supported the formation of the league as a coalition of democratic states that would prosecute the war to a democratic victory. Behind this viewpoint, there was the common belief that Germany was an irremediably militaristic and authoritarian great power that was primarily if not exclusively responsible for the outbreak of conflict. Germany, therefore, had to be punished through defeat to learn to adhere to the civilised values of the democratic powers. In fact, it was more than mere opposition to an immediate peace; in 1918, many league advocates neither saw the prospect that Germany could enter the league in the foreseeable future nor outlined any specific process for its admission. Having recognised that the league could only function if all its members adhered to certain norms, values and goals, the pro-leaguers called for a post-war international order that excluded Germany and any other unqualified state.

Even though pro-leaguers initially aspired to change the norms of international relations, from the rivalry of alliance blocs and armaments to cooperation through a new international organisation, in the final year of the war that aspiration gave way to a vision of the League of Nations as a way to reinforce the war-time alliance against Germany and to continue it into the post-war period. Originally, the pro-league movement had begun, in the form of the Bryce Group, as a reaction against anti-German jingoism, the patriotic fever to support the war and the perils of the balance of power. Identifying the condition of international anarchy, not German aggression, as *the* prime cause of the war, they strove to replace the system of rival alliances and arms races with a league of nations founded on rules and the peaceful resolution of disputes through diplomatic bargaining and judicial mechanisms. In 1917–1918, however, the greatly expanded pro-league movement was united into the League of Nations Union, which came to promote what the original Bryce Group membership had opposed in 1914–1915: a league of victorious powers aligned against Germany and its allies. This vision of the league led to an increase in the popularity of the movement in Britain, and the membership of the League of Nations Union grew to 2,230 by October 1918, and to 3,841 by the end of 1918.[6] Yet, at the same time, it marked the end of the original vision of the Bryce Group as the inspiration for the wider pro–league of nations movement.

---

[4] Ibid., pp. 209–11.   [5] Ibid., pp. 195, 209–11.
[6] Egerton, *Great Britain and the Creation of the League of Nations*, pp. 216, 221; Donald S. Birn, *The League of Nations Union, 1918–1945* (Oxford University Press, 1981), p. 11.

In the course of developing their movement from 1914 to 1918, the original pro-league activists had to undergo critical processes. The more popular and influential they became, the less control over the vision and the foundation of the league they had. In popularising their ideas for mass consumption, their original thinking about world order lost its nuances and sophistication. As Chapter 3 showed, the influence of the pro-league movement reached the critical mass for pushing the league as an important item on the political agenda by the middle of 1917.[7] From late 1917 to 1918, the movement reached its maximum point of influence and war-time popularity. It was an essential process for the pro-leaguers to achieve their aim of creating a new organisation and thereby led to the 'emergence of the new order', which depended on a widespread recognition of the need of a new order.[8] By gaining popularity for the post-war idea, the original pro-leaguers had lost control of what the League would be and how it would be implemented.

Highlighting the change of the pro-leaguers' ideas about a post-war organisation in 1917–1918 reveals a fundamental, yet neglected, backdrop to the formation of the League of Nations. However long and exhausting the war had become, it did not necessarily generate a popular desire for peace that translated directly into public support for a league in accordance with the original ideas of the Bryce Group. Far from being driven by war-weariness or a yearning for peace at any price, many people endorsed a league of nations as an extension of waging the war against Germany by strengthening the anti-German cause. While the wide *variety* of the league plans envisaged by different actors has drawn the attention of historians,[9] there was ultimately *only one* vision of the league – the league of victorious democratic powers arrayed against Germany – that most actors, including the public, politicians and pro-leaguers, upheld in 1918. By tracing the League of Nations Society's split and re-amalgamation into the League of Nations Union in 1918, this chapter will explore this crucial change in pro-league movement's vision of a new international organisation.

The Split in the League of Nations Society

In 1918, the League of Nations Society members' opinions were divided on the question whether Germany should be excluded from the new organisation. Indeed, this was a split between those who advocated for

---

[7] See Chapter 3, n. 5.

[8] Paul W. Schroeder, *Systems, Stability, and Statecraft: Essays on the International History of Modern Europe* (Palgrave Macmillan, 2004), pp. 249, 258.

[9] For example, see Winkler, *The League of Nations Movement in Great Britain*, pp. 255–56.

the idea of the league as an alliance of all the great powers acting in concert to perpetuate peace and those who thought it should be an alliance of victorious powers united against Germany. The former was supported by the original pro-leaguers including Lowes Dickinson and Willoughby Dickinson, who argued that the anarchic international system was the prime cause of the war; the latter view was most vociferously defended by the founders of the breakaway group, the League of Free Nations Association, who regarded German aggression as the primary cause of war. In July 1918, the right wing of the League of Nations Society broke ranks to form the League of Free Nations Association. Led by the Liberal politician and the Welsh 'millionaire major' David Davies, the Association was, as Lowes Dickinson described it, more 'ardent supporters of the war, and good haters of Germany'.[10] Since commanding infantry on the Western Front from December 1915 to June 1916, Davies focused on the issue of peace in international relations.[11] After acting as Lloyd George's parliamentary private secretary from June 1916 to June 1917,[12] he became devoted to the idea of a league, which he believed needed more extensive propaganda to garner 'the whole-hearted support of public opinion'.[13]

In June 1918, some of the Society members, including novelist H. G. Wells, began to demand the immediate establishment of a league of nations without Germany.[14] Wells, who coined the phrase 'The War That Will End War' in 1914,[15] recognised the need for a new world order and worked as a member of the Society.[16] Others, especially the original pro-league leaders such as Lowes Dickinson and Willoughby Dickinson, were more cautious about it.[17] As the Chairman of the

---

[10] Cambridge, King's College, The Papers of Goldsworthy Lowes Dickinson, GLD 1/2/4; Egerton, *Great Britain and the Creation of the League of Nations*, p. 72.

[11] David Steeds, 'David Davies, Llandinam, and International Affairs', *Transactions of the Honourable Society of Cymmrodorion*, vol. 9, (2003), pp. 126.

[12] Brian Porter, 'David Davies: A Hunter after Peace', *Review of International Studies*, vol. 15, no. 1 (January 1989), p. 27–36; Steeds, 'David Davies', p. 125.

[13] Porter, 'David Davies', p. 28.

[14] OBL, Willoughby Dickinson Papers, MS. Eng. hist. c.403, 118, a letter from G. Lowes Dickinson to W. H. Dickinson, June 1918 and 119, a letter from W. H. Dickinson to G. Lowes Dickinson, 5 June 1918. Since Davies expressed his League idea in March 1918, the like-minded people were getting together. See Winkler, *The League of Nations Movement in Great Britain*, p. 71.

[15] Lovat Dickson, *H.G. Wells: His Turbulent Life and Times* (Macmillan, 1969), p. 231; H. G. Wells, *Experiment in Autobiography: Discoveries and Conclusions of a Very Ordinary Brain* (Victor Gollancz Ltd., 1966), p. 667. Also see, Mulligan, *The Great War for Peace*, pp. 8–9.

[16] Dickson, *H.G. Wells*, p. 231; Wells, *Experiment in Autobiography*, pp. 680–81.

[17] Jay Winter (ed.), *The Cambridge History of the First World War*, vol. 2 (Cambridge University Press, 2013), pp. 597–98.

Society, Willoughby Dickinson outlined key points debated inside the Society to his contacts in the United States. Some of the Society's members were in favour of the formation of a league excluding Germany without further delay. Dickinson argued:

(1) That unless some definite action is taken before the time arrives for the discussion of the terms of peace the Allies will not be sufficiently agreed as to the method of forming a league of nations to enable them to put it forward successfully as a part of those terms.

(2) That unless the principal Allied Governments who profess that they are fighting in order to set up a League of Nations that will secure the world from future war, can show to the world a practicable scheme to which they have agreed to submit themselves so as to avoid conflicts amongst themselves their good faith may be doubted ...

(4) ... if the German people desired to enter the League in good faith and reap the advantages of peace and security which the League would provide, they could do so ....[18]

On the other hand, Dickinson described the arguments of those who opposed the immediate formation of such a league as follows:

(1) That the very fact that the Allied Governments had taken this course would be represented to the German people by their Government as being a definite step towards ostracising Germany permanently from all human society, and cutting her off politically and economically...

(2) That a league of nations to be effective in securing a world peace must include the Germans and if so it ought not to be formed except as part of negotiations and discussions to which Germany would be a party, which state of affairs cannot prevail whilst the war is in progress.

(3) That in any case the fact of leaving out Germany, even though it be temporarily, would create an atmosphere in which such a difficult question as the formation of a league of nations could hardly hope to be successfully disposed of.

(4) That the neutral States could not enter a league formed whilst there is uncertainty as to what will be the military outcome of the war.[19]

In fact, those who opposed the idea of excluding Germany were not pacifists. For them, the foundation of the league would come through victory over the Central Powers. Nonetheless, they were cautious about

---

[18] HUHL, League to Enforce Peace Records (Int 6722.8.25*), Box 1, a letter from W. H. Dickinson to Marburg, 27 June 1918.
[19] Ibid.

excluding Germany since they supposed that the formation of the league depended on the situations at the war's end. If, at the end of the war, Germany was defeated and transformed politically and morally, a league of nations could be formed with Germany quickly. On the other hand, if the war did not end in that way, militaristic Germany should not be admitted to a post-war organisation, and such outcomes might still require a defensive alliance. Yet even in 1918, as a leading guardian of the Society and a renowned international lawyer James Bryce put it, 'it is impossible to foresee just how the war will end' and therefore difficult to predict how the league could be formed.[20] More importantly, some of the Society's leaders, such as Lowes Dickinson, still adhered to the original league idea of an international organisation with universal membership. The Bryce Group had originally identified security alliances and competitive blocs, rather than German aggression, as a critical cause of war and attempted to replace them with a new international organisation. If the league excluded Germany and its allies, so ran their logic, then the league would be nothing more than a perpetuation of the great power divide that had been a prime cause of war in the first place.[21]

For those who demanded that Germany be excluded from the league, German militarism, a product of its authoritarianism, had caused the war and therefore a league for peace had to be formed without Germany, although German entry might be possible if, in the future, the public of the transformed Germany wished it 'in good faith'.[22] This difference of opinion caused a split in the League of Nations Society. The new breakaway group, the League of Free Nations Association, in the letter establishing its formation, declared that they were 'in no sense a pacifist or defeatists organisation' and identified 'the need for a vigorous

[20] HUHL, League to Enforce Peace Records (Int 6722.8.25*), Box 1, a letter from Bryce to Taft, 27 June 1918. Also see Victor Rothwell, *British War Aims and Peace Diplomacy, 1914–1918* (Clarendon, 1971), pp.200–201, 249–51; David French, *The Strategy of the Lloyd George Coalition 1916–1918* (Clarendon, 1995), chapter 7; Brock Millman, 'A Counsel of Despair: British Strategy and War Aims 1917–18', *Journal of Contemporary History*, vol. 36 (2001), pp. 260, 269–70; David Stevenson, *1914–1918: The History of the First World War* (Penguin, 2005), p. 466.
[21] OBL, James Bryce Papers, MS. Bryce U.S.A. 23, 112, a letter from Bryce to Lowell, 5 June 1918 and 113–14, a letter from Bryce to Marburg, 5 June 1918; HUHL, League to Enforce Peace Records (Int 6722.8.25*), Box 1, a letter from Bryce to Taft, 27 June 1918 and a letter from Bryce to Marburg, 28 June 1918; The League of Nations Society Publications, no. 17, 'Report of Conference of the Legal Profession', 23 July 1917; The League of Nations Society Publications, no. 22, H. N. Spalding, 'What a League of Nations Means', Jan 1918; The National Library of Wales, Lord Davies of Llandinam Papers, B3/3, 149, 'War Aims and a League of Nations', n.d.; G. Lowes Dickinson, 'A League of Nations Now?', *War & Peace*, no. 60 (September, 1918), pp. 327–28.
[22] HUHL, League to Enforce Peace Records (Int 6722.8.25*), Box 1, a letter from W. H. Dickinson to Marburg, 27 June 1918.

Propaganda of the idea of a League of Free Nations'.[23] According to their definition, a free nation meant 'one which believes in and practises representative government, and whose executive Ministers are responsible for their actions to the elected representatives of the people', namely, a democratic state.[24] The Association emphasised that a current militaristic and autocratic Germany was unqualified to be admitted into the league of free nations.[25] Germany might be admitted in the future, if Germany became democratic, the German public appreciated the value of the peace league and they desired to join.[26] However, since there was 'no immediate prospect' that the war would end soon with the real repentance and the conversion of Germany into a democratic state,[27] the group's object was 'to transform and consolidate the present alliance into a permanent League of free peoples' at once.[28] The British people, the Association claimed, should bind themselves into this great association of free nations that would spread throughout the world, thereby enabling free people to lead the world, destroy Prussian militarism and prevent future war.[29]

Further, the Association was dissatisfied with the Society's activities. Some members of the new group, such as the Conservative MP Arthur Steel-Maitland, believed that 'the direction of the Society was practically collared by the Pacifist section of it'.[30] Indeed, some of the Society's leading members, including Lowes Dickinson, the architect Raymond Unwin and the Liberal MP Aneurin Williams, were labelled by the public

[23] Parliamentary Archives, LG/F/82/8/2, 'the League of Free Nations Association', July 1918.
[24] David Davies, et al., 'League of Free Nations Association: to the Editor of the Times', *The Times*, 18 September 1918, p. 10.
[25] 'The League of Nations: Interview with Prof Gilbert Murray, the Needs and the Difficulties Germany Must be Included', *The Observer*, 11 August 1918, p. 2; David Davies, et al., 'League of Free Nations Association: to the Editor of the Times', *The Times*, 18 September 1918, p. 10.
[26] HUHL, League to Enforce Peace Records (Int 6722.8.25*), Box 1, a letter from W. H. Dickinson to Marburg, 27 June 1918.
[27] NLW, Lord Davies of Llandinam Papers, B3/3, 149, 'War Aims and a League of Nations', n.d.; ibid., B4/1, Box 5, 1917–18, 'Proposal Letter to Manchester Guardian', 8 October 1918.
[28] David Davies, et al., 'League of Free Nations Association: to the Editor of the Times', *The Times*, 18 September 1918, p. 10.
[29] NLW, Lord Davies of Llandinam Papers, B3/2, 2, 'Why an Association is Necessary' and 11, 'The League of Nations: An Urgent Task' (Interview with M. L. Bourgeois), July/August 1918; ibid., B4/1, Box 5, 1917–18, 'Proposal Letter to Manchester Guardian', 8 October 1918.
[30] ORL, Willoughby Dickinson Papers, MS. Eng. hist. c.403, a letter from Steel-Maitland to W. H. Dickinson, 19 and 22 June 1918; OBL, Gilbert Murray Papers, Murray 178, 133–39, to Murray, 5 August 1918.

as pacifists who were sympathetic to Germany.[31] For instance, Gilbert Murray, the Oxford classicist and one of the founders of the new group, received a letter from an Association's member to describe some of the Society's leaders as follows:

> Mr. Aneurin [Williams] is an impossible person to work with. Mr. Lowes Dickinson ... and several of the others are more or less identified with the 'peace by negotiation' movement.[32]

In addition, Davies expressed his discontent at the Society's leaders 'who', in his words, had 'no idea of running a great propagandist campaign, or of how to proceed to raise the necessary funds to do so'.[33] Davies, unlike the leaders of the parent group, was eager to spend more money on propaganda and education. In fact, in the inter-war years, he became even more passionate about peace work and poured money into the league's activities. For instance, Davies established a Chair of International Politics at the University College of Wales, Aberystwyth, to provide the study of international relations with emphasis on the promotion of peace and in 1922 named it as the Woodrow Wilson Chair.[34]

In fact, Davies led this movement along with the Enemy Propaganda Department under the newspaper magnate Lord Northcliffe, at Crewe House. The department, established to transmit British propaganda to neutral and enemy countries in 1918, thought the idea of a league of free nations in propaganda aimed at Germany might effectively threaten the Germans with exclusion from the post-war order if they continued the war.[35] Northcliffe criticised what he perceived to be the pacifistic arguments, such as a negotiated peace,[36] and underlined the constitution of the League of Free Nations as a critical war aim.[37] In practice, Crewe

---

[31] HUHL, League to Enforce Peace Records (Int 6722.8.25*), Box 1, a letter from Holt to Short, 27 April 1918; OBL, Gilbert Murray Papers, Murray 178, 51–52, a letter from W. H. Dickinson to Murray, 15 August 1918; Martin Ceadel, *Semi-Detached Idealists: The British Peace Movement and International Relations, 1854–1945* (Oxford University Press, 2000), pp. 207, 237.

[32] OBL, Gilbert Murray Papers, Murray 178, 133–39, to Murray, 5 August 1918.

[33] Ibid., 149–50, a letter from Davies to Murray, 14 August 1918.

[34] Porter, 'David Davies', pp. 27–28; Steeds, 'David Davies', p. 129.

[35] Egerton, *Great Britain and the Creation of the League of Nations*, pp. 72–73.

[36] J. Lee Thompson, *Politicians, the Press, and Propaganda: Lord Northcliffe and the Great War, 1914–1919* (Kent State University Press, 1999), pp. 120–21, 176–77.

[37] British Library, Add MS 74102, 99, '*The Great Outsiders* Memorandum by the Policy Committee of the British War Mission: Propaganda Peace Policy', 1918 and 102–6, 'Memorandum by the Policy Committee of the British War Mission, 8 October 1918'; BL, Add MS 62162, 17–19, 'Committee for Propaganda in Enemy Countries, Minutes of the Fourth Meeting held at Crewe House, Curzon Street, 11 June 1918 and 20–21, 'Committee of Propaganda in Enemy Countries, Minutes of the Fifth Meeting held at Crewe house, Curzon Street, 25 June 1918.

House was not entirely under Northcliffe's control due to a series of illnesses including influenza.[38] At Crewe House, thinking and writing about the post-war order fell to H. G. Wells – a member of Crewe House, of the League of Nations Society and of the new Association. The outbreak of the war drove Wells to abandon novel-writing and devote himself to journalism and the idea of a new world order.[39] Wells' main task at Crewe House was to set up a league of *free* nations, and he later claimed that, by considering a mere league that lacked clear definition, he inserted the word 'free'.[40] He repeatedly stressed the importance of creating a league of *free* nations in the department's meetings[41] and sought to 'get suitable propaganda' from the League of Nations Society.[42] As a result, Wells reported that 'the Society had been induced to produce a new declaration of aims more in accordance with the policy of Crewe House than was their earlier declaration, and a new League of Free Nations Association, with a considerable endowment, had been formed for the purposes of propaganda and research'.[43] Although Crewe House did not intend to trigger the split in the League of Nations Society, it attempted to move the group in the direction of forming a league of free nations that excluded Germany.[44]

In 1918, there was a growing interest in a post-war organisation inside the British government, and a private secretary of the Prime Minister Philip Kerr and a Conservative MP Robert Cecil pressed a league with the threat of excluding Germany from it.[45] While Lloyd George maintained a vague posture towards their pressure by granting Wilson's wish for private talks on the league issue,[46] Crew House initiated the action for

---

[38] Thompson, *Politicians, the Press, and Propaganda*, p. 197.
[39] Dickson, *H.G. Wells*, p. 231; Wells, *Experiment in Autobiography*, pp. 680–81, 694.
[40] Wells, *Experiment in Autobiography*, pp. 695, 705.
[41] The National Archives, FO371/4364, 202–6, 'Committee for Propaganda in Enemy Countries, Minutes of the Third Meeting held at Crewe House, 31 May 1918; BL, Add MS 62162, 12–16, 'Committee for Propaganda in Enemy Countries, Minutes, 31 May 1918; BL, Add MS 74102, 133–65, 'Report of Work of Committee for Propaganda in Enemy Countries', 1918; BL, Add MS 74101, 149–58, 'Memoranda on War Aim, Prepared by a Select Committee of the Enemy Countries Propaganda for Guidance in the Department of Great Propaganda, 24 May 1918.
[42] BL, Add MS 62162, 20–21, 'Committee of Propaganda in Enemy Countries, Minutes of the Fifth Meeting held at Crewe house, 25 June 1918.
[43] Ibid.
[44] Yearwood, *Guarantee of Peace*, pp. 62–64; Campbell Stuart, *Secrets of Crewe House: The Story of a Famous Campaign* (Hodder and Stoughton, 1920), p. 89.
[45] Yearwood, *Guarantee of Peace*, p. 145; Egerton, *Great Britain and the Creation of the League of Nations*, pp. 72–73.
[46] See Chapter 4; Gaynor Johnson, *Lord Robert Cecil: Politician and Internationalist* (Ashgate Publishing, 2013), pp. 92–93; Peter Yearwood, '"On the Safe and Right Lines": The

a league that excluded Germany.[47] The policy of Crewe House, however, was not directed by the government.[48] The members of Crewe House were aware that they did not have a clear and agreed peace policy as a department because, as Wells complained, 'nothing [about it] could ever be obtained from the Foreign Office'.[49] The League of Free Nations Association did not have close contact with the diplomatic corps either, which is why David Davies asked the Foreign Office about their policy regarding the league of nations from time to time.[50] As Horne has argued, while the government was engaged in a campaign to sustain civil morale in 1917–1918,[51] it was not a simple 'model of state versus society'.[52] The remobilisation of support for the war involved 'voluntary participation' of 'semi-official and private agencies',[53] such as the Association, which supported the cause of fighting on until Germany was defeated.[54]

Both in the League of Free Nations Associations and the League of Nations Society, some of their members criticised the others and were averse to cooperating with them.[55] The two groups, therefore, worked separately during the summer of 1918. As a new group, the Association was recruiting members fast. It grew to 987 by October 1918.[56] The Association also contacted similar organisations in the United States and France by emphasising the need for an active international propaganda campaign for the league of free nations.[57] Meanwhile, within only a

---

Lloyd George Government and the Origins of the League of Nations, 1916–1918', *The Historical Journal*, vol. 32, no. 1 (1989), p. 145.

[47] Egerton, *Great Britain and the Creation of the League of Nations*, pp. 72–73.

[48] Crew House's idea was taken up by the political intelligence department, which 'was entrusted with the development of foreign office thinking on the league question'. But those who were responsible for the post-war proposals, Alfred Zimmern and Eustace Percy, mostly focused on the political use of the economic weapon, not the post-war system of war prevention. See, Yearwood, *Guarantee of Peace*, pp. 64–6; Yearwood, 'On the Safe and Right Lines', pp. 146–47.

[49] BL, Add MS 62162, 82–90, 'Committee for Propaganda in Enemy Countries, Minutes of the Fourteenth Meeting', 29 October 1918; also see Wells, *Experiment in Autobiography*, p 704.

[50] TNA, FO 371/3439, 40–41, 11 March 1918, 92–93, 3 June 1918, 394, 19 June 1918, 563, 14 March 1918 and 564–65, 19 March 1918.

[51] Horne, *State, Society and Mobilization*, p. 198.   [52] Ibid., p. 209.

[53] Ibid., pp. 195, 209.   [54] Ibid., pp. 210–11.

[55] OBL, Gilbert Murray Papers, Murray 178, 133–39, to Murray, 5 August 1918 and 161, a letter from G. Lowes Dickinson to Murray, 6 Sept [1918].

[56] Egerton, *Great Britain and the Creation of the League of Nations*, p. 221.

[57] PA, LG/F/82/8/4, a letter from D. Davies to Adams, 22 July 1918; PA, LG/F/82/8/1, a letter from D. Davies to Adams, 5 July 1918; PA, LG/F/82/8/2, a letter from G. Murray to Adams, n.d.; NLW, *Lord Davies of Llandinam Papers*, B3/2, 11, 'The League of Nations: An Urgent Task' (Interview with M. L. Bourgeois), July/August 1918; OBL, Gilbert Murray Papers, Murray 125, 56, a letter from Bryce to Murray, 2 August 1918;

month of the Association's formation, the two groups began to negotiate amalgamation. They agreed to a common platform including the immediate formation of the league among the Allies and were united into the League of Nations Union in October 1918.[58] Why, then, they amalgamated so quickly, is the question we now examine.

Amalgamation for the League without Germany

Even though neither the League of Nations Society nor the League of Free Nations Association recorded any specific reasons why they amalgamated, there were two major elements to be considered. First, one unified group would reinforce their pro-league campaign; second, and more strikingly, the majority opinion favoured the exclusion of Germany. Both groups concluded the movement required politicians' – especially famous and powerful ones – support to create a league. Indeed, at the beginning of August 1918, one ideal political figure for the movement, the former Foreign Secretary Edward Grey, accepted the offer to be the president of the amalgamated body.[59] Grey had been interested in the league from 1914 and in touch with the pro-league groups including the League of Nations Society,[60] although he had withdrawn from

ibid., Murray 178, 154, a letter from Davies to Murray, 16 August 1918 and 133–39, to Murray, 5 August 1918; HUHL, LEPR (Int 6722.8.25*), Box 3, Letters from Foreign Peace Organizations, England, 'the League of Free Nations Association', July 1918 and a letter from Davies to the League to Enforce Peace, 13 September 1918; ibid., Box 2, England, a letter from Davies to Taft, 15 September 1918.

[58] OBL, Gilbert Murray Papers, Murray 178, a letter from W. H. Dickinson to Murray, 8 August 1918, 215–16, "'Forming the League Now'', from the League of Nations Society and the League of Free Nations Association to the Editor of the Times'' and 189–91, 'Joint Meeting of Representatives of the League of Nations Society and the League of Free Nations Association to Consider Amalgamation'; ibid., Murray 125, 61, a letter from Bryce to Murray, 11 September 1918; ibid., Murray 179, 238–39, 'Report on Proposed Amalgamation of the League of Free Nations Association and the League of Nations Society; 'League of Nations Union: a Proposed Amalgamation', *The Manchester Guardian*, 9 November 1918, p. 8; 'League of Nations Union: An Amalgamation of Societies', *The Times*, 9 November 1918, p. 8.

[59] OBL, Gilbert Murray Papers, Murray 178, 154–59, a letter from Davies to Murray, 2 August 1918; Winkler, *The League of Nations Movement in Great Britain*, p. 74; Birn, *The League of Nations Union*, pp. 10–11; Ceadel, *Semi-Detached Idealists*, p. 237.

[60] A. J. P. Taylor, *The Trouble Makers: Dissent over Foreign Policy, 1792–1939* (H. Hamilton, 1957), p. 127; Egerton, *Great Britain and the Creation of the League of Nations*, p.25; *The Nation*, 14 March 1914; CKC, the Papers of Charles Robert Ashbee, CRA 3/3, July 1914, p. 337; ibid., CRA3/4, 153–56, 12 February 1915; BL, Add MS 50908, 202, a letter from G. Lowes Dickinson to Scott, 10 June 1916; HUHL, League to Enforce Peace Records (Int 6722.8.25*), Box 2, 2 Foreign Peace Organizations, Marburg, 11 September 1916; ibid., Box 1, a letter from Bryce to Marburg, 7 December 1916; OBL, James Bryce Papers, MS. Bryce U.S.A. 8, 68–69, a letter from Lowell to Bryce, 4 November 1916; ibid., MS. Bryce 158, 73–74, a letter from Bryce to Grey, 10 August

Westminster and the public eye since December 1916 when he had left the government. Sympathetic to the pro-leaguers' post-war plan, Grey stressed in public that a league could only be formed as a result of military victory.[61] His support for the league was widely reported in newspapers, which boosted the pro-league campaign.[62] Although some leaders of the League of Free Nations Association, such as David Davies and Gilbert Murray, triggered the split in the pro-league group, they preferred cooperation to competition.[63] Equally, the League of Nations Society leadership, shortly after negotiations started with the Association in August 1918, saw the logic of uniting their efforts.[64] The two groups agreed that one unified group would strengthen their activities, including the recruitment of members, fundraising and above all, securing political support and influence.[65]

More significantly, the two groups amalgamated quickly because by August 1918 the League of Nations Society had learnt that opinions outside the pro-league circles did not favour the inclusion of Germany. In 1918, the question whether Germany would be admitted to the league attracted widespread attention not only from pro-league activists but also from the public and the press. Most argued that a post-war organisation needed to exclude Germany due to its militaristic and authoritarian character, which propelled the League of Nations Society to advocate the restricted league among the Allies. Along with those who were inside the government, a political figure such as Grey, before receiving the offer

---

1917; ibid., MS. Bryce U.S.A.10, 200–201, a letter from Grey to Bryce, 1 January 1918; OBL, Gilbert Murray Papers, Murray 178, a letter from Jones to Murray, 9 February 1918.

[61] 'Lord Grey on the League of Nations', *The Manchester Guardian*, 11 October 1918, p. 5; PA, STR/7/8/34, a letter from Grey to Strachy, 30 October 1918(7?); OBL, Willoughby Dickinson Papers, MS. Eng. hist. c.407, 88–95, 'Grey's Message "the League of Nations"', (speech by Grey, 10 October 1918).

[62] 'The League of Nations: Viscount Grey's Essential Conditions', *The Manchester Guardian*, 20 June 1918, p. 4; 'League of Nations: Viscount Grey's Pamphlet', *The Times*, 20 June 1918, p. 5; 'Viscount Grey on a League of Nations', *The Observer*, 23 June 1918, p. 4; Winkler, *The League of Nations Movement in Great Britain*, p. 76.

[63] OBL, Gilbert Murray Papers, Murray 178, 149–50, a letter from Davies to Murray, 14 August 1918 and 146, a letter from Dickinson to Murray, 12 August 1918; PA, LG/F/82/8/2, 'League of Free Nations Association' by G. Murray; Also see Birn, *The League of Nations Union*, p. 9.

[64] OBL, Gilbert Murray Papers, Murray 178, 122, 'Conference between Representatives of the League of Nations Society and the League of Free Nations Association', 26 July 1918, 124–26, a letter from W. H. Dickinson to Murray, 31 July 1918 and 166, 27 September 1918.

[65] OBL, Gilbert Murray Papers, Murray 179, 240–43, 'Amalgamation with League of Nations Society, Corrected Draft Submitted by C. A. McCurdy, MP. Also, Birn has argued that 'the movement was too small to be divided', in Donald Birn, *The League of Nations Union, 1918–1945* (Oxford University Press, 1981), pp. 9–10.

to become the president of the amalgamated group, also favoured excluding Germany from the league until it became democratic.[66] Newspapers featured the question of German admission into the league from time to time during 1918.[67] Even though their articles covered both positive and negative views on the matter, the majority opinion was decidedly against German inclusion:

German militarism must disappear. It will not disappear unless it is totally beaten in the field. To be safe themselves and to promote more effective action for the larger purpose the Allies must form their own League, making it as solid and comprehensive as possible.[68]

This feeling against Germany was also shared by the public. As Kate Courtney, a social worker and the wife of a Liberal politician Leonard Henry Courtney, described in her diary, 'half the people who advocate a League of Nations speak either of compelling Germany to come in as one of our terms – or refusing to admit her except as a conscious penitent and suppliant'.[69] Even after the armistice, public opinion did not necessarily want mere peace in Europe but demanded that Germany be punished. Kate Courtney noted in November 1918:

Yesterday I took up the banner I had been embroidering – large blue silk one with a dove in the centre and olive branch – to ask if they would like to put among their many flags on the Town Hall. I went to-day and was told by the Town Clerk they thought it wholly unsuitable. 'You have put an olive branch in', he said, 'and we are not ready to offer Germany the olive branch', and added with a nasty sneer: 'We are not pro-Germans here.' 'Nor Christians either apparently', I said (perhaps unwisely) and walked out. But that spirit hurts me.[70]

Many people, politicians or the public, longed not for a league with Germany, potentially through a negotiated settlement, but for a league that would be a continuation of the war-time alliance against Germany, which would strengthen the cause of victory over Germany and the

---

[66] OBL, Willoughby Dickinson Papers, MS. Eng. hist. c.407, 99–105, 'The League of Nations' by E. Grey, 11 May 1918.

[67] 'A League of Nations: Immediate Beginning by the Allies Mr. Barnes's Suggestion', *The Manchester Guardian*, 17 June 1918, p. 8; 'League of Nations: Mr. Barnes on Inclusion of Germany', *The Times*, 6 August 1918, p. 6; 'Foreign Policy Control', *The Times*, 20 March 1918, p. 7; 'The League of Nations: Professor Murray and Its Necessity', *The Manchester Guardian*, 12 October 1918, p. 4; Denbigh Sydenham and E. Maddison, 'League of Nations: A Misleading Ideal', *The Times*, 5 April 1918, p. 8; 'League of Nations: Sir John Simon on Mr. Wilson's Ideal', *The Observer*, 28 July 1918, p. 8; 'The League of Nations Meeting', *The Times*, 11 October 1918, p. 9.

[68] 'The League of Nations', *The Observer*, 30 June 1918, p. 6.

[69] Kate Courtney, *Extracts from a Diary during the War* (Victor Press, 1927), 29 September 1918, pp. 168–69. Also see Gregory, *The Last Great War*, pp. 234–38.

[70] Courtney, *Extracts from a Diary*, 12 November 1918, p. 174.

militarism and authoritarianism that the German empire had come to embody. The prevalence of this view clearly compelled the leadership of the Society to shift its stance and amalgamate with the Association for the common goal of founding a league of nations.

The League As a Result of Victory and Abolishing Militarism

In fact, examining why many people wanted the league that excluded Germany reveals the logic behind the popularity of the league in Britain in 1917–1918. As historians have argued, war-weariness was largely evident in Britain at this stage of the war,[71] yet that did not necessarily mean that the public or politicians desired the league as the product of their craving for peace at any price. Rather, to many people, the league was an extension of fighting the ongoing war. There was what Horne has called the 'self-mobilisation' of civil society to support for the war in 1917–1918, which reactivated the public commitment to war aims such as fighting until victory had been achieved.[72] The self-mobilisation was successful and most of the league advocates presumed that a league, as a British war aim, could only be established through victory. What Grey proclaimed in the first meeting of the amalgamated League of Nations Union in October 1918 illustrated one of the most fundamental conditions of creating the league:[73] 'a League of Nations cannot be a substitute for a successful termination of this war. It must arise out of the successful termination'.[74] Even Lowes Dickinson, a leading member of the Society who was labelled a pacifist by the public, admitted the following, in a rather resigned tone: 'once war had broken out it was "inevitable" that every means would be adopted, at every cost to everything, to win the war'.[75] Indeed, this determination to win the war as the ultimate goal was

---

[71] See n. 1.   [72] Horne, *State, Society and Mobilization*, pp. 209–11.

[73] For example, the president of the League of Nations Society, Lord Shaw of Dunfermline, stated that 'the war must go on until this [German militaristic] state of mind is changed', in NLW, Lord Davies of Llandinam Papers, B3/3, 149, 'War Aims and a League of Nations', n.d.

[74] The League of Nations Society Publications, no. 44, 'Viscount Grey on a League of Nations: At a Meeting Held at Central Hall, Westminster, 10 Oct 1918', October 1918; 'Lord Grey on the League of Nations: Some Crucial Points Examined', *The Manchester Guardian*, 11 October 1918, p. 5; Also, before taking up the post of president of the League of Nations Union, Grey declared 'complete victory over Germany' was needed in advance of the creation of the League, in OBL, Willoughby Dickinson Papers, MS. Eng. hist. c.407, 99–105, 'The League of Nations' by Grey, 11 May 1918.

[75] OBL, Gilbert Murray Papers, Murray 178, 100, a letter from G. Lowes Dickinson to Murray, 1918?

also shared by those who were outside the pro-league circles, such as a private secretary of the Prime Minister Philip Kerr.[76]

Of course it was true that once war began people had to fight for victory; yet many British people, either in favour of the league or not, deemed that they were not just fighting for victory but also for a higher ideal – abolishing militarism. For instance, it was undergirded by the propaganda of the National War Aim Committee, 'a cross-party parliamentary organisation' that began operations in July 1917 'to conduct propaganda within Britain, aimed at maintaining civilian morale'.[77] The Committee claimed that the post-war world should be a peaceful one without war, which required complete victory and the eradication of German militarism.[78] Indeed, 'to destroy Prussian militarism' was not merely advocated as a war aim[79] but also repeatedly highlighted even by pro-leaguers during the war.[80] As we will see, especially after the Russian Revolution and American entry into the war in 1917, the character of the war became ideological: democracy versus autocracy. In this context, pro-leaguers also supposed that the league should be established to promote democracy after eradicating militarism. Frequently, abolishing militarism was equivalent to defeating Germany[81] and included the thinking that Germany had to be punished.[82] Thus, the logic of supporting the league was almost the same as that of supporting the war: Britain needed to fight to vanquish Germany *and* militarism.

---

[76] 'The Speaker on War Aims: Speech at Carlisle No Shining Swords in the League', *The Observer*, 30 December 1917, p. 8; PA, LG/89/1/10, 'Lansdowne Speech', from Kerr to Prime Minister, 5 December 1917. Also see British Library of Economic and Political Science (hereafter BLEPS), MOREL/F13/6, Norman Angell, 'Shall This War End German Militarism', the Union of Democratic Control Pamphlet, n.d., p. 3.

[77] Monger, *Patriotism and Propaganda in First World War Britain*, p. 1.

[78] Ibid., pp. 95, 202.

[79] 'League of Nations: General Smuts on War Aims', *The Times*, 25 October 1917, p. 6.

[80] The League of Nations Society Publications, no. 22, 'What a League of Nations Means', January 1918; The League of Nations Society Publications, no. 39, 'League of Nations Speech by the Right Hon Lord Shaw of Dunfermline', 26 June 1918. Also see BLEPS, MOREL/F13/6, Norman Angell, 'Shall This War End German Militarism', the Union of Democratic Control Pamphlet, n.d., pp. 3, 19.

[81] PA, LG/89/1, 'Manchester District', 1 December 1917; 'The League of Nations', *The Observer*, 30 June 1918, p. 6; The League of Nations Society Publications, no. 15, Noel Buxton, '"America and the League", The Project of a League of Nations', August 1917; The League of Nations Society Publications, no. 28, W. H. Dickinson, 'Disarmament and A League of Nations, March 1918; NLW, Lord Davies of Llandinam Papers, B3/2, 11, 'The League of Nations: An Urgent Task' (Interview with M. L. Bourgeois), July/August 1918; ibid., B4/1, Box 5, 1917–18, 'Proposal Letter to Manchester Guardian', 8 October 1918.

[82] PA, LG/89/1/10, 'Lansdowne Speech', Kerr to Prime Minister, 5 December 1917; 'The League of Nations', *The Observer*, 23 December 1917, p. 6.

Whereas winning the war was essential for the creation of the league, it did not necessarily mean that militarism would be abolished altogether. Hence, the condition of public support for the league was that Germany had to be transformed into a non-militaristic state. As newspapers frequently reported, most people recognised that the league provided 'no room for a Kaiser-ridden Germany, represented by triumphant military and naval figures'.[83] It was, therefore, 'plainly impossible to admit Germany to a League of peace until she has given proofs of complete regeneration'.[84] The National War Aim Committee, for example, argued that the league should be based on the Allies' superior values and that if it included Germany, which was responsible for the development of militarism, it would not last as a new peaceful organisation.[85] Similarly, those who advocated for the league in public proclaimed that Germany had to learn the lesson that militarism would only jeopardise world peace.[86] This view was also endorsed by one of the Society's very powerful backers, the Christian church, especially the Church of England.[87]

Christian Blessings upon a League without Germany

In 1917–1918, the Church of England was the most influential and enthusiastic supporter of the league among religious groups. Yet, here again, it came not only from their preaching peace but also from their supporting the war effort. The connection between the Society and the Church of England began with the former's approach to the Archbishop of Canterbury Randall Davidson to attend the first meeting of the League of Nations Society in May 1917.[88] After this successful meeting, from time to time, the Society directly asked the Archbishop for his support, such as financial assistance, attending or organising meetings and writing

[83] 'The League of Nations: M. Thomas on Duty of Entente Nations', *The Times*, 5 March 1918, p. 5.
[84] Denbigh Sydenham and E. Maddison, 'League of Nations: A Misleading Ideal', *The Times*, 5 April 1918, p. 8.
[85] Monger, *Patriotism and Propaganda in First World War Britain*, pp. 92–5, 202.
[86] 'League of Nations: General Smuts on War Aims', *The Times*, 25 October 1917, p. 6; OBL, Willoughby Dickinson Papers, MS. Eng. hist. c.407, 99–105, 'The League of Nations' by Grey, 11 May 1918; 'The League of Nations: Interview with Prof Gilbert Murray, the Needs and the Difficulties Germany Must be Included', *The Observer*, 11 August 1918, p. 2.
[87] The church's advocacy included almost all the most important churches in the United Kingdom. For example, when churches published an appeal for Christians' support for the League in December 1918, all except the Roman Catholic Church joined. See 'League of Nations: Churches' Appeal to All Christians', *The Times*, 5 December 1918, p. 8.
[88] See Chapter 3.

an open letter to endorse the league idea.[89] The Archbishop, who was aware of his influence as well as of many other peace activists seeking his blessing, was cautious about his involvement with the Society.[90] He endeavoured to avoid the appearance of being perceived as one of the Society's leaders, and on several occasions he declined to speak at the Society's events and to contribute to its publications.[91] Still, the Archbishop sympathised with the pro-league movement and was involved in the church's campaign to promote a league of nations.

In 1918, the church's support for the league became stronger and more pronounced. Behind this change in attitude lay the church's ambition to influence government policy and to shape public opinion. During the war, religion was very important to individuals who sought the assurance of their fighting on the 'right side'.[92] From the perspective of the church in 1914, the war provided an unparalleled chance for a spiritual awakening as well as for the creation of a genuinely Christian nation.[93] Thus, the church supported the war by preaching the virtues of self-sacrifice for a just cause.[94] Yet, by late 1917, some Christian leaders began to proclaim that their failure to prevent the war and their approval of it were fatal mistakes that diminished their dignity and standing.[95] For them, the issue of a league of nations provided a great opportunity to regain their influence and legitimacy as the true voice of peace and reason

---

[89] Lambeth Palace Library, Davidson 409, 23, letters from Magwern Garrett-Jones (an organising Secretary of the League of Nations Society) to G. K. A. Bell, 25 July 1917, and 34, 9 December 1917, and 116, n.d., and 112, a letter from Lord Shaw of Dunfermline to the Archbishop, 7 March 1918, and 55, the League of Nations Society, January 1918; OBL, Willoughby Dickinson Papers, MS. Eng. hist. c.403, a letter from W. H. Dickinson to the Archbishop, 14 June 1918; OBL, James Bryce Papers, MS. Bryce 55, 203, a letter from the Archbishop to Bryce, 21 September 1918.

[90] 'In so far as Davidson consistently avoided supporting any group which tried to enlist his support for a peace initiative, he was thoroughly representative of the majority opinion in Church and State', in Alan Wilkinson, *The Church of England and the First World War* (SPCK, 1978), p. 227.

[91] OBL, Willoughby Dickinson Papers, MS. Eng. hist. c.403, 78, a letter from the Archbishop of Canterbury to W. H. Dickinson, 5 June 1916 and 122, a letter from the Archbishop of Canterbury to W. H. Dickinson, 15 June 1918; LPL, Davidson 409, 129, a letter from the Archbishop to Lord Shaw, 2 April 1918 and 135, a letter from the Archbishop to W. H. Dickinson, 11 April 1918; OBL, James Bryce Papers, MS. Bryce 55, 203, a letter from the Archbishop to Bryce, 21 September 1918.

[92] Gregory, *The Last Great War*, pp. 183–84.   [93] Ibid., pp. 161, 163, 165, 167.

[94] Ibid., pp. 156, 163; David L. Edwards, *Christian England, Vol. 3: From the Eighteenth Century to the First World War* (Collins, 1984), p. 359; Albert Marrin, *The Last Crusade: The Church of England in the First World War* (Duke University Press, 1974), p. 81.

[95] 'A League Of Nations', *The Times*, 18 July 1917, p. 3; 'The Free Churches and A League of Nations', *The Manchester Guardian*, 20 February 1918, p. 8.

in world affairs.[96] As the Bishop of Oxford Charles Gore declared, it was the church's opportunity 'to lead public opinion in a Christian direction'[97] and 'to make its own spirit felt in national policy such as has not occurred heretofore since the outbreak of this war'.[98]

The Church of England's ambition to retain their influence in Britain not only encouraged them to highlight their endorsement of the league but also enabled the idea of the league to perfectly fit the church's rhetoric of justice and Christian ideals of peace among nations. The church stressed that the idea of a post-war organisation already had wide support among representatives of Christian communions[99] and publicly appealed for even a stronger adherence of Christians.[100] Their official reason for supporting the foundation of a league was that its object was to ensure world peace; as this object naturally conformed to Christian doctrines, the church equated the effort of creating the league with the Christian mission.[101] Comments by the Chairman of the Sussex Congregational Union, Reverend S. Maddock, vividly described such attitudes and were cited in one of the official publications of the League of Nations Society.

(1) The aims of the League are visions of the oracles of God.
(2) The basis of the League ... is the Christian basis of all human relationship[s.]
(3) The methods of the League are those of justice and reason.
(4) The conditions – the driving force of the League – are those of the will to peace, freedom and brotherhood.[102]

Many Christian leaders expanded the notion of the brotherhood of men into that of nations and underlined brotherhood as the key for a league of nations.[103] The Archbishop of Canterbury proclaimed that future wars could only be prevented 'by creating the Christian spirit and the growth

[96] Marrin, *The Last Crusade*, pp. 242–43.
[97] The League of Nations Society Publications, no. 33, 'the Demand of the Churches for a League of Nations', June 1918.
[98] LPL, Davidson 409, 87–88, a letter from the Bishop of Oxford to Bell, 14 February 1918.
[99] Randall Cantuar, et al., 'Christianity and The League of Nations: to the Editor or the Times', *The Times*, 23 February 1918, p. 5.
[100] The League of Nations Society Publications, no. 33, 'the Demand of the Churches for a League of Nations', June 1918; 'League of Nations: Churches' Appeal to All Christians', *The Times*, 5 December 1918, p. 8.
[101] 'League of Nations: Churches' Appeal to All Christians', *The Times*, 5 December 1918, p. 8.
[102] The League of Nations Society Publications, no. 33, 'the Demand of the Churches for a League of Nations', June 1918.
[103] Ibid.; 'A League of Nations', *The Times*, 8 February 1918, p. 3.

of the spirit of brotherhood' and by forming an international organisation for peace, namely, a league of nations.[104] Not only did the league of nations idea fit Christian ideals, but the church also preached that it was a duty for all the Christians to unite in establishing it in accordance with Christian doctrines.[105] Since lasting peace could only be assured by an international order based upon Christian principles, 'the Churches were destined to play an important part in the formation' of the league.[106] Embedding the league into their religious causes, the church underlined Christian responsibility to contribute to the league that would realise a Pax Christi.[107]

The League of Nations Society echoed the church's call for a Christian peace to enhance its public appeal.[108] For instance, claims by Lord Parmoor, one of the Society members and a lawyer who was also prominent in ecclesiastical circles, resonated with the church's rhetoric:

Christianity taught a common brotherhood under a common Father, and inculcated the spirit of reconciliation and peace. It was therefore our duty to enunciate the spirit of reconciliation and peace.[109]

One of the leaders of the League of Free Nations Association, David Davies, put pressure on the church by repeating its appeal that the church 'should insist that the new structure should be based upon the principles of Christianity'.[110] Meanwhile, politicians, who were not a member of the Society or Association but approved the idea of the league, spoke approvingly of the league by associating it with Christian themes.[111] For

---

[104] 'A League of Nations', *The Times*, 8 February 1918, p. 3.

[105] The League of Nations Society Publications, no. 33, 'the Demand of the Churches for a League of Nations', June 1918; 'A League of Nations: Action by Christian Churches', *The Times*, 30 October 1918, p. 10.

[106] 'A League of Nations: Action by Christian Churches', *The Times*, 30 October 1918, p. 10.

[107] The League of Nations Society Publications, no. 41, 'Sermon on "the League of Nations" Preached at Holy Trinity, Sloane Street, on July 7th 1918 by Father Paul B. Bull, M.A. (Community of the Resurrection)', Mirfield, August 1918; 'League of Nations: Churches' Appeal to All Christians', *The Times*, 5 December 1918, p. 8.

[108] OBL, James Bryce Papers, MS. Bryce U.S.A. 23, 127–28, a letter from Bryce to Lowell, 30 October 1918.

[109] 'A League of Nations: Discussion in the House of Laymen', *The Times*, 21 February 1918, p. 3; Lord Parmoor also said that 'the object of the war to a Christian Church could not be mistaken, and that the League of Nations merely embraced in a practical form the Christian ethic of the common brotherhood of mankind'. In 'League of Nations: Lord Parmoor in a Leeds Pulpit', *The Manchester Guardian*, 9 December 1918, p. 3.

[110] NLW, Lord Davies of Llandinam Papers, B3/3, 9, 'The Church and the League of Nations', n.d.

[111] For example, the Conservative MP Hugh Cecil said that 'what was wanted was to substitute the general world-wide patriotism of the whole of cosmopolitan Christendom

example, Lord Lansdowne, who became well known for his 'peace letter' to call for a negotiated peace in November 1917,[112] endorsed the creation of the league as it 'was not a mirage; it was a Promised Land'.[113]

Although the church did not provide any substantial ideas about a post-war order, it was clear that the league for a Pax Christi excluded a militaristic Germany. Also, in the church's rhetoric, militarism had to be abolished and Germany had to be punished for causing the war. As the Bishop of Oxford declared in July 1917, the Church of England endorsed fighting until completely defeating Germany:

I am confident that it was our duty to enter into it [the war], and I am confident also that it is our duty to prosecute it until the military power of Germany – the military Government of Germany – is publicly and signally discredited. I am among those who feel that before peace you must put victory.[114]

Stressing 'our' – not individual – duty to fight, the Church of England advocated that people should be united in defeating Germany and thereafter a league of peace could be established.[115]

The League of Democratic States

Moreover, closer inspection of the sources reveals that many people had more demands than simply defeating Germany and abolishing militarism. Pro-league activists, politicians, the church and newspapers all tended to agree that the league should comprise civilised, peace-loving states and would be founded on the Christian doctrine of brotherhood.[116] Hence Germany, in order to enter the league, needed to possess such qualities. While one of the leading members of the League of Nations Society, Aneurin Williams, noted that which states qualified as

for the older patriotism', in 'A League of Nations: Discussion in the House of Laymen', *The Times*, 21 February 1918, p. 3.

[112] Winkler, *The League of Nations Movement in Great Britain*, pp. 112–15.

[113] 'A League of Nations: Lord Lansdowne on the Inclusion of Germany', *The Manchester Guardian*, 20 March 1918, p. 5.

[114] 'The League of Nations: Bishop Gore and German Militarism What the German', *The Manchester Guardian*, 18 July 1917.

[115] Gregory, *The Last Great War*, pp. 163, 168.

[116] The League of Nations Society Publications, no. 17, 'Report of Conference of the Legal Profession', 23 July 1917; PA, LG/89/1/10, 'Lansdowne Speech', Kerr to Prime Minister, 5 December 1917; The League of Nations Society Publications, no. 41, 'Sermon on "the League of Nations" Preached at Holy Trinity, Sloane Street, on July 7th 1918 by Father Paul B. Bull, M.A.(Community of the Resurrection)', Mirfield, Aug 1918; NLW, Lord Davies of Llandinam Papers, B4/1, Box 5, 1917–18, 'Proposal Letter to Manchester Guardian', 8 October 1918; 'Towards a League of Nations', *The Times*, 5 October 1918, p. 7; OBL, Willoughby Dickinson Papers, MS. Eng. hist. c.403, a letter from Bryce to W. H. Dickinson, 24 August 1917.

civilised 'would be for the States already members [of the league] to decide',[117] what 'civilised states' meant was not clearly defined by anyone. Still, one of the key criteria for judging it should be whether a state was democratic. As Philip Kerr pointed out, after the Russian Revolution and American entry into the war in 1917, the war became not simply for the liberation of Belgium. 'The war has taken on openly the character of a war democracy versus autocracy.'[118] Especially in 1917–1918, those who advocated a league believed that it should be created to promote democracy as well as peace.[119]

This is particularly striking when we look into politicians' reaction to the issue of a post-war organisation. As previous chapters discussed, the most important aim of the League of Nations Society was to influence the government so that the goal of the activists – to establish a league and transform post-war international relations – would be achieved. Especially from May 1917 onwards, when the Society held its first public meeting, British politicians began to approve the league in public.[120] The Society was also in touch with the Foreign Office to lobby for its support,[121] and the league finally became an important political goal.

From May 1917, the League of Nations Society urged the governments to take more practical steps to establish the League, not just to pay lip service to it. Specifically, they strove to persuade the British

---

[117] The League of Nations Society Publications, no. 17, 'Report of Conference of the Legal Profession', 23 July 1917.

[118] The National Records of Scotland, Private and Political Papers of Philip Kerr, 11th Marquess of Lothian, GD40/17/866, 'Memorandum (with Amendments) on Need for New Declaration of Policy Following the Russian Revolution and Entry of the U.S. into the War, Which Have Transformed the Diplomatic Situation as Registered in the Allied Reply of [10] Jan. 1917 to [Proposals to the Warring Powers, 18 Dec. 1916 by] President Wilson', April 1917. Also see Stevenson, *1914–1918*, p. 462.

[119] 'The League of Nations', *The Observer*, 23 December 1917, p. 6. Also see BLEPS, MOREL/F13/6, the Union of Democratic Control, 'The Morrow of the War', p. 19, Bertrand Russell, 'War the Offspring of Fear', the Union of Democratic Control Pamphlet, n.d., p. 67 and H. N. Brailsford, 'The Origins of the Great War', the Union of Democratic Control Pamphlet, 17 September 1914, p. 20.

[120] The League of Nations Society Publications, no. 12, 'Pronouncements of Leading Statesmen', June 1917; The League of Nations Society Publications, no. 21, 'A Durable Settlement After the War by Means of a League of Nations', November 1917; OBL, Willoughby Dickinson Papers, MS. Eng. hist. c.403, a letter to Bryce, 16 May 1917. Also see the Labour Party repeatedly supported the League in public, see 'A League of Free Nations: Mr. Arthur Henderson on Brotherhood', *The Times*, 17 September 1917, p. 5; 'The League of Nations: Why Labour Supports the Proposal', *The Manchester Guardian*, 3 January 1918, p. 6; PA, LG/F/23/2/7, a letter from M. P. A. Hankey to Prime Minister, 12 January 1918; 'League of Nations: Approval of Labour Mr. Henderson on the Future of Industry', *The Observer*, 23 June 1918, p. 8.

[121] OBL, James Bryce Papers, MS. Bryce 58, 37, a letter from Dickinson to Bryce, 23 March 1918.

government to set up an international or at least Anglo-American committee to study the league.[122] Although they submitted a letter to the government with several signatures of prominent figures, including the Archbishop of Canterbury, the government was not moved to act. Like South African General Jan C. Smuts, many politicians justified avoiding detailed discussion about the league due to the fact that Britain was still waging the war.[123] Even those who agreed with the creation of the league declined to become members of the Society or to sign the Society's letter because they thought it inopportune.[124] Robert Cecil, a Conservative politician and the most well-known defender of the League of Nations, expressed his agreement with the Society's plans from time to time, yet was not actively engaged with the war-time movement.[125] Reasoning that the discussion about the league entailed delicate as well as difficult problems during the war, he was reluctant to speak about a post-war organisation in public.[126] Neither did he want to be involved in the Society because he preferred avoiding any responsibilities that his official approval might cause.[127] Many politicians such as Cecil supported the league in principle but distanced themselves from the Society by stating that, just as the league opponents criticised, it was premature and inappropriate to speak of peace.[128]

Indeed, what made politicians including Cecil unwilling to publicly advocate a league could be found in their reactions against Lansdowne's letter to call for a negotiated peace in November 1917.[129] Many criticised his opinion as pacifistic nonsense that might promote a settlement with

---

[122] See Chapter 4.

[123] OBL, James Bryce Papers, MS. Bryce 138, 6, 27 October and 26 November 1917, a letter from Smuts to Bryce.

[124] OBL, Willoughby Dickinson Papers, MS. Eng. hist. c.403, letters from H. Cecil to W. H. Dickinson, 8 June 1917 and 25 July 1917, 193, a letter from Bryce to W. H. Dickinson, 24 July 1917, a letter from Seurne to W. H. Dickinson, 23 June 1917 and 97, a letter from W. Phillimore to W. H. Dickinson, 1 August 1917.

[125] Johnson, *Lord Robert Cecil*, pp. 76–79.

[126] 'The League of Nations: Lord Robert Cecil on the Difficulties', *The Manchester Guardian*, 18 February 1918, p. 6; OBL, James Bryce Papers, MS. Bryce 243, 144, a letter from Cecil to Bryce, 8 April 1918.

[127] 'The League of Nations: Lord Robert Cecil on the Difficulties', *The Manchester Guardian*, 18 February 1918, p. 6; OBL, Willoughby Dickinson Papers, MS. Eng. hist. c.403, a letter from R. Cecil to W. H. Dickinson, 13 April 1918.

[128] OBL, Willoughby Dickinson Papers, MS. Eng. hist. c.403, a letter from Bourne to W. H. Dickinson, 19 April 1918, 218, a letter from E. Drummond to Marburg, 21 May 1917 and a letter from Aiubero Pell to W. H. Dickinson, 25 June 1917; Ralph Williams, 'A League of Nations', *The Times*, 22 July 1918, p. 4; W. H. D. Rouse, 'A League of Nations: to the Editor of the Times', *The Times*, 9 August 1918, p. 8.

[129] Winkler, *The League of Nations Movement in Great Britain*, pp. 112–15.

Germany and its allies without a definite victory.[130] For instance, Philip Kerr advised the Prime Minister to refute Lansdowne's letter as 'unmistakeably a plea for compromise with Germany'.[131] Many politicians were afraid that discussing the post-war settlement, whatever character it might possess, made them appear not to intend to fight the war to outright victory over Germany. This was critical to them because the British government anticipated that victory was not yet within sight and the war would last at least into 1919.[132] As David Stevenson has argued, statesmen in 1917–1918 had 'a long-war illusion' in contrast to the 'short war illusion' of 1914, and therefore victory in 1918 came as a surprise.[133]

In connection with the long-war illusion, another reason for statesmen's unwillingness to advocate a league of nations lay in their principal objective, military victory. The British government insisted upon the Allies' achieving a complete victory over Germany as an essential precondition for a new post-war order. In his suggestion to the Prime Minister, Kerr continued:

I am a League of Nations man, but a League which has succeeded in defending right and defeating wrong in this war .... This is in truth a war against war. But that can only be attained through victory for our cause.[134]

Since military victory was perceived as crucially important,[135] even at Germany's request for an armistice in 1918, the British government wondered if they should continue the war until Germany was completely beaten.[136] Indeed, the government assumed that the league had to offer not only short-term but also a long-term solution to the blight of war.[137] To this end, the league needed to be an organisation of democratic

---

[130] LPL, Davidson 13, 192–201, dictated on Sunday 9 December 1917 and 315–23, 4 August 1918; PA, LG/89/1, 'Manchester District' (Special Note from Forthergill), 1 December 1917; NLW, Lord Davies of Llandinam Papers, B3/3, 149, 'War Aims and a League of Nations', n.d.; PA, LG/89/1/9, 'Re. the Lansdowne Letter', 4 December 1917; Mulligan, *The Great War for Peace*, p. 230.

[131] PA, LG/89/1/10–11, 'Lansdowne Speech', Kerr to Prime Minister, 5 December 1917.

[132] Rothwell, *British War Aims and Peace Diplomacy*, pp. 200–201, 249–51; French, *The Strategy of the Lloyd George Coalition*, chapter 7; Millman, 'A Counsel of Despair', *Journal of Contemporary History*, pp. 260.

[133] Stevenson, *1914–1918*, p. 466; Also see French, *The Strategy of the Lloyd George Coalition*, p. 12; Millman, 'A Counsel of Despair', pp. 269–70.

[134] PA, LG/89/1/11, 'Lansdowne Speech', Kerr to Prime Minister.

[135] French, *The Strategy of the Lloyd George Coalition*, p. 268.

[136] Manfred F. Boemeke, Gerald D. Feldman and Elisabeth Glaser (eds.), *The Treaty of Versailles: A Reassessment after 75 Years* (Cambridge University Press, 2006), p. 72; French, *The Strategy of the Lloyd George Coalition*, pp. 192, 202–4; Millman, 'A Counsel of Despair', p. 260.

[137] Johnson, *Lord Robert Cecil*, p. 87.

states, which Germany could not enter unless it was defeated and transformed into a democracy.[138]

The concept of a league of victorious, democratic states was also publicly employed by the Allied governments. From the early stage of the war, the new international order was upheld by each belligerent in order to mobilise the public and also win the support of neutral and uncommitted powers.[139] In 1917, war-weariness, the Russian Revolution and American pressure urged the Allies to revise their joint war aims and for the first time to associate themselves with the plan of forming a post-war organisation.[140] Indeed, it was Wilson's Fourteen Points speech of January 1918 that fully launched the liberal ideological manifesto of the war.[141] The US president called for a new international order centred on a league of nations that would guarantee a lasting peace with principles such as open diplomacy, arms limitations and self-determination.[142] Like the original British pro-leaguers at the beginning of the war, Wilson saw the international system as the primary cause of war in 1914–1917. Yet, he later turned to blame Germany as the peace-breaker and emphasised the abolition of German militarism. Thus, the post-war league he envisioned would monitor Germany's progress towards a democratic state.[143]

In Britain, the league question already received attention in the Imperial War Cabinet's study of war aims in 1917,[144] and the Lloyd George government endorsed a post-war organisation to guarantee peace.[145] In principle, the Prime Minister approved its creation on the basis that the defeat of Germany would serve as a warning to future

---

[138] PA, LG/89/1/10–11, 'Lansdowne Speech' Kerr to Prime Minister, 5 December 1917; The League of Nations Society Publications, no. 24, 'Recent Pronouncements on a League of Nations', Jan 1918; Winkler, *The League of Nations Movement in Great Britain*, pp. 248–49.

[139] Yearwood, 'On the Safe and Right Lines', p. 131.

[140] David Stevenson, *Cataclysm: The First World War As Political Tragedy* (Basic Books, 2004), p. 375; Egerton, *Great Britain and the Creation of the League of Nations*, p. 45.

[141] Egerton, *Great Britain and the Creation of the League of Nations*, p. 61.

[142] Ibid., p. 61–62.

[143] Ross Kennedy, *The Will to Believe: Woodrow Wilson, World War I, and America's Strategy for Peace and Security* (Kent State University Press, 2009), pp. xiii–xiv, 29–30, 65, chapter 1; Ross A. Kennedy, 'Woodrow Wilson, World War I, and an American Conception of National Security', *Diplomatic History*, vol. 25, no. 1 (2001), pp. 1–31; Stevenson, *1914–1918*, pp. 311–12; Alan Sharp, *The Versailles Settlement: Peacemaking in Paris 1919* (Basingstoke, 1991), p. 11; Boemeke et al. (eds.), *The Treaty of Versailles*, p. 610.

[144] Egerton, *Great Britain and the Creation of the League of Nations*, pp. 47, 57; Yearwood, 'On the Safe and Right Lines', p. 131.

[145] Yearwood, 'On the Safe and Right Lines', pp. 131–32.

potential aggressors.[146] The destruction of German militarism was a fundamental requirement of securing democracy and achieving stable peace.[147] On 5 January 1918, Lloyd George's Caxton Hall speech officially expressed the creation of a post-war organisation as a war aim of Britain.[148] Having draft statements of war aims prepared by Cecil, Smuts and Philip Kerr,[149] the Prime Minister stressed that Britain was fighting a crusade against autocracy for the establishment of a just and lasting peace.[150] The advocacy of a league of nations by Wilson and Lloyd George helped boost the Allies' morale by pointing to a liberal internationalist order that could justify waging the war until victory.[151] As the war was becoming more ideological in 1918, the Allied and Associated Powers declared the defence of democracy, as well as the abolition of militarism, to be the central war aims.[152]

While the French government was aligned with the British and Americans, its war aims were built more on the nation's self-image and their contrasts with the German character. France defined its unique role as the defender of civilisation, law, freedom and humanity,[153] which brought a conviction that security for France 'meant the preservation of civilisation'.[154] From the early years of the war, the French used binary categories to distinguish themselves from the Germans: 'civilisation versus barbarism, humanity versus inhumanity, the rule of law versus the rule of force'.[155] Their aim to break Prussian militarism included the destruction of German industrial and demographic power[156] – a necessary condition for post-war European security.[157] Founded on these projections, the French war aims were to defend civilisation, democracy and law against Germany.[158] Especially as an 'evangelist of the new rule

---

[146] Ibid., p. 132; Egerton, *Great Britain and the Creation of the League of* Nations, pp. 47, 57.

[147] David French, *The Strategy of the Lloyd George Coalition, 1916–1918* (Clarendon, 1995), pp. 35–36, 200–201; Yearwood, *Guarantee of Peace*, pp. 45–46, 48–49, 145.

[148] Stevenson, *Cataclysm*, p. 375; Egerton, *Great Britain and the Creation of the League of Nations*, pp. 60–61; George W. Egerton, 'The Lloyd George Government and the Creation of the League of Nations', *The American Historical Review*, vol. 79, no. 2 (April 1974), pp. 426–27.

[149] Mulligan, *The Great War for Peace*, p. 230; Egerton, *Great Britain and the Creation of the League of Nations*, pp. 57–59; Egerton, 'The Lloyd George Government and the Creation of the League of Nations', pp. 426–27.

[150] Horne, *State, Society and Mobilization*, pp. 203–4; Egerton, 'The Lloyd George Government and the Creation of the League of Nations', pp. 426–27.

[151] Egerton, *Great Britain and the Creation of the League of Nations*, p. 62.

[152] Stevenson, *1914–1918*, p. 462; Peter Jackson, *Beyond the Balance of Power: France and the Politics of National Security in the Era of the First World War* (Cambridge University Press 2013), p. 83.

[153] Jackson, *Beyond the Balance of Power*, pp. 79–81. [154] Ibid., pp. 79–81.

[155] Ibid., pp. 80–81. [156] Ibid., p. 83. [157] Ibid., pp. 82–83.

[158] Ibid., pp. 81, 83, 209–10, 517; Horne, *State, Society and Mobilization*, pp. 203–4.

of law', the French deemed the rule of law to be the basis of a new international organisation as well as of the war aims.[159] It was formally endorsed by the Ribot government when it established a study commission for 'a society of nations' under the leadership of French lawyer and internationalist Léon Bourgeois in 1918.[160]

Since 1916, Bourgeois had already outlined a proposal for a post-war organisation that rested on the juridical conception of international order and the need for the German transformation.[161] Preconditions for achieving a league of 'democratic peoples' were the Allies' victory and the overthrow of Prussian militarism.[162] Bourgeois argued that Germany could be eligible for membership in a league, after it was punished for its violation of law, made to pay for the damage it had inflicted, underwent a moral revolution and became democratised.[163] The objective was to bind Germany into an international organisation and to encourage its evolution towards peace and democracy as a responsible member in it.[164] Most senior policymakers in France, including President Raymond Poincaré and Prime Minister Georges Clemenceau, agreed that Germany was 'unfit for immediate membership', although a democratised Germany could eventually enter a league.[165]

While politicians did not agree about how Germany could be democratised, most of them, including Cecil and even the US President Woodrow Wilson, viewed defeating Germany as an absolute prerequisite.[166] Otherwise, any post-war leagues would be irreconcilable with official war aims and unable to justify the fight and the enormous sacrifices made to achieve victory.[167] Such thinking was well summarised by Smuts:

If you ask me what, in the first place, the people are fighting for, I should say the people are fighting the war for peace, to put an end to war, and to rid the world of the danger of militarism and Prussianism which is hanging over it to-day.[168]

Having emphasised that peace would only be realised by the defeat of Germany, Smuts continued:

---

[159] Jackson, *Beyond the Balance of Power*, pp. 79–82, 209–10; Horne, *State, Society and Mobilization*, pp. 203–4.
[160] Jackson, *Beyond the Balance of Power*, pp. 209–10, 517.
[161] Ibid., pp. 180–81, 187–88, 273–74.   [162] Ibid., pp. 180–81, 187–88.
[163] Ibid., p. 181.   [164] Ibid., pp. 181, 184, 263–64.   [165] Ibid., p. 273.
[166] Johnson, *Lord Robert Cecil*, p. 90; Kennedy, *The Will to Believe*, p. 139.
[167] Rothwell, *British War Aims and Peace Diplomacy*, p. 206.
[168] 'League of Nations: General Smuts on War Aims', *The Times*, 25 October 1917, p. 6.

We could not make peace while Germany sat with the fruits of her sin. She planned this deed of shame against Europe, she schemed in the dark and prepared. Germany must realize that this thing must not be.[169]

Also at the first meeting of the League of Nations Union in October 1918, Grey articulated the idea of a democratic league. Having mentioned that the US President Wilson had the same opinion, Grey stated that 'you can trust no Government which does not come to you with the credentials that it exists with the confidence of the people behind it, and is responsible to that people, and to no one else'.[170] He also demanded 'proof' that German authorities 'truly represent[ed] a regenerate and articulate nation' before being 'admitted to membership of any League', although he did not suggest what type of proof was required.[171] Hence, the wide support for the league in Britain did not necessarily come from their craving for peace but was conditioned upon the Allies' victory and the abolition of militarism. By recasting the war as an ideological struggle of democracy versus authoritarian militarism, and as a moral crusade of right versus wrong, justice versus injustice, those who supported the league required that Germany like any member state must be civilised and democratic. In other words, they hoped member states would become like Britain – civilised, democratic, peace-loving, adhering to Christian doctrines and credible as a part of the international community. Attaching these conditions to the creation of the league also had a non-negligible impact on the pro-league movement in Britain.[172]

The End of the War and of the Original Ideas about the League of Nations

The amalgamation in October 1918 of the two pro-league groups in Britain on the basis of promoting the exclusive league marked, in effect, the final break with the ideals that had been inspired by the Bryce Group. The Bryce Group members had originally identified the alliance system and international anarchy as the principal causes of the war and sought to replace them with an international organisation to promote peace. In 1914, moreover, the pro-league movement began as a counter to anti-German jingoism.[173] Nonetheless, as a result of the amalgamation of the

---

[169] Ibid.
[170] OBL, Willoughby Dickinson Papers, MS. Eng. hist. c.407, 88–95, 'Grey's Message "the League of Nations"', Speech by Grey, 10 October 1918.
[171] 'The League of Nations Meeting', *The Times*, 11 October 1918, p. 9.
[172] Zara Steiner, *The Lights That Failed: European International History, 1919–1933* (Clarendon Press, 2005), chapter 1.
[173] See Chapter 2.

two pro-league groups in 1918, the League of Nations Union adopted the militant vision of the league as a continuation of the war-time democratic alliance aligned against Germany. This shift in policy would have consequences in the way the peace was framed and the League of Nations formed.[174]

If we look at this in the wider context of the movement, we can see the essential process of its development. In 1915–1917, in the face of the challenge of galvanising widespread support, the League of Nations Society had to simplify the official league scheme for mass consumption. It avoided going into the details in public by stressing only the creation of the league and allowed different ideas about the organisation of the league to be expressed even inside the Society. As a result of this, while the Society succeeded in gaining support, it lost the detailed discussions about the league – such as how war could be prevented in practice and what sort of problems they might have in a new organisation.[175] Now, in 1917–1918, in order to obtain even wider support, it promoted the league as an extension of waging the war. Although historians have tended to pay attention to the *variety* of the league plans by various league advocates,[176] there was ultimately *only one* vision of the league that people both inside and outside the pro-league circles in 1918 upheld: the league of victorious free allies fighting against German militarism and authoritarianism to the bitter end.

Further, the League of Nations Union came to acquire a different character from the League of Nations Society because the end of the war and the establishment of the League shifted the focus of the pro-league campaign. To begin with, the amalgamation was substantially the takeover by the anti-German League of Free Nations Association, which was keen to invest in propaganda and education more vigorously than the Society had done. After the war, the League of Nations Union became more engaged in educating the public about the ideal of the League, democracy and citizenship.[177] As Helen McCarthy has argued, their work 'nourished a rich conversation about the rights and responsibilities of democratic citizenship', thereby taking root in the inter-war British society rather than affecting the organisation of the League of Nations.[178]

---

[174] Boemeke et al. (eds.), *The Treaty of Versailles*, pp. 79–80, 85–86; Steiner, *The Lights that Failed*, pp. 19–22.

[175] See Chapter 3.

[176] For example, see Winkler, *The League of Nations Movement in Great Britain*, pp. 255–56.

[177] Helen McCarthy, *The British People and the League of Nations: Democracy, Citizenship and Internationalism, c. 1918–45* (Manchester University Press, 2011), pp. 1–2, 6, 9, 20–21.

[178] McCarthy, *The British People and the League of Nations*, pp. 1–2, 6.

The League of Nations Covenant disappointed several war-time pro-league activists and Lowes Dickinson resigned from the executive committee of the group.[179] Meanwhile, the Union became more closely associated with names such as Robert Cecil rather than the original war-time leaders including Willoughby Dickinson or Bryce.[180]

Although many leading members of the League of Nations Society eventually adopted the exclusive league as the League of Free Nations Association devised it, the very first initiator of the pro-league movement, Goldsworthy Lowes Dickinson, warned against the movement deviating from its original aim to change the norms of international relations. In June 1918, having noted that the idea of the league was now attracting widespread support including officials, he expressed regret:

the idea of a league now between the allies was treated by everyday as destroying the very idea of a true league and as practically substituting for such an alliance against the central powers. I have no reason to think that anyone on our committee desires that, but I feel sure that a number of influential people are waiting for an opportunity to divert the league movement into that channel.[181]

Despite Dickinson's concern, the negotiations between the Society and the new Association drove the former to steer in the direction of the exclusive league of democratic states aligned against Germany. Before the amalgamation, Dickinson predicted that the new body would 'fall into Davies hands' due to his capability to provide 'the funds, and office, and organiser, and all the rest of it', and moaned about the incompatible views between the original league idea and Davies' stand.[182] Dickinson criticised Davies' anti-German claim for hindering German people from fostering the right thinking for future peace. It should be encouraged, not hindered, by 'regard[ing] the willingness of Germany to enter a league as a proof that she has abandoned militarism and a sign that the only victory we need to win has been won'.[183]

---

[179] For example, 'The Peace Treaty', *The Manchester Guardian*, 24 May 1919, p. 8; CKC, *the Papers of Goldsworthy Lowes Dickinson*, GLD 1/2/4, 'Autobiography of G. Lowes Dickinson' (London, 1973), p. 303–6 (246–9); Birn, *The League of Nations Union*, p.18.

[180] Birn, *The League of Nations Union*, pp. 2, 17–18, 23; 'The Peace Treaty', *The Manchester Guardian*, 24 May 1919, p. 8.

[181] OBL, Willoughby Dickinson Papers, MS. Eng. hist. c.403, 118, a letter from G. Lowes Dickinson to W. H. Dickinson, June 1918.

[182] OBL, Gilbert Murray Papers, Murray 178, 161, a letter from G. Lowes Dickinson to Murray, 6 September 1918; ibid., Murray 179, 63, a letter from G. Lowes Dickinson to Murray, 1918?

[183] OBL, Gilbert Murray Papers, Murray 178, 161, a letter from G. Lowes Dickinson to Murray, 6 September [1918]. See also, G. Lowes Dickinson, 'A League of Nations Now?', *War & Peace*, no. 60 (September, 1918), pp. 327–28.

This remark of Dickinson's clearly shows that he, as many pro-league leaders initially did, adhered to the original ideal articulated by the Bryce Group that the league should include all the great powers and replace the old system of competitive alliances and arms races. Having identified inter-national anarchy and its consequences as the primary cause of the war, Dickinson believed that unless the league included all the major powers it would produce a repeat of the rampant, unregulated great power competition of the pre-1914 years and trigger great wars again. Hence, Dickinson was never convinced of the direction that the amalgamated Union took. Yet the public and politicians preferred a league of free nations that excluded Germany, in other words, the goal of a moral victory against Germany, which depressed him even more. After the armistice in October 1918, he lamented:

A kind of despair comes over me as I realise how the events of the last five years have made it almost impossible for the governments or peoples at war with [G]ermany to believe in or understand that spirit [of creating the league]. The orgy or suspicion and contempt and hate, the mere determination to trample on the man that is down, which occupies our whole press, and even apparently the minds of our statesm[e]n, is terrible at a moment which will determine the whole future of mankind.[184]

To Dickinson's disappointment, not just the public and the government but also pro-league activists wanted victory over Germany and for the Germans to be punished.[185] While Dickinson only had to accept the settlement established by the Peace Conference,[186] he remained con-vinced that having Germany inside rather than outside the new organisa-tion would work better both for educating the Germans about democracy and for the true path to peace.

At the establishment of the League of Nations, its Covenant stipulated any self-governing state might become a member, 'provided that it shall give effective guarantees of its sincere intention to observe its inter-national obligations, and shall accept such regulations as may be pre-scribed by the League in regard to its military, naval and air forces and armaments'.[187] In practice, the League excluded Germany from

---

[184] BL, Add MS 50909, 135, a letter from G. Lowes Dickinson to Scott, 24 October 1918.
[185] As Bryce stated, even pro-leaguers, 'peace lovers' not 'Jingoes', were determined 'to fight on' until defeating Germany, in OBL, James Bryce Papers, MS. Bryce U.S.A. 23, 38, letters from Bryce to House, 26 November 1915 and 67–68, 27 December 1916; also see Stevenson, *1914–1918*, pp. 36–37, 41, 271.
[186] Stuart Wallace, *War and the Image of Germany: British Academics 1914–1918* (Donald, 1988), pp. 121–24.
[187] 'The Covenant of the League of Nations', The Avalon Project: Documents in Law, History and Diplomacy, Yale Law School, Lilian Goldman Law Library, http://avalon .law.yale.edu/20th_century/leagcov.asp.

membership as league supporters in 1917–18 envisaged and buttressed the structure to enforce incoming members to have desirable qualities. During the Paris Peace Conference, pro-league leaders were in contact with Robert Cecil, who participated in the Peace Conference and also held an Inter-Allied Societies Conference with pro-league groups of several Allied states in January 1919.[188] This Conference, under Bourgeois' presidency, agreed on proposals that added armaments limitation and renunciation of secret treaties to the programme of the League of Nations Union. Headed by Bourgeois, the Conference deputation presented its proposals to the Big Four at the Paris Peace Conference.[189] Yet British pro-league leaders hoped in vain to influence the foundation of the League of Nations.[190] On 24 May 1919, several leading members of the League of Nations Union, including Gilbert Murray, Leonard Woolf and H. G. Wells, published an open letter to request the Allied governments to reconsider the Treaty.[191] While emphasising that defeating Germany and its militarism were absolutely necessary, the letter indicated the peace terms belied the spirit of Wilson's Fourteen Points and put Germany in the position of 'a helot nation'.[192] It even proclaimed that the Draft Treaty of May, probably 'inspired by vindictiveness and fear', would 'have no endurance' but 'only initiate a renewed epoch of mutual aggression and suspicion', which would provoke future wars. Pro-league leaders could, however, only wish to be of use in Paris since 'great men do not welcome assistance from outside the immediate governmental circle'.[193] Although some pro-leaguers complained about it, there was little they could do. The idea of the league of nations was no longer in the control of a few elite liberal internationalists, the small circle of thinkers who had formed the Bryce Group back in 1914. At the Paris Peace Conference, the fate of the

---

[188] Birn, *The League of Nations Union*, pp. 11–15. Also in Brussels from 1 to 3 December 1919, a Conference of Associated Societies had over 100 delegates from 16 countries.

[189] Ibid., pp. 11–13.

[190] OBL, Gilbert Murray Papers, Murray 179, 63, a letter from G. Lowes Dickinson to Murray, 1918?; OBL, Willoughby Dickinson Papers, MS. Eng. hist. c.403, 130, a letter from R. Cecil to W. H. Dickinson, 2 January 1919 and 131, R. Cecil to W. H. Dickinson, 4 January 1919; OBL, James Bryce Papers, MS. Bryce U.S.A. 23, 136–37, a letter from Bryce to Lowell, 15 January 1919, and 143–44, 27 March 1919; BL Add MS 60664, 151–52, 'To the Big Four', n.d.

[191] 'The Peace Treaty: to the Editor of the Manchester Guardian', *The Manchester Guardian*, 24 May 1919, p. 8; Birn, *The League of Nations Union*, p. 17.

[192] Ibid. See also 'The I.L.P and the League of Nations', Independent Labour Party, National Administrative Council, 10 March 1919, IPM/IPB/306, 14207, General Correspondence, 1911–1950.

[193] OBL, Willoughby Dickinson Papers, MS. Eng. hist. c.403, 212, a letter from W. H. Dickinson to Bryce, 4 February 1919.

league idea was in the hands of leading statesmen and officials,[194] and ultimately their league plans triumphed.

The transformation of the pro-league movement into a popular one, for the prosecution of the war to a just victory over German militarism and authoritarianism, diverted it from fundamental thinking about the causes of war and the conditions of peace. On the other hand, the intellectual backbone of the movement – liberal internationalism, especially their belief in social and political progress – remained the underlying ideal.[195] Many pro-leaguers were optimistic: once the league was established, it would evolve over time into something closer to their original vision, however imperfect at the time of its formation. Throughout their war-time campaign, setting up the league after the war was the activists' most important goal; the details of its organisation, constitution and mechanisms came to be secondary considerations. Bryce, an unofficial but de facto guardian of the war-time pro-league movement, never softened his cautious stance and even after the armistice thought that the movement 'must not attempt too much at first' because he supposed that 'the more you ask the less you may get'.[196] 'Advance must be gradual .... We must not let slip the present opportunity of achieving something, and if that something is on right lines... we can build upon it afterwards.'[197] To pro-leaguers in 1918, the league was still to some extent 'a germ which might develop by degrees into an international polity', as Lowes Dickinson portrayed in 1915.[198] That was why, when the Versailles Peace Treaty was signed in June 1919, Willoughby Dickinson noted that in a sense it was a new beginning for those who worked for the league: 'Peace has been agreed to-day but peace has not been made .... Now is the time for our work, the remaking of goodwill.'[199] Despite such an expectation, the League of Nations did not evolve as they wished.

[194] For example, see Margaret MacMillan, *Peacemakers: The Paris Conference of 1919 and Its Attempt to End War* (J. Murray, 2001); Steiner, *The Lights That Failed*, chapter 1.

[195] Casper Sylvest, *British Liberal Internationalism, 1880–1930: Making Progress?* (Manchester University Press, 2009), pp. 3–4, 11, 26, 139, 197.

[196] HUHL, League to Enforce Peace Records (Int 6722.8.25*), Box 1, a letter from Bryce to Marburg, 20 December 1918.

[197] Ibid.

[198] British Library of Economic and Political Science, CANNAN 970, *Proposals for the Avoidance of War, with a Prefatory Note by Viscount Bryce, As Revised up to 24 February 1915*.

[199] Hope Costley White, *Willoughby Hyett Dickinson, 1859–1943: A Memoir, etc.* (Gloucester: Privately Printed, 1956), pp. 152, 148.

Conclusion

In 1920, the League of Nations was established as the first international organisation for the purpose of preventing war as the original pro-leaguers such as the Bryce Group members of 1915 had dreamed, thereby realising their ultimate goal. The war-time pro–league of nations movement succeeded in bringing public attention to the idea of a post-war organisation for peace and making it one of the critical political issues. Yet in reality, pro-leaguers came to promote the league idea that the original Bryce Group membership in 1914–1915 had opposed: a league of victorious powers aligned against Germany and its allies. In 1914–1915, they aspired to change the norms of international relations and quell international anarchy through the creation of a new international organisation based on collective security, the rule of law and justice for all nations. The pro-league movement began, in the form of the Bryce Group, as a reaction against anti-German jingoism as well as balance-of-power politics. International anarchy, not German aggression, was *the* cause of the war.[200]

In 1918, however, the League of Nations Union, the pro-league body that united the League of Nations Society and the League of Free Nations Association, promoted the league as a continuation of the war-time alliance against Germany because the 'self-mobilisation' of civil society successfully reinforced the argument to fight until defeating Germany.[201] Most advocates of the league, including the public, politicians, the churches and even pro-league leaders, supposed that the league should be formed as a coalition of democratic states to prosecute the war to a democratic victory. Considering Germany the militaristic and authoritarian state that was responsible for the war, they thought that the current Germany could not be a league member until the Germans learned to adhere to the civilised values of the democratic nations. This vision of a post-war organisation led the League of Nations Society to adopt an international organisation that excluded Germany. While such a league idea helped increase the popularity of the movement, it simultaneously marked a break with the original vision of the pro-league movement that had started with the Bryce Group in 1914. This was an inevitable consequence of the pro-league movement, which sought to establish a new organisation, reform the international system and make the 'emergence of the new order' possible.[202]

---

[200] G. Lowes Dickinson, *The European Anarchy* (George Allen & Unwin, 1916); G. Lowes Dickinson, *The International Anarchy, 1904–1914* (George Allen & Unwin, 1926).
[201] Horne, *State, Society and Mobilization*, pp. 209–11.
[202] Schroeder, *Systems, Stability, and Statecraft*, pp. 249, 258.

Across the Atlantic, the League to Enforce Peace had a similar course of development.[203] As with the British group, the American counterpart also attempted to increase its influence even though it had to abandon its original ideas about the league of all the states. In order to go along with government policy, after American entry of the war in April 1917, the League to Enforce Peace gradually adopted the idea of the league as a continuation of the war-time alliance. As Charles Eliot, a former president of Harvard University, criticised, the League to Enforce Peace publicly abandoned their original propositions, such as the one 'that the League should include all the nations of the world'.[204] Highlighting military victory over Germany, the American group changed its post-war plan from the league of all the states to the league of victorious allies.[205] In the end, the pro-league groups in Britain and the United States promoted the league as an extension of fighting the war. The league became a just war aim in a fight for freedom against militarism and tyranny, which became a means of mobilising, sustaining and legitimising the goal of final victory. The support of creating the league, therefore, was in tandem with the support of waging the war. The promotion of the league in this way prepared the way to legitimise the harsh terms imposed on Germany at the Paris Peace Conference as something desired by the public as well as peacemakers.[206]

---

[203] See Chapter 4. See also John Bew, *Realpolitik: A History* (Oxford University Press, 2016), p. 130.

[204] HUHL, League to Enforce Peace Records (Int 6722.8.25*), Box 1, a letter from Charles Eliot to Taft, 23 April 1918.

[205] Roland Marchand, *The American Peace Movement and Social Reform, 1898–1918* (Princeton University Press, 1972), pp. 158–60; HUHL, Abbott Lawrence Lowell Peace Papers (*2005-481), Box 10, 833, 'Platform Adopted by the League to Enforce Peace at the "Win the War for Permanent Peace" Convention', Philadelphia, 17 May 1918.

[206] Alan Sharp, *Consequences of Peace: The Versailles Settlement: Aftermath and Legacy 1919–2010* (Haus, 2010), chapter 2.

Conclusion

In 1942, twenty-four years after the end of the First World War, the world was fighting another great war. Willoughby Dickinson, the ex-chairman of the League of Nations Society, reflected on the pro–league of nations movement during the Great War in a letter to a war-time pro-leaguer F. N. Keen:

> I do think that it is a pity that the rising generation should have to tackle the problem in ignorance of what has happened in the past and I have been wondering whether something might not be done to give a picture of what happened in the years 1915 to 1919? ... Your letter has made me wonder whether you might not perhaps be induced to put together quite a short account of what we did do and why what we did came to nothing.[1]

After the Great War, the pro-league movement realised its goal of creating a new international organisation for peace. Yet, the outbreak of the Second World War, another global conflict that the pro-league activists had worked hard to prevent, led their contemporaries, including many League supporters and subsequent generations of internationalists, to a damning conclusion: the pro-league movement of 1914–1918 and the League of Nations had failed.

This book has traced the original ideas and the little-appreciated development of the pro–league of nations movement in Britain from 1914 to 1919, particularly focusing on the Bryce Group and the League of Nations Society. The war-time pro-league movement, as well as the influence of the US President Woodrow Wilson and public reaction to the horrors of war, culminated in the establishment of the League of Nations. Having succeeded in pushing the issue of the league onto the political agenda and garnering support for its formation, the pro-league activists fulfilled the ultimate goal of their war-time campaign – the foundation of a post-war organisation. Nonetheless, the process

---

[1] BLEP, Papers of Frank Noel Keen, folder 11, a letter from W. H. Dickinson to F. N. Keen, 5 March 1942.

of developing the movement was not straightforward nor entirely successful.

As this book illustrated, building upon the intellectual tradition of war and peace in European thought, the idea of a league of nations emerged from the Bryce Group at the outbreak of the war in 1914 and produced the pro–league of nations movement. It was not a pacifist or anti-war campaign but a popular movement organised to establish a new institution to counteract the condition of international anarchy through international cooperation and the rule of law. Identifying balance-of-power politics induced by anarchy in the international system as the primary cause of war, the Bryce Group aimed to change the norms of international relations, from the rivalry of alliance blocs to great power cooperation and management exercised through a new permanent international organisation. In the drafting process of their *Proposals for the Avoidance of War*, the members of the Bryce Group debated the possible mechanisms for the prevention of war from what would now be described by international relations scholars as both 'realistic' and 'idealistic' points of view. In fact, their thinking was a rich mixture of various perspectives and intellectual traditions that defied such clear-cut categories as realistic and idealistic. Although the concept of collective security, including military sanctions, was one of the central pillars of its *Proposals*, the Bryce Group also recognised that the future application of military sanctions to prevent war might escalate into general war, as the war in the Balkans had in the summer of 1914. Because of the perils of escalation, the group suggested that military sanctions should only be implemented after exhausting all other war prevention measures such as the judicial settlement of disputes. In the *Proposals*, the Bryce Group merged both realistic and idealistic means of preventing war, attempting to maintain a fine balance between them. While the group acknowledged the weaknesses of both pacific and potentially violent approaches to war prevention, its members found no magic formula to avoid the pitfalls and problems of both approaches. They simply concluded that a fine balance between such measures had to be maintained in practice and left the balance unstable and ambiguous in their plan. It should come as no surprise to us today that precisely the same dilemmas of maintaining international peace plague world politics to this very day.

Inspired by the Bryce Group's *Proposals*, with all its fine balances and complexity, the League of Nations Society campaigned for the foundation of a post-war organisation. In 1915–1916, the Society worked undercover to avoid being denounced as a pacifist organisation and having its ideas and ideals discredited in that way. In May 1917, however, the Society held its first public meeting and the idea of a league obtained widespread public support. Thus, the League of Nations Society made great strides in making its case popular and legitimate, yet that year also marked the time when the originators of the pro-league movement began to lose control of the debate about what the league would look like. In the process of gaining popular support for the creation of an international organisation, much of the nuance, sophistication and complexity of the Bryce Group's 1914 *Proposals* was lost. The constitution and the make-up of the League of Nations were eventually determined by politicians. The pro-league movement exerted little direct influence on them. Abandoning any detailed public discussion about the complexity and ambiguities about the post-war order, however, also served as a source of strength for the movement. It allowed many actors outside the pro-league circle to adopt the idea and to project their own images and aspirations for the future upon it in the political and public spheres, thereby helping to pave the way for the emergence of a new order centred on a league of nations after the war.

Towards the same goal, the League of Nations Society worked with another body inspired by the Bryce Group: the League to Enforce Peace in the United States. Because both groups operated in very different political contexts and emerged from different liberal internationalist traditions, they failed to collaborate in a close and constructive way. Ultimately, both pro-league groups saw the other more as a means of gaining top-level political influence in each other's country to realise their own vision of the League, than as a genuine transnational collaborator. In 1918, the final year of the war, the League of Nations Society split and re-amalgamated with another pro-league group, the League of Free Nations Associations, into the League of Nations Union. When the Union was formed, the pro-league leaders came to adopt what the original Bryce Group membership had opposed in 1914: the league was no longer presented as a replacement for the alliance system and the balance of power but as a continuation of the war-time alliance against Germany and its allies into the post-war peace. Behind this important shift, there was a widely shared belief that the league should be formed as a coalition of democratic states to prosecute the war for a democratic victory. Previous accounts have often assumed that the ideas about a league garnered wide support because the pro-leaguers appealed to the public's longing for peace.[2] In contrast, by examining both manuscripts and

---

[2] George W. Egerton, *Great Britain and the Creation of the League of Nations: Strategy, Politics, and International Organization, 1914–1919* (Scolar Press, 1978), p. 49; Henry R. Winkler, *The League of Nations Movement in Great Britain, 1914–1919* (Rutgers University Press, 1952), pp. 82–83, 255–56; David Monger, *Patriotism and Propaganda*

printed sources, this book has revealed that the pro-leaguers won support because they co-opted public concerns such as the yearning for victory and the expanding ideological nature of the conflict with Germany, which was increasingly framed as a war of free and peace-loving peoples over the excesses of Germanic authoritarianism and militarism. While the ideas about a league had to be transformed into something very different from what had been originally conceived, its ideas became a rallying cry for a moral and ideological crusade, which had serious implications for how the league would be received after the war in the defeated countries.[3]

Originally identifying the international system based on the balance of power and the rivalry of alliance blocs as the prime cause of war, the movement sought to reform international relations by introducing a new post-war organisation for peace. Yet, by the end of the war, its principal claim became not international reform but a perpetuation of the war-time alliance against Germany into peacetime. Many league advocates opposed Germany's entry into the league for the foreseeable future and promoted the idea of an exclusive league of what they saw as peaceful democracies without specifying admission procedures into it. This development of the pro-league movement also faced the underlying dilemma that bedevilled Woodrow Wilson's war-time diplomacy, which was, as Ross Kennedy has put it, 'the paradox at the heart of Wilson's national security strategy – that of practicing power politics to end power politics'.[4] The pro-league movement worked to reform international relations and eradicate rival alliance blocs, characterised by nationalistic hatred; eventually, however, the ideas and ideals of the league were subsumed into the allies' war effort as a means of mobilising popular support for victory in the final phase of the war. As the Bryce Group had anticipated in 1914, this war-time shift in the conception of the organisation had negative consequences for it after the armistice – for instance, the perception that the League was an alliance of the victors. Unavoidably, the League of Nations embodied the paradox of seeking world peace through

in *First World War Britain: The National War Aims Committee and Civilian Morale* (Liverpool University Press, 2012); Martin Ceadel, *Semi-Detached Idealists: The British Peace Movement and International Relations, 1854–1945* (Oxford University Press, 2000), p. 187; Adrian Gregory, *The Last Great War: British Society and the First World War* (Cambridge University Press, 2008); Peter Yearwood, *Guarantee of Peace: The League of Nations in British Policy, 1914–1925* (Oxford University Press, 2009), pp. 1–2; William Mulligan, *The Great War for Peace* (Yale University Press, 2014), chapter 6.

[3] Mark Mazower, *Governing the World: The History of An Idea* (Penguin Books, 2012), pp. 182–86.

[4] Ross A. Kennedy, *The Will to Believe: Woodrow Wilson, World War I, and America's Strategy for Peace and Security* (Kent State University Press, 2009), pp. xiii–xiv.

military victory, because peace and war were 'mutually dependent', not opposed.[5] As William Mulligan has suggested, war was not only 'an instrument to achieve peace' but also 'interwoven' with peace in 1914–1919.[6]

Despite all these complicated political issues and conceptual dilemmas, there was perhaps no way forward other than the one the pro-leaguers took. G. Lowes Dickinson, the very initiator of the pro-league movement, articulated the problem that it had to confront:

> I see the trouble with our organisation is going to be that while we may advocate a league in the abstract, we shall be held up whenever we want to advocate anything consequential and essential. There's no one like an englishman [sic] for wanting everything good in the abstract and everything bad in the concrete.[7]

This development was inevitable: high ideals and the hope of reconciliation evolved, or were deformed, beyond recognition into instruments of national policy.

As this book has illustrated, it was the pro–league of nations activists, not politicians, that first raised the issue of the post-war order and put the league on the political agenda. The pro-leaguers obtained broad support for a post-war organisation, provided the intellectual foundations of the League and played a significant role in its creation. Yet simultaneously, it is true that the power to shape what the actual League would be was in the hands of politicians. Hence, before re-evaluating the pro-leaguers' ideas and movement, this book reviews how the post-war order was discussed by decision-makers at the war's end.[8] In Britain, from the armistice to the Paris Peace Conference, the government held discussions with the aim of moulding their policy regarding the League. Robert Cecil, who was appointed as the head of a league of nations section in the

---

[5] Mazower, *Governing the World*, pp. 154–55; Mulligan, *The Great War for Peace*, pp. 8–9.

[6] Mulligan, *The Great War for Peace*, pp. 375–57.

[7] OBL, Gilbert Murray Papers, Murray 179, a letter from G. Lowes Dickinson to Murray, 1918?

[8] This section reviews how decision-makers discussed the new order at the Paris Peace Conference only briefly due to the accumulation of intense research on this topic for almost a century. For example, see Manfred F. Boemeke, Gerald D. Feldman and Elisabeth Glaser (eds.), *The Treaty of Versailles: A Reassessment after 75 Years* (German Historical Institute; Cambridge University Press, 2006); Alan Sharp, *Consequences of Peace: The Versailles Settlement: Aftermath and Legacy 1919–2010* (Haus, 2010); Alan Sharp, *The Versailles Settlement: Peacemaking after the First World War, 1919–1923* (Palgrave Macmillan, 2018); Margaret MacMillan, *Peacemakers: The Paris Conference of 1919 and Its Attempt to End War* (J. Murray, 2001); 'World Politics 100 Years after the Paris Peace Conference', *International Affairs*, vol. 95, no. 1 (January 2019); Leonard V. Smith, *Sovereignty at the Paris Peace Conference of 1919* (Oxford University Press, 2018).

Foreign Office, and Jan Smuts, who represented South Africa in Paris, respectively published their post-war plans in December 1918,[9] in addition to reports from the Phillimore Committee, an official study group of the Foreign Office.[10] These plans provided the basis for debate at the Imperial War Cabinet.[11] The cabinet had two options for negotiation at the Peace Conference: one was a partnership with France to support Clemenceau's proposals of strengthening France by shaping a favourable balance of power against Germany, the other was cooperation with the United States to accept Wilson's ideas about international order. The cabinet decisively favoured the latter position,[12] but the choice was never a simple binary one. Even though the British population warmly responded to Wilson's vision of a new world order with a shared tradition of liberal internationalism,[13] British politicians were conscious that the United States was 'a long way off' while France sat 'at our door'.[14] The British Prime Minister supported the creation of the League since, in addition to the need to reform the old order, it would help gain American underwriting for European stability and reinforce Britain's global position.[15] At the Peace Conference, Lloyd George also sought to satisfy French security demands, because London would not want to become the guarantor of the European order nor the protector of France in the event of an attack on France by Germany. For British officials, prioritising cooperation with the United States was also a logical consequence of this policy.[16]

During the Paris Peace Conference, the British did not completely agree among themselves on their approach to the new organisation. At the breakfast meeting on 20 January 1919, Cecil realised Lloyd George

---

[9] Cecil submitted the 'Cecil plan', which envisaged the league with five great powers in charge of a new system, excluding Germany until 'it complied with the victors' terms. Smuts also published his post-war plan, 'The League of Nations: A Practical Suggestion'. See Zara Steiner, *The Lights That Failed: European International History, 1919–1933* (Oxford University Press, 2005), pp. 32–33; Patrick Cohrs, *The Unfinished Peace after World War I: America, Britain and the Stabilisation of Europe, 1919–1932* (Cambridge University Press, 2006), p. 42.

[10] On 20 March 1918, the Phillimore Committee proposed in its report that a post-war league would be an alliance of victors pledged not to go to war without submitting a case to arbitration or to a conference of member states. Member states would impose sanctions against non-complying countries. See Steiner, *The Lights That Failed*, pp. 32–33.

[11] The Imperial War Cabinet rejected guarantees of peace, namely, collective security and the automatic sanctions in the plans of the Phillimore Committee, Cecil and Smuts. See Steiner, *The Lights That Failed*, pp. 32–33.

[12] Steiner, *The Lights That Failed*, pp. 32–33.   [13] Ibid., pp. 33–34.   [14] Ibid.

[15] Ibid.; Cohrs, *The Unfinished Peace*, pp. 41–42.   [16] Cohrs, *The Unfinished Peace*, p. 57.

had 'no real interest'[17] in the League. The British premier was advised by several figures such as Philip Kerr to adopt a different approach from that of Cecil, whose plan they considered as going too far.[18] Lloyd George himself also preferred a more functional League based on the experience and practice of the Supreme War Council.[19] In a meeting with Cecil and Smuts on 31 January, the Prime Minister read out a memorandum prepared by Kerr and attacked their post-war plans.[20] He particularly criticised the idea of collective security, because he presumed the effective means of ensuring peace would be an expansion of the peace conference into a league where nations could 'remain in continual consultation'.[21] This memorandum underlined the differences of opinion that Cecil could hardly digest before meeting Wilson on the same day.[22] Cecil decided to ignore Lloyd George's intervention by claiming that the Prime Minister's views were likely to result in a breakdown of the negotiations and that he lacked any knowledge of prior discussions.[23] The British position on the post-war league was far from united.

In January 1919, before the opening of the Peace Conference, the British and American delegations privately held meetings in Paris to coordinate an Anglo-American plan about the post-war organisation.[24] For this purpose, Cecil and David Hunter Miller, an American legal expert, began discussions on 21 January[25] and reached an agreement on a revision of the US president's draft proposal for the League Covenant

---

[17] Egerton, *Great Britain and the Creation of the League of Nations*, pp. 111, 120; Yearwood, *Guarantee of Peace*, pp. 108–10; Gaynor Johnson, *Lord Robert Cecil: Politician and Internationalist* (Ashgate Publishing, 2013), p. 102.

[18] While Cecil indicated that his draft of the League was based on plans of Phillimore and Smuts, Kerr and Hanky considered Cecil's plan was not on sound lines. See, Johnson, *Lord Robert Cecil*, p. 102; Yearwood, *Guarantee of Peace*, pp. 108–11.

[19] Sharp, *The Versailles Settlement*, pp. 54–55.

[20] Johnson, *Lord Robert Cecil*, p. 102; Yearwood, *Guarantee of Peace*, p. 110; Egerton, *Great Britain and the Creation of the League of Nations*, pp. 121–24.

[21] Johnson, *Lord Robert Cecil*, p. 102; Yearwood, *Guarantee of Peace*, p. 110; Sharp, *The Versailles Settlement*, pp. 54–55.

[22] Johnson, *Lord Robert Cecil*, p. 103; Sharp, *The Versailles Settlement*, pp. 54–55.

[23] Egerton, *Great Britain and the Creation of the League of Nations*, pp. 125–26; Yearwood, *Guarantee of Peace*, pp. 110–11; Johnson, *Lord Robert Cecil*, p. 103; Sharp, *The Versailles Settlement*, pp. 54–55.

[24] Egerton, *Great Britain and the Creation of the League of Nations*, p. 114; Steiner, *The Lights That Failed*, pp. 40–41.

[25] Cecil had little idea about Wilson's post-war plan until he discussed it with House and Lansing of the American delegation. The American plan involved a universal system of compulsory arbitration, which Cecil realised would be disputed by British circles due to their objection to applying it to the British Empire. See Johnson, *Lord Robert Cecil*, chapter 5; Egerton, *Great Britain and the Creation of the League of Nations*, pp. 114, 118.

on 27 January.[26] This Cecil-Miller draft was further modified at a meeting with Wilson on 31 January. On 1–2 February, Miller and Cecil Hurst, a British legal advisor, prepared a working draft for the conference that reflected the results of the negotiations in January.[27] This plan, called the Hurst-Miller draft, was used as the basis of negotiations at the Paris Conference. US and British officials asserted that, in order to complete the task of designing the first international organisation in a short period, there should only be minimum debate about basic principles.[28] Although Wilson and Cecil disagreed on some issues, as Steiner has argued, the Covenant of the League of Nations was 'very much the product' of the Anglo-American partnership.[29]

One of the most well-known episodes at the Paris Conference relating to the prevention of a future war was the French demand for an international army.[30] Léon Bourgeois, a French delegate on the League of Nations Commission, argued that a worthwhile league must provide 'iron-fast guarantees for national security'.[31] He quoted Wilson's phrase: 'a force must be created, a force so superior to that of all nations or to that of all alliances, that no nation or combination of nations can challenge or resist it'.[32] Bourgeois' proposal arose from the French premier's scepticism about the utility of a League that 'had no ultimate weapon of enforcement but would be dependent on the goodwill of its members'.[33] Given that Germany had invaded France twice in living memory,[34] it is no surprise that Clemenceau remained 'faithful' to the old system of alliances and the balance of power.[35] While distrusting Wilson, 'utopian theorists' and the Anglo-American vision of the league, Clemenceau wanted American and British assurance of his country's security. The French attempted to achieve 'the firmest possible alliance guarantees

---

[26] For example, a proposed Council of small and middle powers was abandoned in favour of the British idea that the Great Powers should run the League. See, Egerton, *Great Britain and the Creation of the League of Nations*, p. 118.

[27] Ibid., pp. 125–28; Steiner, *The Lights That Failed*, p. 41.

[28] Egerton, *Great Britain and the Creation of the League of Nations*, p. 129.

[29] Steiner, *The Lights That Failed*, p. 41.

[30] Ibid., pp. 42–43; Egerton, *Great Britain and the Creation of the League of Nations*, pp. 134–35.

[31] Egerton, *Great Britain and the Creation of the League of Nations*, pp. 135–36.   [32] Ibid.

[33] Steiner, *The Lights That Failed*, p. 43; Mulligan, *The Great War for Peace*, p. 273.

[34] Cohrs, *The Unfinished Peace*, p. 49. Peter Jackson, *Beyond the Balance of Power: France and the Politics of National Security in the Era of the First World War* (Cambridge University Press, 2013), p. 5.

[35] Cohrs, *The Unfinished Peace*, pp. 28, 49; Alan Sharp, 'The New Diplomacy and the New Europe, 1916–1922', in Nicholas Doumanis (ed.), *The Oxford Handbook of European History, 1914–1945* (Oxford University Press, 2016), p. 125.

against future German attacks' that could be 'supplemented, but not replaced' by the League's collective security.[36]

The French delegation aimed 'to ensure that France would never again be threatened' by Germany, supposing its domestic public opinion also demanded it.[37] According to the French proposal, no nation would be admitted into the League unless it had a democratic government and a sincere intention to abide by international rules; this was to ensure that only a thoroughly reformed and disarmed Germany would join the League.[38] Wilson and Lloyd George agreed that Germany would only be admitted to the League after 'a period of probation'.[39] Eventually, the Treaty of Versailles decided that Germany could join the organisation if it 'showed good faith in fulfilling the peace terms', which left the French leverage over Berlin's entry.[40]

In fact, as Peter Jackson has demonstrated, French post-war policy was more sophisticated and open-ended than has been widely recognised.[41] The traditional approach – advocated by Clemenceau, the foreign ministry and army high command in France[42] – presumed that the pursuit of power and an adversarial relationship with Germany were permanent features of international politics.[43] That traditional approach rested on the balance of power and alliance politics, with the aim of weakening and isolating Germany.[44] By the end of the war, however, the alliances and the balance of power had been discredited as features of the 'old diplomacy' of pre-1914 Europe,[45] and military force had become increasingly seen by many as an illegitimate tool of foreign policy in European politics.[46] These normative changes and the unprecedented scale of the war allowed an alternative, namely, internationalists', idea to influence French policy.[47] Hence, not only the traditional ideas of achieving a favourable balance of power, but also the internationalists' plans for a new order based on collective security and the rule of law, came to shape the French peace programme.[48]

---

[36] Cohrs, *The Unfinished Peace*, pp. 49, 57; Steiner, *The Lights That Failed*, pp. 22, 43; Jackson, *Beyond the Balance of Power*, p. 262.

[37] Cohrs, *The Unfinished Peace*, pp. 48–49.

[38] Egerton, *Great Britain and the Creation of the League of Nations*, pp. 134–35; Cohrs, *The Unfinished Peace*, p. 57.

[39] Cohrs, *The Unfinished Peace*, pp. 36, 43–44.   [40] Ibid., p. 57.

[41] Jackson, *Beyond the Balance of Power*, pp. 5, 198.   [42] Ibid., pp. 5–6.   [43] Ibid.

[44] Ibid.

[45] Cohrs, *The Unfinished Peace*, pp. 28, 49; Sharp, 'The New Diplomacy and the New Europe', p. 125.

[46] Jackson, *Beyond the Balance of Power*, p. 518. Yet the idea of 'imperial policing' remained legitimate in the colonial sphere.

[47] Ibid., p. 6.   [48] Ibid., pp. 5, 14, 195–96.

Indeed, the French proposal for the international force in Paris relied on the internationalists' ideas rather than the traditional notion of a preponderance of military power.[49] French internationalists called for a new system based on the rule of law, with emphasis on compulsory international arbitration and collective force.[50] Sanctions supported by an international armed force were essential, which established common ground between their view and that of the traditionalists.[51] Bourgeois, as a leading internationalist, proposed a juridical conception of the new order that would impose mutual obligations on all the member states to maintain peace.[52] In this post-war plan, security risks were mutualised and the enforcement had to rest on a union of the member states' forces.[53] By accepting duties and obligations, member states had also to accept infringements of their sovereignty.[54] French internationalists assumed that political leaders would be willing to sacrifice a measure of state sovereignty in return for greater international security.[55]

Even though Bourgeois insisted that the French programme was designed by 'realism', informed by the experience of the war,[56] the plan for a powerful defensive institution and the surrender of sovereignty were rejected by the British and American delegates.[57] Cecil, facing the French demand for an international army, privately warned the French delegation that the Anglo-American plan for the league was 'their only means' of getting British and American assistance; the alternative would be an alliance between Britain and the United States.[58] Wilson also argued against the French proposal, stressing that France should accept the following promise: 'When danger comes, we too will come, and we will help you, but you must trust us. We must all depend on our mutual good faith.'[59] In fact, as Clemenceau suspected, Wilson admitted military force was 'in the background' of his post-war plan, since the League was 'intended as a constitution of peace' not of war.[60] If moral force would not suffice, armed force would be employed as a last resort. Yet

---

[49] Ibid., p. 273.   [50] Ibid., pp. 5–6, 181–82, 187–88, 263.
[51] Ibid., pp. 6, 184, 187–88.
[52] Ibid., pp. 188–89, 262, 520; Glenda Sluga, *Internationalism in the Age of Nationalism* (University of Pennsylvania Press, 2013), pp. 35–37.
[53] Jackson, *Beyond the Balance of Power*, p. 273.   [54] Ibid., pp. 182, 184–86, 273.
[55] Ibid., pp. 188–89, 520.   [56] Ibid., pp. 181–82.
[57] Ibid., p. 520; Steiner, *The Lights That Failed*, pp. 40–41; Egerton, *Great Britain and the Creation of the League of Nations*, pp. 140.
[58] Egerton, *Great Britain and the Creation of the League of Nations*, pp. 136–37; Johnson, *Lord Robert Cecil*, pp. 106–7.
[59] Yearwood, *Guarantee of Peace*, p. 115; Egerton, *Great Britain and the Creation of the League of Nations*, p. 139.
[60] Ibid.

the league relied 'primarily and chiefly' on 'the moral force of the public opinion of the world'.[61] Similarly, Cecil also emphasised public opinion as the weapon to replace physical force in the future.[62] Even though Clemenceau managed to convince the peacemakers to compensate for France's sacrifices with security guarantees,[63] France could not sustain its position without American and British backing, especially in the manner of enforcing peace.[64]

On 7 May 1919, the Allied draft of the peace treaty was presented to the Germans at the Trianon Palace in Versailles, giving them fifteen days to reply; this was later extended to 29 May. Having believed they could negotiate a 'Wilsonian treaty', the Germans were dismayed at 'the last dreadful triumph' of the old power politics.[65] Undoubtedly, Wilson had some very utopian ideas. By employing the word 'covenants', he stressed the spiritual underpinnings of the League – not only a new social contract to replace the old international system[66] but also 'a mission to give international expression to a social gospel of peace'.[67] While the US president never spelt out his post-war scheme in detail and had arrived in Europe with only the vaguest of ideas about it,[68] he saw himself as 'the impartial judge' who would punish the wrongdoers and assist the victors throughout the Conference.[69] Yet in Paris, Wilson also realistically sought to secure agreement on a new order, taking advantage of the fact that the other leaders needed American support for the reconstruction of

---

[61] Ibid.; Stephen Wertheim, 'Reading the International Mind: International Public Opinion in Early Twentieth Century Anglo-American Thought', in Daniel Bessner and Nicolas Guilhot (eds.), *The Decisionist Imagination: Democracy, Sovereignty, and Social Science in the 20th Century* (Berghahn Books, 2018).

[62] Yearwood, *Guarantee of Peace*, pp. 111–12, 115–16.

[63] For example, Wilson and Lloyd George agreed that Germany should significantly lose its military power and territories. See Steiner, *The Lights That Failed*, pp. 69–70.

[64] Ibid.

[65] Steiner, *The Lights That Failed*, p. 62; Cohrs, *The Unfinished Peace*, p. 52; Peter Weber, 'Ernst Jäckh and the National Internationalism of Interwar Germany', *Central European History*, vol. 52, no. 3 (September 2019), pp. 402–23.

[66] Wilson's most crucial aim at the Conference was to establish a new world order, after the Great War confirmed for him that the old balance of power and the alliance systems were bankrupt. He was convinced that the mission of America, as a state that 'had escaped the cycles of war ... which had marked European history', was to redeem Europe and teach it the American successful experience. See Steiner, *The Lights That Failed*, p. 35. See Chapter 5.

[67] Steiner, *The Lights That Failed*, pp. 36–37; Egerton, *Great Britain and the Creation of the League of Nations*, p. 201.

[68] Wilson let his adviser Colonel Edward House prepare the post-war scheme. See Steiner, *The Lights That Failed*, pp. 36–7.

[69] Ibid., pp. 64–65. Also, Wilson's European tour made him confident that his league plan received strong popular support. See Egerton, *Great Britain and the Creation of the League of Nations*, p. 111.

Europe, both politically and financially.[70] At the same time, he had to reckon with the political situation at home, where the league plan would arouse opposition.[71] Especially after the defeat of the Democratic Party in the November 1918 elections, President Wilson foresaw that he would have to defend the treaty in the Senate. This situation forced the President to take a tougher line towards Germany,[72] although he did not doubt that Germany, as the 'guilty party', had to be punished and could not immediately be admitted into the league.[73]

On the other hand, Lloyd George was much more willing than Wilson to revise the treaty in light of German objections. The British Prime Minister believed, like the US President, that the peace treaty should be harsh enough to punish, constrain and teach Germany 'an unforgettable lesson'.[74] He was, nevertheless, worried that Germany might reject the proposed treaty,[75] so he pursued a settlement that the Germans would accept. Under pressure for revision from British delegates such as John Maynard Keynes,[76] the Prime Minister agreed to request modifications to the proposed occupation of the Rhineland and ask for the swift admission of Germany to the League if the country fulfilled the treaty obligations.[77] His post-war vision was to construct a stable Europe that would 'operate a self-regulating mechanism to keep the peace that would not require outside intervention',[78] because, if Europe were at peace, Britain could look to its 'imperial interests'.[79] Lloyd George and certain British officials probably shared the view expressed by Maurice Hankey, the British Cabinet Secretary, in his diary: 'the British Empire is worth a thousand League of Nations. They are a sound nation over there – the sheet anchor of the world. I can do more for the peace of the world there than in Geneva'.[80]

The German demands and Lloyd George's requests for revision irritated Wilson, who insisted there could be 'no concessions merely to get the Germans to sign the treaty'.[81] Even though the president admitted the treaty was very severe, he stressed 'justice had been done' to Germany's offence against civilisation, which made it unsuitable for readmission to the ranks of civilised states until it was chastised.[82]

---

[70] Steiner, *The Lights That Failed*, pp. 39–40. See Chapter 5.
[71] Steiner, *The Lights That Failed*, pp. 36–37, 39–40. See Chapter 5.
[72] Steiner, *The Lights That Failed*, pp. 39–40, 64–65.   [73] Ibid., pp. 39–40.
[74] Ibid., p. 29.   [75] Ibid., pp. 63–66.   [76] Ibid., pp. 63–64.   [77] Ibid.
[78] Ibid., pp 29.   [79] Ibid; also see Mazower, *Governing the World*, p. 128.
[80] Yearwood, *Guarantee of Peace*, p. 132.
[81] Steiner, *The Lights That Failed*, p. 64–65; Marc Trachtenberg, 'Versailles after Sixty Years', *Journal of Contemporary History*, vol. 17, no. 3 (July 1982), pp. 487–506.
[82] Steiner, *The Lights That Failed*, pp. 64–65, 69.

Following the Council of Four's rejection of the German reservations, Wilson set a twenty-four-hour ultimatum; the German cabinet signed the treaty, although it did not give up protesting and condemning the treaty's injustice.[83] On 28 June 1919, the final ceremony took place in the Hall of Mirrors at Versailles, 'staged to celebrate the French triumph and underline the enemy's humiliation', as Steiner has described it.[84] Germany was neither downgraded to a second rank power nor prevented from regaining great power status.[85] Nonetheless, the settlement was undeniably a victors' peace for punishing and constraining Germany,[86] as well as a flawed treaty that could not conciliate Germany and stabilise post-war Europe.[87] As Cohrs has pointed out, stabilising European security required a new form of great power cooperation, for which the League could not become a core instrument.[88] While it did not provide for an international armed force as the French had hoped,[89] the Covenant for the first time institutionalised the concept of collective security and thereby the League became the legal and institutional embodiment of something more than just the Concert of Europe.[90] The foundation of the League of Nations, however, remained firmly embedded in the ideological vision of victory pursued by the victors and an outcome understood as part of the moral crusade against enemy countries.

Having reviewed the political ending of the war-time project to create a league, we now analyse the weakness and limits of the war-time ideas about a league of nations. First, throughout the war, the pro-league movement was caught in the seeming paradox that its activists condemned war in general, yet simultaneously supported the ongoing war. From the very outset of the conflict in the summer of 1914, the blueprint for an international organisation had been prepared on the premise of the Allies' victory.[91] One of the leading pro-league thinkers, the Liberal MP Aneurin Williams, argued that a new post-war organisation would only be possible as a result of the Entente powers' winning the war.

When I speak of 'after the war', I am assuming, of course, that we and our Allies are eventually victorious. In the opposite event it is scarcely possible for an Englishman to imagine what would result, certainly not possible for him to

---

[83] Ibid., pp. 66–67.   [84] Ibid.   [85] Ibid., pp. 67–68.   [86] Ibid., p. 69.

[87] Ibid., p. 68; Cohrs, *The Unfinished Peace*, pp. 23–24.

[88] Cohrs, *The Unfinished Peace*, p. 67.   [89] Steiner, *The Lights That Failed*, pp. 42–43.

[90] Ibid., p. 41; Egerton, *Great Britain and the Creation of the League of Nations*, pp. 131–32; Yearwood, *Guarantee of Peace*, pp. 111–12.

[91] For instance, in a meeting of the Bryce Group, Graham Wallace said that 'we have found it best to assume that the Allied forces will be successful, and have considered what are the results which we should desire to follow from that success'. See OBL, Willoughby Dickinson Papers, MS. Eng. hist. c.402, 'Mr. Graham Wallas's Notes'.

hope for any good result. A victorious Germany would presumably be more militarist .... We look forward with confidence to a victory for ourselves and our Allies, and we intend to make that victory subserve the interests of the world and of the world's peace.[92]

Since many leading pro-leaguers presupposed military victory was a precondition for 'the world's peace' to be achieved by a new international organisation, their support for the war was hardly in conflict with their ideas about the post-war project.[93] For many of the pro-league leaders, who wondered what they could do on the home front, struggling for the formation of a league was their part in fighting the war.

Nonetheless, in the early years of the war, the efforts of the pro-leaguers prompted accusations that they were organising a stop-the-war campaign under the cloak of support for victory.[94] Even among intellectuals, the ideas about a post-war organisation occasionally invited the criticism that the pro-leaguers hoped for victory but did nothing for it, simply pointing to the wickedness of conducting war and the need for a new order after the conflict ended.[95] In fact, some of the pro-league thinkers were uncertain of their support for waging the war, while publicly advocating victory. The Oxford classicist and one of the leading pro-league thinkers, Gilbert Murray, for example, continued to defend the Entente's cause in public, yet privately expressed his horror at the reality of the fighting. Whatever higher goals the Allies fought for, the actual war was 'merely one of the ordinary sordid and bloody struggles of nation against nation'.[96] It might even lead Britain to become 'a nation like Germany without its discipline – a nation which scarcely deserves to win'.[97] The paradox of supporting the current war and simultaneously opposing future war posed a personal dilemma for some of the pro-leaguers.

Second, even though the pro-leaguers strove to deny that their ideas were utopian, the idealistic assumptions of their thinking persisted throughout the war. G. Lowes Dickinson was criticised by some of his fellow intellectuals for being naïve.[98] Since Dickinson remained a true believer of moral internationalists' arguments that stressed the moral

---

[92] Aneurin Williams, 'Proposals for a League of Peace and Mutual Protection among Nations' (reprinted from the *Contemporary Review*, November 1914), March 1915, pp. 3–4.

[93] See Chapter 3.   [94] Ibid.

[95] Stuart Wallace, *War and the Image of Germany: British Academics 1914–1918* (Donald, 1988), p. 117.

[96] Gilbert Murray, *Faith, War, and Policy: Addresses and Essays on the European War* (Houghton Mifflin Company, 1917), p. 17; Wallace, *War and the Image of Germany*, p. 107.

[97] Wallace, *War and the Image of Germany*, p. 107.   [98] Ibid., p. 117.

progress of humanity, his fundamental ideas about the post-war order rested on an optimistic conception of human nature.[99] Although the jingoism of war-time Britain disappointed him, Dickinson remained faithful to the possibility that the public might be properly educated to see beyond aggressive patriotism and to act rationally for the collective good. In 1918, Dickinson disagreed with the plan that the newly formed league should exclude Germany, claiming its anti-German vision could discourage the evolution of the German people's thinking towards peace.[100] In a way, his intellectual focus on the impersonal force of international anarchy and institutional arguments of liberal internationalism in the later years of the war perhaps helped him to sustain his convictions about moral progress and human rationality.[101] In international anarchy, the international system imposed its own compelling forces and norms to induce even high-minded statesmen to pursue policies conducive to war. Dickinson's thinking, centred on these impersonal forces, led him to downplay Germany's war guilt, in other words, the agency of Germany's leaders in 1914. He remained convinced of the future possibility of moral progress in and through the power of international public opinion.[102] Although after the war he became more sceptical about public opinion as a promoter of peace, he still believed that the moral education of the public would enable the League of Nations to be effective.[103]

The concept of progress also represented a weakness of the pro-leaguers' ideas and liberal internationalism more generally. First, despite their strong belief in the progress of humanity and society, the pro-leaguers' thinking itself did not 'progress' to a noticeable degree beyond that of their intellectual predecessors, the nineteenth century international lawyers. As this study has illustrated, the advocates of a league saw it as a union of 'civilised' and 'democratic' countries. Most of the pro-leaguers took the morality of empire and the domination of Europeans for granted, rarely considering non-European peoples and places as integral sovereign parts of the post-war international system. Such thinking affirmed in the League of Nations the right of the civilised powers to share in leadership for the maintenance of public order and their responsibility for the uncivilised states by positing that these latter

---

[99] Ibid., p. 115.
[100] See Chapter 5; OBL, Gilbert Murray Papers, Murray 178, 161, a letter from G. Lowes Dickinson to Murray, 6 September [1918].
[101] See Chapters 1 and 2.   [102] Ibid.; Wallace, *War and the Image of Germany*, p. 91.
[103] G. Lowes Dickinson, *Causes of International War* (Swarthmore Press, 1920).

were 'not yet able to stand' for themselves.[104] Similarly, international law in the nineteenth century was not regarded as 'universal' but as a regional 'droit public d'Europe',[105] grounded in the European and Christian tradition.[106] While some studies have illustrated that non-European regions also had their own versions of international, civilisational law before the European one was universalised in the twentieth century, such traditions were frequently ignored.[107] International law would apply only between 'civilized, European and Christian peoples' with common values and history,[108] not between non-European and non-Christian states nor between European/Christian and non-European/Christian states.[109]

In the nineteenth century, the concept of 'civilisation' gradually came to play a critical role in international law. It was based on the arguments of the eighteenth-century Scottish Enlightenment, which posited Europe's progress from the uncivilised to the civilised.[110] This concept prompted international law to promote a global norm for achieving the full judicial unity of humanity, as well as a 'moral justification of the European expansion'.[111] Many international lawyers of those days

---

[104] Thomas Hippler and Miloš Vec (eds.), *Paradoxes of Peace in Nineteenth Century Europe* (Oxford University Press, 2015), p. 236; Gunther Hellman (ed.), *The Transformation of Foreign Policy: Drawing and Managing Boundaries from Antiquity to the Present* (Oxford University Press, 2016), pp. 289–90; Susan Pedersen, *The Guardians: The League of Nations and the Crisis of Empire* (Oxford University Press, 2015).

[105] Besson and d'Aspremont (eds.), *The Oxford Handbook*, pp. 132, 148–49; Hellman (ed.), *The Transformation of Foreign Policy*, p. 151.

[106] Hippler and Vec (eds.), *Paradoxes of Peace*, pp. 38, 172, 241–42, 245–46; Hellman (ed.), *The Transformation of Foreign Policy*, p. 150; Samantha Besson and Jean d'Aspremont (eds.), *The Oxford Handbook of the Sources of International Law* (Oxford University Press, 2018), p. 149.

[107] See Besson and d'Aspremont (eds.), *The Oxford Handbook*, p. 149; Arnulf Becker Lorca, *Mestizo International Law: A Global Intellectual History 1842–1933* (Cambridge University Press, 2014), pp. 4, 49–50, 69; Antony Anghie, *Imperialism, Sovereignty and the Making of International Law* (Cambridge University Press, 2004), p. 32.

[108] Hellman (ed.), *The Transformation of Foreign Policy*, pp. 144–45; Martti Koskenniemi, *The Gentle Civilizer of Nations: The Rise and Fall of International Law 1870–1960* (Cambridge University Press, 2004), p. 63; Hippler and Vec (eds.), *Paradoxes of Peace*, p. 38.

[109] Besson and d'Aspremont (eds.), *The Oxford Handbook*, pp. 148–49; Anghie, *Imperialism, Sovereignty and the Making of International Law*, pp. 59–60, 103; Martin H. Geyer and Johannes Paulmann, *The Mechanics of Internationalism: Culture, Society, and Politics From the 1840s to the First World War* (Oxford University Press, 2001), chapter 9.

[110] Lorca, *Mestizo International Law*, pp. 3–4; Anghie, *Imperialism, Sovereignty and the Making of International Law*, pp. 4, 55–56, 102–3; Hippler and Vec (eds.), *Paradoxes of Peace*, pp. 219–21; also see, Ian Clark, *Legitimacy in International Society* (Oxford University Press, 2005), pp. 4, 7, 248–9.

[111] Hippler and Vec (eds.), *Paradoxes of Peace*, pp. 245–46, 249; Hellman (ed.), *The Transformation of Foreign Policy*, p. 150.

supposed, as a powerful vehicle of civilisation, international law was capable of liberating humanity from barbarism and violence.[112] Since regions outside the Western legal and political system – where societies seemed like children who lacked moderation and education[113] – would not soon achieve a sufficient degree of civilisation,[114] the official aims of Europe's civilising mission to these places were 'education and enlightenment'.[115] On this premise, international lawyers asserted that the use of violence in dealing with 'barbarians' was driven by moral values and therefore no breach of international law.[116] Given that international law and arbitration could only apply to warfare between civilised states,[117] war with uncivilised ones was not war but intervention.[118] Peace, moreover, was the outcome of civilisational progress and hence only possible among the civilised[119] – a narrative that also endorsed the violent spread of European civilisation.[120] The more global diplomatic relations became, the more a discriminatory boundary was set,[121] with the consequence that the boundary became a criterion of belonging to the West or the rest.[122] International law neither set the standard of civilisation, nor included any procedures for determining civilised status;[123] as in the twentieth century, the League did not clarify what 'democracy' meant. As this book has suggested, the concept of 'civilised/uncivilised' began to be replaced by 'democratic/undemocratic' and 'liberal/non-liberal' from the Great War onwards, reflecting the ideas of the league of nations movement.[124]

Another weakness of the pro-leaguers' post-war ideas and liberal internationalism lay in their optimistic assumption about the future evolution of the league of nations. Based on their belief in social and

---

[112] Hellman (ed.), *The Transformation of Foreign Policy*, p. 150.

[113] Koskenniemi, *The Gentle Civilizer of Nations*, p. 66; also see Lorca, *Mestizo International Law*, pp. 43–44, 48–49, 51; Anghie, *Imperialism, Sovereignty and the Making of International Law*, pp. 5–6; also see, Nazli Pinar Kaymaz, 'From Imperialism to Internationalism: British Idealism and Human Rights', *The International History Review*, vol. 41, no. 6 (2019), pp. 1235–55.

[114] Hellman (ed.), *The Transformation of Foreign Policy*, pp. 141–42,151; Koskenniemi, *The Gentle Civilizer of Nations*, p. 61.

[115] Hippler and Vec (eds.), *Paradoxes of Peace*, pp. 248, 280.   [116] Ibid., p. 248.

[117] Ibid., pp. 177, 219, 235, 246–47; Besson and d'Aspremont (eds.), *The Oxford Handbook*, p. 155.

[118] Hippler and Vec (eds.), *Paradoxes of Peace*, pp. 220–21.   [119] Ibid., pp. 219, 277.

[120] Ibid., pp. 219–22, 277.

[121] Hellman (ed.), *The Transformation of Foreign Policy*, pp. 289–90.

[122] Ibid., pp. 150, 289; Hippler and Vec (eds.), *Paradoxes of Peace*, pp. 178, 220–21.

[123] Lorca, *Mestizo International Law*, pp. 7, 66–67, 73; Anghie, *Imperialism, Sovereignty and the Making of International Law*, pp. 59–60, 84–85.

[124] Hippler and Vec (eds.), *Paradoxes of Peace*, pp. 219–21; also see Mulligan, *The Great War for Peace*, p. 10.

political progress,[125] the pro-leaguers assumed that once the league was founded it would evolve over time into a better organisation, one closer to their original conception, however imperfect at the time of its formation. Yet the evolution of a league, not completely but still critically, depended on the moral progress of the public. While the emphasis of the pro-leaguers' thinking shifted during the war from individual morality to how institutions could support moral order,[126] the pro-leaguers still considered the moral and rational progress of humanity as an important element in the prevention of future wars. Just as the journalist Henry Brailsford longed for a league comprising peoples not states,[127] so many of his fellow pro-league leaders expected that a post-war league would evolve into an international organisation that drew strength from the morality of the public. To them, a league should be buttressed by morality and human reason and, in crisis, as Gilbert Murray remarked, should 'stand up against violence for the sake of right'.[128] Lowes Dickinson also believed in future moral progress and supposed that the interplay of moral and institutional elements would maintain the new liberal world order, however slow and gradual the process of educating the public would be.[129]

This reliance upon moral progress was not purely a weakness but also a part of the pro-league movement's strength. By expecting the future progress of the organisation, the pro-leaguers avoided a dogmatic approach to its foundation. This enabled them to develop the post-war plan, to make political compromises and to celebrate the creation of the League in 1919 despite its imperfections. Yet, at worst, the wager on future progress to perfect the new international order was precisely the kind of optimism that could threaten peace,[130] leaving the problem of how, and whether, the public could be educated largely unanswered. The Fabian writer Leonard Woolf pointed out the difficulties of assuming

---

[125] Casper Sylvest, *British Liberal Internationalism, 1880–1930: Making Progress?* (Manchester University Press, 2009), pp. 3–4, 11, 26, 139, 197.

[126] Sylvest, *British Liberal Internationalism*, pp. 198–99, 267–70; Sylvest, 'Continuity and Change in British Liberal Internationalism, c. 1900–1930', *Review of International Studies*, vol. 31, no. 2 (2005), pp. 266–67.

[127] Henry Noel Brailsford, *A League of Nations* (Macmillan, 1917), pp. 317–22.

[128] Wallace, *War and the Image of Germany*, p. 110–11.

[129] See Chapter 2; Casper Sylvest, 'Continuity and Change in British Liberal Internationalism, c. 1900–1930', *Review of International Studies*, vol. 31, no. 2 (2005), pp. 281.

[130] Paul W. Schroeder, *Systems, Stability, and Statecraft: Essays on the International History of Modern Europe* (Palgrave Macmillan, 2004), p. 264.

that the establishment of an international organisation would change the public mind or promote a higher standard of morality:[131]

That machinery, to be effective, must at every moment be exactly fitted to the international consciousness of the moment .... No people exist in the world in which the international mind is in anything but an immature state, and the machinery of any international council, established in the next twenty years, would have to reflect this immaturity.... Machinery cannot create mind. It can only translate it into action. The only way to build is from the bottom upwards, whether you are building a house or a democracy.[132]

Witnessing the widespread enthusiasm for battle at the outbreak of the war, John A. Hobson, a journalist as well as an economist who was a member of the Bryce Group, came to view his pre-war assumption – that most civilised men were rational – as a mere illusion.[133] This led him to emphasise the fallibility of the public and to presuppose that it was 'idle' to imagine that an organisation 'starting with so little inner unity of status and of purpose can dispense entirely with the backing of physical force with which the most highly evolved of national societies has been unable to dispense'.[134] Many pro-leaguers were appalled by the aggressive nationalism engendered by the war and suspicious of the role of 'the people' in politics. Some of them believed that the popular control of foreign policy advocated by the anti-war Union of Democratic Control might simply empower 'general ignorance'.[135] Gilbert Murray argued that greater democratic control might cause violence and irrationality, since at war the public could be 'stupid', 'dishonest' and 'brutal' and might 'transform your imagined crusade into a very different reality'.[136] The jingoistic upheaval of the public compelled many pro-leaguers to recognise that an organisation alone would not educate the public nor unite the world.[137] Despite their recognition of the difficulty of promoting moral progress, pro-league leaders could not, or did not, overcome it.

---

[131] Sylvest, 'Continuity and Change in British Liberal Internationalism', p. 278; Wallace, *War and the Image of Germany*, p. 98.
[132] Leonard Woolf, 'The International Mind', *The Nation*, 7 August 1915, p. 614; Sylvest, 'Continuity and Change in British Liberal Internationalism', p. 280.
[133] See Chapter 1; John A. Hobson, *Confessions of an Economic Heretic* (G. Allen & Unwin 1938), pp. 93–94, 104; Peter F. Clarke, *Liberals and Social Democrats* (Cambridge University Press, 1978), pp. 166, 170.
[134] John A. Hobson, *Towards International Government* (Macmillan, 1915), p. 96; Sylvest, 'Continuity and Change in British Liberal Internationalism', p. 281–82.
[135] Wallace, *War and the Image of Germany*, pp. 90–91.
[136] Murray, *Faith, War, and Policy*, p. 240; Wallace, *War and the Image of Germany*, pp. 108–9.
[137] Henry Noel Brailsford, *A League of Nations* (Macmillan, 1917), p. 317

Reassessing the league of nations movement and its ideas compels us to look at the aftermath of its endeavor to reform international society. After the armistice, the formation of the League of Nations introduced a new set of international norms and conceptions of legitimacy, such as the assumption that 'war was no longer a legitimate tool of foreign policy in Europe'.[138] While norms and values in international society were to be 'negotiated and re-negotiated',[139] the opposition to war and the promotion of peace – the core of liberal internationalism – failed to become universal values, at least in the inter-war years. On the contrary, war was occasionally considered to have a positive value.[140] During the First World War, for example, Social Darwinism reinforced progressive history in parallel with the biological analogy[141] and the view that military power and war would prompt state construction.[142] In this theory, violence was required for evolution, progress and the formation of a state since it constituted a process of selection in the human species.[143] Meanwhile, on the battlefield, trench warfare impressed some soldiers with the camaraderie of soldiers, which seemed to be a 'meaningful community' of a variety of men for the same end, even though they confronted mass death and fear everywhere.[144] Such a view was in fact shared by some British intellectuals who admitted war could be a meaningful form of human engagement. Richard H. Tawney, an economic historian who was a friend of many of the pro-league leaders, enlisted as a

---

[138] Jackson, *Beyond the Balance of Power*, pp. 209, 520–21; Pedersen, *The Guardians*, p. 357; Zara Steiner, *The Triumph of the Dark: European International History 1933–1939* (Oxford University Press, 2010), pp. 1039–40; Steiner, *The Lights That Failed*, pp. 624–25; Mulligan, *The Great War for Peace*, pp. 7–8, 218.

[139] Jackson, *Beyond the Balance of Power*, pp. 207–8.

[140] Peter Jackson, 'Europe: The Failure of Diplomacy, 1933–1940', in Richard Bosworth and Joseph A. Maiolo (eds.), *Cambridge History of the Second World War*, vol. 2 (Cambridge University Press, 2015), pp. 219, 222, 241.

[141] See Chapter 4; Lloyd E. Ambrosius, *Wilsonian Statecraft: Theory and Practice of Liberal Internationalism during World War I* (Scholarly Resources Books, 1991), p. 9.

[142] J. Adam Tooze, *The Deluge: The Great War and the Remaking of Global Order, 1916–1931* (Allen Lane, 2014), p. 28. See also, Akira Iriye, *War and Peace in the Twentieth Century* (Tokyo University Press, 1986) [in Japanese], pp.24–27; Ambrosius, *Woodrow Wilson and American Internationalism*, p. 87.

[143] George Nasmyth, *Social Progress and the Darwinian Theory: A Study of Force As a Factor in Human Relations* (G. P. Putnam's Sons, 1916), pp. 7, 17, 140; Tooze, *The Deluge*, pp. 28–29; Charles E. Merriam, *American Political Ideas: Studies in the Development of American Political Thought, 1865–1917* (Macmillan, 1920), p, 371; Koch, 'Social Darwinism As a Factor in the "New Imperialism"', in Koch (ed.), *The Origins of the First World War*, p. 336; Paul Crook, *Darwinism, War, and History: The Debate over the Biology of War from the 'Origin of Species' to the First World War* (Cambridge University Press, 1994), pp. 130, 136–37.

[144] George L. Mosse, *Fallen Soldiers: Reshaping the Memory of the World Wars* (Oxford University Press, 1991), pp. 5–6.

soldier and experienced trench warfare on the Somme in 1914–1916. Throughout the war, Tawney kept his faith in the moral quality of war and presumed the 'war could be used to usher in social change'.[145] Furthermore, in the inter-war period, Fascists and Communists highlighted war's potential for national unification and progress, as well as for the creation of revolutionary conditions.[146] In Italian Fascism, war was not only the 'inevitable' trial but also an important unifying concept.[147] The leader of Italian Fascism, Benito Mussolini, stressed that 'the Italian nation could realize its historic mission only through war'.[148] When in the 1930s the rise of Fascism undermined the international society that the pro-leaguers envisaged would become united under the League of Nations, liberal internationalists' vision of peace could not be a viable alternative. As Alan Cassels has argued, liberal internationalism was 'hardly conducive to ideological fervour' and could not arouse 'the emotional commitment' as Fascism and Nazism did.[149]

Thus, the long, horrible experience of the First World War neither transformed the public attitude into absolute opposition to war, nor did it stimulate the development of the pro-league movement in ways that early advocates had hoped for. In reality, the experience of the war led people to require legitimate, moral and ideological reasons for fighting in the future. Prior to 1914, war was advocated for reasons of conquest, defence or honour. In the early years of the war, generally speaking, the defence of the nation and the image of war as heroic, romantic and even enjoyable mobilised people to the great cause.[150] By the end of the war, however, the most legitimate reason to wage war in liberal-democratic states, in Britain particularly, became the preservation of peace. The British public supported the creation of an international organisation to prevent war, not simply because of war-weariness or a longing for peace but because of their recognition that the League would be an alliance against German militarism and aggression. Philosopher and political campaigner

---

[145] Jay M. Winter, *Socialism and the Challenge of War: Ideas and Politics in Britain, 1912–18* (Routledge and Kegan Paul, 1974), p. 170; Wallace, *War and the Image of Germany*, pp. 86–88.

[146] Alan Cassels, *Ideology and International Relations in the Modern World* (Routledge, 1996), p. 139.

[147] Peter Jackson, 'Europe: The Failure of Diplomacy', in Bosworth and Maiolo (eds.), *Cambridge History of the Second World War*, vol. 2, pp. 228, 231. Also see Reto Hofmann, *The Fascist Effect: Japan and Italy, 1915–1952* (Cornell University Press, 2015).

[148] Jackson, 'Europe', p. 228.

[149] Cassels, *Ideology and International Relations*, pp. 243–44.

[150] I. F. Clarke, *Voices Prophesying War, 1763–1984* (Oxford University Press, 1966), pp. 131, 162.

Bertrand Russell, for instance, opposed the First World War because 'no great principle is at stake no great human purpose is involved on either side'. 'The supposed ideal ends for which it is being fought are merely part of the myth.'[151] Yet, in the Second World War, he did not oppose fighting the war because Hitler's Germany was a different case. Russell deemed 'the Nazis utterly revolting – cruel, bigoted, and stupid. Morally and intellectually they were alike odious', which made his pacifists convictions difficult to cling to'.[152] The Great War did not necessarily lead the public to an unconditional rejection of war but instead recast the way in which popular support for mass participation in total war would be mobilised, specifically around a great moral cause. At the end of the First World War in Britain (and also in the United States), the idea of destroying German militarism and authoritarianism, as well as the establishment of the League as a democratic alliance of peace-loving nations, provided just such an ideological basis for the final push to victory.[153]

Indeed, ideas about a league of nations, as this book has illustrated, developed in tandem with the First World War. Due to its unprecedented scale, the war had to be justified by appealing to the higher cause of establishing a future peace-sustaining organisation – a war aim that helped to legitimise the continuation of the war and to intensify the violence.[154] The idea of a league of nations, in turn, needed to be framed as a war aim, part of the moral crusade of the Western powers against German barbarism; it was essential for the idea to become politically legitimate and popular enough to form a league. Such an evolution of post-war ideas under the pressures of politics and public opinion highlighted a fundamental problem that pro-league leaders had to acknowledge. That is, war was in essence 'an act of violence' that entailed the shedding of blood, fostering passions and hatred of the enemy, whatever higher ideals people entertained.[155] Even though the pro-leaguers hoped for a new peaceful organisation and fought for a higher cause such as 'a war against war', in reality they fought for victory over enemy states, not the abstract idea of war. Fighting against states entailed military victory as well as political and ideological victory, something that required the mobilisation of the public and their hatred of the enemy. In addition to the realities of war time, the change in the ideals of the pro-league movement mirrored a larger transformation in European international

[151] Bertrand Russell, *Justice in War-Time* (The Open Court Publishing, 1916), pp. 13–14.
[152] Bertrand Russell, *Autobiography* (Routledge, 2009), p. 410.
[153] See Chapter 5. Also see John Horne (ed.), *State, Society and Mobilization in Europe during the First World War* (Cambridge University Press, 1997).
[154] Mulligan, *The Great War for Peace*, pp. 7–9.
[155] Carl von Clausewitz, *On War* (Start Pub. LLC, 2013), pp. 41–42.

relations. In the nineteenth century, international politics was based on
the Concert of European Powers, in which limited war was deemed as a
continuation of politics.[156] From the Great War to the Cold War, what
constituted the legitimate use of military force was transformed, and the
concept of peace itself became the focal point for intensifying ideological
antagonism in the international and transnational spheres.[157]

The central findings of this book help us to understand more precisely
why the League of Nations could not prevent the Second World War.[158]
In 1919, the preamble of the Covenant of the League of Nations stipulated the obligation of member states not to resort to war.[159]
Nevertheless, as Willoughby Dickinson's letter quoted at the beginning
of this conclusion indicated, the outbreak of another world war within
one generation led many to conclude that the pro-league movement and
the League had failed[160] and that those who had conceived of the League
and founded it had been utopian dreamers detached from the realities of
power politics. Indeed, some crucial elements of the League's failure lay
in the facts that the League had been created as an extension of the Great
War and embodied the liberal ideals of the war-time Allies. As Chapter 5
argued, people's desire for a democratic victory and for the punishment
of Germany and its allies, not their longing for peace, shaped the creation
of the League of Nations. Even most of the pro-league movement's
leadership, who had originally determined to work for international
reform for lasting peace, came to see the league as an effective way to
continue the war-time alliance into peacetime. The aim of creating a

---

[156] Ibid.; F. H. Hinsley, *Power and the Pursuit of Peace: Theory and Practice in the History of Relations between States* (Cambridge University Press 1967), chapter 14; Michael Eliot Howard, *War and the Liberal Conscience* (Oxford University Press, 1981); Masataka Kosaka, *International Politics* (Chuo Koronsha, 2017) [In Japanese], pp. 12, 34.

[157] Sharp, 'The New Diplomacy and the New Europe'; Robert W. Tucker, 'Woodrow Wilson's "New Diplomacy"', *World Policy Journal*, vol. 21, no. 2 (Summer, 2004), pp. 92–107; Arno J. Mayer, *Wilson vs. Lenin: Political Origins of the New Diplomacy 1917–1918* (Meridian Books, 1969). For the Concert of Europe of the nineteenth century, see Paul W. Schroeder, *The Transformation of European Politics, 1763–1848* (Clarendon Press, 1996); Schroeder, *Systems, Stability, and Statecraft*; Cohrs, *The Unfinished Peace*. For the shift to ideological polarity in the twentieth century, see Cassels, *Ideology and International Relations*, pp. 139–56; Mark Mazower, 'Violence and the State in the Twentieth Century', *The American Historical Review*, vol. 107, no. 4 (October 2002), pp. 1158–78.

[158] Cassels, *Ideology and International Relations*, chapter 7.

[159] *The Covenant of the League of Nations*, the Avalon Project, http://avalon.law.yale.edu/20th_century/leagcov.asp.

[160] Hinsley, *Power and the Pursuit of Peace*, chapter 14. Also see Pedersen, *The Guardians*, pp. 356–57; Steiner, *The Triumph of the Dark*, p. 95; Susan Pedersen, 'Back to the League of Nations: Review Essay', *The American Historical Review*, vol. 112, no. 4 (October 2007), pp. 1094–95.

league of nations for a just and lasting peace, as Schroeder has pointed out, could perhaps contain a conceptual confusion. Peace and order would not be established by treaties or politics but should be conceived as something organic, constantly changing, always 'being created and recreated',[161] an insight about which the pro-leaguers remained rather optimistic.

From the outset, the League as a security institution had innate weaknesses. First, as Steiner has argued, the League could not substitute collective security for great power politics but acted as an adjunct to it – a mechanism for 'multinational diplomacy whose success or failure depended on the willingness of the states, and particularly the most powerful states'.[162] The new international order was inherently unstable, not only because of 'unanimous opposition to the idea of a super-state that would compromise the national sovereignty of its member states'[163] but also because of 'the temporary weakness of Germany and Russia', which meant 'the balance of power upon which it [the new order] was founded was essentially artificial and would come under increasing strain as those two states regained their strength'.[164] Although the absence of the United States left only two of the Great Powers, Britain and France, committed to the values of liberal internationalism,[165] neither British nor French political leaders regarded the League as an optimal solution for international stabilisation.[166]

As the Bryce Group had already discussed in 1914–1915, collective security itself relied on several idealistic assumptions from the beginning: for example, that aggression would be deterred by sanctions, that member states would be united against an aggressor, that an aggressor would be clearly defined, that concerted action would be taken by member states when necessary, that most disputes would be resolved before initiating collective security.[167] Post-1945 critics of the League as well as political leaders such as President Wilson condemned the League as an organisation without the teeth – the military sanctions that the pro-

---

[161] Schroeder, *Systems, Stability, and Statecraft*, p. 266.

[162] Steiner, *The Lights That Failed*, p. 349; Steiner, *The Triumph of the Dark*, pp. 1039–40.

[163] Jackson, *Beyond the Balance of Power*, p. 188; David Armstrong, Lorna Lloyd and John Redmond, *International Organisation in World Politics* (Palgrave Macmillan, 2004), p. 22.

[164] Armstrong, Lloyd and Redmond, *International Organisation in World Politics*, p. 22.

[165] Ibid.

[166] Pedersen, *The Guardians*, pp. 8–9; Steiner, *The Lights That Failed*, pp. 135, 350.

[167] Armstrong, Lloyd and Redmond, *International Organisation in World Politics*, p. 22; Steiner, *The Lights That Failed*, p. 352.

leaguers proposed – to enforce peace in crisis.[168] Nevertheless, even with teeth, the League of Nations would have failed to implement joint military actions by all of the, or at least the major, member states and provide reliable sanctions.

Furthermore, collective security, whether or not it was adopted and implemented as a peace mechanism, posed an innate, fundamental problem in the first place. In the Covenant of the League of Nations, war was regulated but neither outlawed nor excluded. Article 11 stipulated:

> any war or threat of war, whether immediately affecting any of the members of the League or not, is hereby declared a matter of concern to the whole League, and the League shall take any action that may be deemed wise and effectual to safeguard the peace of nations.[169]

Member states agreed not to go to war against any state, had to submit 'any dispute likely to lead to a rupture' to arbitration, judicial settlement or the Council and were forbidden from resorting to war within three months after any decision.[170] Nonetheless, there were no enforcement provisions and, if arbitration failed, states could resort to war after a cooling-off period.[171] As sanctions, Article 16 stated an immediate economic, financial and diplomatic boycott; if these were unsuccessful, the Council could recommend to the member states what military forces they might severally contribute to.[172] Whereas the members still enjoyed the freedoms pertaining to sovereign states, the League wished for collective action without acknowledging superior authority.[173] The formation of the League as an organisation of 'democratic' states also affected the function of collective security. In the League, as this book has shown, the adoption of democratic institutions was demanded both domestically and internationally, and democratic values became key for the membership requirements.[174] The League's imposition and promotion of democracy brought the exclusion and selectivity of rightful membership,

---

[168] President Wilson, for example, criticised the Phillimore plan as 'it has no teeth'. See Lloyd E. Ambrosius, *Woodrow Wilson and the American Diplomatic Tradition: The Treaty Fight in Perspective* (Cambridge University Press, 1990), p. 45.

[169] Steiner, *The Lights That Failed*, p. 42; Egerton, *Great Britain and the Creation of the League of Nations*, pp. 131–32; *The Covenant of the League of Nations*, the Avalon Project, http://avalon.law.yale.edu/20th_century/leagcov.asp.

[170] Steiner, *The Lights That Failed*, pp. 42–3; *The Covenant of the League of Nations*, the Avalon Project, http://avalon.law.yale.edu/20th_century/leagcov.asp.

[171] *The Covenant of the League of Nations*, the Avalon Project, http://avalon.law.yale.edu/20th_century/leagcov.asp; Steiner, *The Lights That Failed*, p. 351.

[172] See n. 171.   [173] Steiner, *The Lights That Failed*, pp. 40–43.

[174] Clark, *Legitimacy in International Society*, pp. 112, 251; Jackson, *Beyond the Balance of Power*, p. 207.

which limited the universality that the ideals of collective security required.[175]

As the pro-league thinkers discussed at the early planning stage of the league, collective security, based on their intellectual foundation of liberal internationalism, contained a profound paradox: in seeking to prevent war, it incorporated the collective use of force as an indispensable element for the maintenance of peace. Pro-leaguers also acknowledged the possibility that war in the name of sanctions might easily escalate into worldwide war, contrary to their aim to prevent or at least limit war. Apart from the warning that military sanctions should be implemented only as a final resort, the pro-league activists and subsequent promoters presented few practical safeguards. While this optimism was vital for the evolution of the league project, pro-leaguers were mostly content to suggest that the league would gradually develop into a perfect organisation. Indeed, as Steiner has observed, 'the gap between the normative rules in the Covenant and the realities of international behaviour was recognized from the start' – not only from the establishment of the League of Nations but from its very planning stage during the Great War.[176]

Nevertheless, it would be unjustifiable to attribute all these problems and limits of the war prevention system to the mechanisms peculiar to the League of Nations. Rather, they derived from the intrinsic nature of international relations: the condition of anarchy. Many criticisms of the League and its war prevention scheme, such as an insufficient power to compel member states to act in unison, stemmed from the lack of the supreme authority in international politics, in other words, its defining characteristic. Hence, the problems that the League of Nations as a peace-inducing organisation exposed and which the war-time pro-leaguers readily acknowledged persist to this day.[177] Almost a century has passed since the Bryce Group discussed possible ways to prevent war. Yet the central ideas and paradoxes about how to maintain peace in international politics have made little progress since then. A similar sobering view was expressed in Leonard Woolf's review of a new translation of Kant's *Perpetual Peace* in 1915:

---

[175] Clark, *Legitimacy in International Society*, p. 251.   [176] Ibid., p. 352.

[177] Koskenniemi, *The Gentle Civilizer of Nations*, pp. 471 73; Cassels, *Ideology and International Relations*, pp. 9, 13, 120–21; Hedley Bull, *The Anarchical Society: A Study of Order in World Politics* (Macmillan, 1995); G. Lowes Dickinson, *The European Anarchy* (George Allen & Unwin, 1916); G. Lowes Dickinson, *The International Anarchy, 1904–1914* (George Allen & Unwin, 1926).

There remains, however, the main problem to haunt the philosopher. Why, if these are the conditions have we made so small progress to their attainment in the 120 years since the Treaty of Basle? Is the answer to be found still in the answer of Leibniz: 'The mightiest among the living have little respect for tribunals'?[178]

That same observation could be repeated today.

---

[178] Leonard Woolf, 'Perpetual Peace', *New Statesman*, 31 July 1915, pp. 398–89; Sylvest, 'Continuity and Change in British Liberal Internationalism', *Review of International Studies*, p. 279.

Appendix

Key Figures

James Bryce

The renowned jurist, historian and the former British ambassador in Washington. He chaired the Bryce Group and directed behind-the-scenes lobbying of the League of Nations Society. He had wide academic and political networks both in Britain and the United States and also acted as the pro-league groups' go-between in communication with the American group, the League to Enforce Peace.

Goldsworthy Lowes Dickinson

The Cambridge classicist who first sketched out the league of nations scheme a few weeks after the British entry into the Great War in 1914. He brought together those who were interested in a post-war plan and launched the pro–league of nations movement. He is now best known as the author of *European Anarchy* (1916).

Willoughby Dickinson

The Liberal MP who led the pro-league movement as the chairman of the League of Nations Society. Inspired by his Anglican faith, he had already engaged in peace work in Europe before the war.

Aneurin Williams

The Liberal MP who wrote one of the first post-war plans titled *Proposals for a League of Peace and Mutual Protection among Nations,* published in November 1914. In public, he was frequently labelled a pacifist. As one of the leading pro-league members, he also corresponded with the League to Enforce Peace in the United States.

188

David Davies

The Welsh Liberal politician and philanthropist who organised a new pro-league, anti-German group, the League of Free Nations Association, in 1918. In the early years of the war, he commanded infantry on the Western Front and after that acted as Lloyd George's parliamentary private secretary. Davies established a Chair of International Politics at the University College of Wales, Aberystwyth, and in 1922 named it as the Woodrow Wilson Chair.

Gilbert Murray

The renowned classicist and scholar of international studies at the University of Oxford. He became the vice-president of the League of Nations Society in 1916 and also participated in founding the League of Free Nations Association in 1918.

H. G. Wells

The famous novelist and social commentator who was a member of the Fabian Society. After the outbreak of the Great War, he coined the phrase 'The War That Will End War' and devoted himself to journalism. Wells was a member of the League of Nations Society, the League of Free Nations Association and the Enemy Propaganda Department Crewe House.

Arthur Ponsonby

A Liberal (later Labour) MP who was one of the core members of the Union of Democratic Control from 1914. He was also a member of the Bryce Group and contributed to the discussion about its post-war plan, *Proposals for the Avoidance of War* of 1915.

The Bryce Group's *Proposals for the Avoidance of War* (Transcript)

BLEPS, CANNAN 970, *Proposals for the Avoidance of War, with a Prefatory Note by Viscount Bryce, As Revised up to 24 February 1915.*

Prefatory Note

The frightful catastrophe of the present War, involving more than half the human race, and bringing grave evils on neutral nation also, has driven thoughtful men to reflect on the possibility of finding means by which the risk of future wars may be dispelled, or at least largely reduced. The only effective and permanent remedy would be to convince the several peoples of the world that they have far more to lose than to gain from strife, and to replace by a sentiment of mutual international goodwill the violent national antagonisms that now exist. But this, we may well fear, would be a slow process. Meantime that which may be done, and which it seems possible to do at once, is to provide machinery by and through which that great body of international public opinion which favours peace may express itself, and bring its power to bear upon the governments of those nations in which there may, from time to time, exist a spirit of aggression, or a readiness to embark on war in pursuit of selfish interests or at the bidding of national pride. The public opinion of the world would surely prove to possess a greater force than it has yet shewn if it could but find an effective organ through which to act.

A group of men in England who have long been seeking for some method by which this aim might be attained has recently tried to draft a scheme embodying, in outline, such a method. It is briefly set forth in the document which follows, and is explained in the Introduction prefixed thereto. It is now circulated privately to a small number of persons believed to be in general accord as to the object in view, with the hope that those of them who can find the time will criticize it fully and freely, and will append such alternative suggestions as may seem likely to be helpful. Those who have drafted the scheme are aware that it deals with only one branch of a very large subject, and they are duly sensible of the difficulties to be overcome before even these limited and tentative proposals could be likely to find acceptance with those who direct the policy of States. But there are some advantages in submitting and bespeaking attention for one particular plan, especially as the practical measures it points to would be the extension and development of an institution (the Hague Tribunal) which has so far worked for good.

Everyone seems to feel the approach of a supremely important moment. The reason and the conscience of mankind have been roused, as never before, to a sense of the moral as well as the material evil wrought by war. If the opportunity which the close of the present conflict will offer for the provision of means to avert future wars be lost, another such may never reappear, and the condition of the world will have grown worse, because the recurrence of like calamities will have been recognized as a thing to be expected, and their causes as beyond all human cure.

BRYCE

Introduction

The feeling that the present war is a disastrous failure of civilization, and that at its close all should be done, that human wisdom and foresight can devise, to prevent the recurrence of such a catastrophe, is, we believe, general, if not universal, among all the nations concerned. But to concentrate this feeling upon definite and practicable measures is not an easy task. It is clear that the reforms to be introduced must be drastic if they are to be effective, For, as John Stuart Mill has said: 'Small remedies for great evils do not produce small effects. They produce no effects.' On the other hand, there must be continuity; for proposals involving too violent a breach with the established order are not likely to be seriously considered. What is attempted here is to put forward a scheme which, while it involves a real and radical advance upon the present organization of international relations, yet does not break so violently with the course of historical development as to be fairly described as Utopian.

With the deep underlying causes of war we do not here concern ourselves. Those causes, mainly connected, in the modern world, with false ideas and wrong feelings about the moral and economic relations of States, of classes, and of individuals, can only be gradually dissipated by the spread there can be no complete security for peace. Meantime, however, we think it possible, by such an arrangement as we suggest, to diminish very considerably the risk of war, and so to give time for the development of that educational process upon which we mainly rely.

Proposals for the reform of international relations vary in range and extent from complete schemes for a world-State, to improvements in the conduct of diplomacy. The project of a world-State, or even of a European Federation, we do not here advocate. It is perhaps a possibility of the distant future, and it well deserves the discussion it has provoked. But we do not believe it to be practicable at any near date. Our aim is a more modest one. We desire to give definite shape to that idea of an association or union of Sovereign States which is being advocated by many leading men both in Europe and in America, and which, we believe, could be realized immediately at the conclusion of the war.

Such an arrangement would not make war impossible, but it would, we think, make it much less probably than it would otherwise be. And it would be a germ which might develop by degrees into an international polity.

We propose then that existing States, retaining their sovereignty, should unite themselves by treaty to preserve peace. What we contemplate is not a league of some States against others, but a union of as many as possible in their common interests. The success of the Union will depend upon the number and importance of the State entering into it. To achieve its purpose it should include at least the Great Powers of Europe. And it would be enormously strengthened if the United States of America should be willing to join. We suggest that the members should be, in the first instance, the eight Great Powers (the United States of America, Austria-Hungary, France, Germany, Great Britain, Italy, Japan and Russia) and any of the other States of Europe that are willing to join. The Union might ultimately grow into a World-Union, but it does not seem probably, nor is it necessary that it should be inaugurated on so wide a basis.

The members of the Union would bind themselves by treaty:

(1) To refer all disputes that might arise between them, if diplomatic methods of adjustment had failed, either to a court of arbitration for judicial decision, or to a council of conciliation for investigation and report.
(2) Not to declare war or begin hostilities until the court had decided or the council had reported.
(3) To put pressure, diplomatic, economic or forcible, upon any signatory power that should act in violation of the preceding conditions.

Concerted pressure by the Members of the Union is contemplated only in the case where one of them has resorted to force, or the threat of force, in breach of the moratorium imposed by the treaty The measures required would be taken by the Powers as sovereign States acting through their ordinary diplomatic and governmental machinery, and would be supported, if necessary, by their national armaments. We so not propose an international force, nor an international executive. These may be desirable and may come in time. It is doubtful whether they would be accepted at present, or whether, if accepted, they would be used with effect. In concerting the measures that may be necessary in this contingency, we suggest that the Powers should be bound by the vote of a majority. We do so in order to avoid the paralysis which might occur (and which is said to occur under present conditions when the Powers meet in concert) were unanimity to be required for common action. It may be objected that, under such an arrangement, a majority of small Powers might attempt to override a minority of great ones. Bur we think such a bound, by their interest as well as by the treaty, to put sufficient pressure upon the Power offending. Their discussions would turn merely upon the question of ways and means. And it is not likely that proposals would be made and pushed through which were obviously unreasonable or impracticable. This, however, is one of the many points on which we should be glad to receive suggestions.

In suggesting economic, as an alternative to forcible, pressure, we have in mind such measures as the refusal of financial aid or of commercial intercourse. This, if practicable, might be a very effective weapon. And it is one which some Powers, for example the United States, might be more able and willing to employ than actual armed force.

Our proposal is that disputed between the treaty Powers should be referred either to arbitration or to conciliation. We distinguish, therefore, two classes of disputes, and two processes of settlement.

(1) The first class of disputes we call 'justiciable'. They are such as are capable of settlement by judicial determination; for example, the interpretation of a treaty, or any question of international law or of fact, where the fact in dispute is one which, if proved, would constitute a breach of international duty. In case of disagreement as to whether a dispute is justiciable or not, the Council of Conciliation proposed below, is to decide.

All disputes of a justiciable character, including those that involve honour and vital interests, are to be referred to the Hague Court, as it now is, or may in future be constituted, or to some other arbitral court. We so not think it necessary to exclude cases involving honour and vital interests, first because it cannot be conductive to the honour of a State to break the terms of a treaty or the rules of international law, and secondly, because most disputes involving vital interests belong to the other category and will go to conciliation. It may be urged that it may be contrary to the vital interests of a State to observe a treaty of old date when the circumstances are radically changes; this possibility should be met by an arrangement whereby existing treaties come up periodically for prolongation, amendment or abrogation, but in no case ought the right to break a treaty to be admitted.

(2) The other class of disputes, and, of course, the class most likely to lead to war, includes those which are not justiciable, and which arise out of the general economic and political rivalry of States, or, it may be, from the discontent of nationalities within a State, which commands the sympathy of a kindred people. Any settlement of such disputes must aim at the removal of their causes, and for this purpose a judicial tribunal is not the best authority. We propose a judicial tribunal is not the best authority. We propose, therefore, to institute for this purpose a new international body which we call the Council of Conciliation. The functions of the Council would be similar to those hitherto performed by the diplomatic representatives of the Powers when they meet in concert to discuss difficult questions, but it is intended that the composition of the Council should enable its members to take a more impartial and international view, and to suggest a radical settlement rather than a mere temporary compromise, likely to be broken as soon as some Power is ready to risk war. No mere machinery can secure the right type of man. But we think the desired result would be promoted if

the appointments to the Council were made for a fixed term of years, and not for each particular issue as it arises, nor with a view to the supposed pinions of the member on that issue. The members should deliberate and decide freely according to their best judgement, and not under instructions from their governments, though they should, of course, be and keep in touch with public opinion in their country. In countries having representative institutions, their appointment should be subject to approval by the Legislature.

In this way it should be possible to secure men who will act with an international outlook, and who will not be mere agents of possibly reactionary and absolute governments.

The question arises whether the Powers should be equally represented on the Council. This does not seem to be a point of fundamental importance, since the functions of the Council are conciliatory only, and not executive. But since it is likely that the greater Powers would have a larger number of men qualifies to be members, they might be given a greater representation: say three to each of the Great Powers, and one at least to each of the rest.

The Council would publish a Report or Reports on every dispute of which it took cognizance, and make recommendations for a settlement. These reports and recommendations would focus public opinion upon the issue and its settlement, and it is reasonable to hope that the best opinion of all countries would support the Council in pressing for an amicable solution on the lines suggested.

It is proposed further, that the Council should have power to take cognizance of any circumstances which seemed likely to endanger the amicable relations of the signatory Powers, whether or not an actual dispute had arisen, and to make recommendations, which need not in all cases be published, towards the casing of the situation.

With the publication of its Report, the function of the Council would end. It would not be an international executive and would have no power to enforce its recommendations. Nor would the Powers be under treaty obligation to enforce them. In case the recommendations were not accepted by any of the Powers concerned, the question would become one for diplomacy. The signatory Powers would be under treaty obligation to consider in concert the situation that would then have arisen, but would not be bound to take collective action.

It is no doubt possible that for such a situation in the last resort, war might arise. It is not claimed that the Union would make war impossible, but it is believed that the enforced period of delay, the consideration by an impartial Council and the publicity given to its recommendations would be very likely to prevent war by rallying the public opinion of the world in favour of peace; and that in the worst case the area of war would be likely to be restricted, for a Power making war in defiance of the recommendations of the Council could not rely on support from the other signatory Powers.

In addition to its primary function of dealing with disputes that have actually arisen, we propose that power should be given to the Council to take cognizance of any circumstances likely to endanger in the future the good relations between the signatory Powers; and to recommend solutions. As examples of such circumstances may be mentioned the problems of immigration which arise from marked racial dissimilarities and those which are due to the competing economic and commercial interests of different Powers in undeveloped territory. The elaboration and acceptance beforehand of clear general principles, to be applied to particular cases when they arise, might obviate many dangerous disputes.

The limitation or reduction of armaments is so generally felt to be one of the objects to be pursued with an earnest purpose in the future, that we propose to give the Council power to frame a scheme for that end, if they think fit, on their own initiative. Such measures would clearly be facilitated by any arrangement giving security to States against sudden and unprovoked attack. We think, therefore, that our proposed Union would form a good basis for endeavours in that direction.

It will be observed further that our plan implies and presupposes such a measure of popular control over international relations as is involved in the publication of the results of impartial inquiry, and their discussion in representative assemblies and in the press. Without pretending that public opinion is always and everywhere pacific, we believe that, when properly instructed, it is more likely to favour peace than do the secret operations of diplomacy.

It may be worth while to emphasize the difference between the Union we are proposing and what has been known as the Concert of Europe. In the first place, the Union if not confined to European Powers. In the second place, it binds the signatory Powers, under the sanction, in the last resort, of force, to submit their disputes to peaceable settlement, before having recourse to military measures. In the third place, it creates for the discussion of the most difficult and contentious questions, an impartial and permanent Council, which would have some advantages over the present machinery of the Concert. We attach much importance to the creation of such a permanent international organ, and believe that it ultimate and indirect effects may be even more important than its operations in particular cases.

Finally, in confining ourselves, in this paper, to the question of an International Union, we wish it to be understood that we are not indifferent to the many other questions and proposals which must come up for consideration at the peace. But we have thought it convenient to put forward this one project, for separate discussion, in the hope of contributing to form a public opinion in favour of a definite proposal. And we suggest that other questions might be usefully treated in a similar way.

'I should like, if I might for a moment, beyond this enquiry into causes and motives, to ask your attention and hat of my fellow countrymen to the end which in this war we ought to keep in view. Forty-four years ago, at the time of the war of 1870, Mr. Gladstone used these words. He said 'The greatest triumph of our time will be the enthronement of the idea of public right as the governing idea of European politics.' Nearly fifty years have passed. Little progress it seems has yet been made towards that great and beneficent change, but it seems to me to be now at this moment as good a definition as we can have of our European policy. The idea of public right, what does it mean when translated into concrete terms? It means first and foremost the clearing of the ground by the definite repudiation of militarism as the governing factor in the relation of States, and of the future moulding of the European world. It means next that room must be found and kept for the independent existence and the free development of the smaller nationalities-each with a corporate consciousness of its own. Belgium, Holland, and Switzerland and the Scandinavian countries, Greece and the Balkan States, they must be recognized as having exactly as good a title as their more powerful neighbours- more powerful in strength as in wealth-exactly as good a title to a place in the sun.

And it means, finally, or it ought to mean, perhaps by a slow and gradual process, the substitution for force, for the clash of competing ambitions, for groupings and alliances and precarious equipoise, the substitution for all these things of a real European partnership, based on the recognition of equal right and established and enforced by a common will. A year ago that would have sounded like a Utopian idea. It is probably one that may not or will not be realized either to-day or to-morrow. If and when this war is decided in favour of the Allies, it will at once come whthin the range, and before long within the grasp, of European statesmanship.' (Mr. Asquith, at Dublin, 25 September 1914)

Proposals for the Avoidance of War

(1) The parties to the treaty arrangement contemplated in the succeeding clauses to be the Great Powers (i.e., the six great Powers of Europe, the United States and Japan), and all other European Powers which may be willing to adhere to the arrangement.

Justiciable Disputes

(2) The signatory Powers to agree to refer to the Permanent Court of Arbitration at the Hague, or to some other arbitral tribunal, all disputes between them (including those affecting honour and vital interests),

which are of a justiciable character and which the Powers concerned have failed to settle by diplomatic methods.

(3) The signatory Powers to agree to accept and give effect to the award of the arbitral tribunal.

(4) 'Disputes of a justiciable character' to be defined as 'disputes as to the interpretation of a treaty, as to any question of international law, as to the existence of any fact which, if established, would constitute a breach of any international obligation, or as to the nature and extent of the reparation to be made for any such breach'.

(5) Any question which may arise as to whether a dispute is of a justiciable character, to be referred for decision to the Council of Conciliation proposed below.

N.B.-It has been suggested, as an alternative, that the determination of this question should be left to the Hague Court.

Permanent Council of Conciliation

(6) With a view to the prevention and settlement of disputes between the signatory Powers which are not of a justiciable character, a permanent Council of Conciliation to be constituted.

(7) The members of the Council to be appointed by the several signatory Powers for a fixed term of years, and vacancies to be filled up by the appointing Powers, so that the Council shall always be complete and in being. Each of the Great Powers to appoint three members; the other Powers each to appoint at least one member.

(8) The signatory Powers to agree that every party to a dispute, not of a justiciable ultimately endanger friendly relations with another Power or Powers, will submit its case to the Council with a view to conciliation.

(9) Where, in the opinion of the Council, any dispute exists between any of the signatory Powers which appears likely to endanger their good relations with each other, the each Power concerned to submit its case with a view to conciliation.

(10) The Council to make and publish, with regard to every dispute considered by it, a report or reports, containing recommendations for the amicable settlement of the dispute.

(11) When it appears to the Council that, from any cause within its knowledge the good relations between any of the signatory Powers are likely to be endangered, the Council to be at liberty to make suggestions to them with a view to conciliation, whether or not any dispute has actually arisen, and, if it considers it expedient to do so, to publish such suggestions.

(12) The Council to be at liberty to make and submit for the consideration of the signatory Powers, suggestions for the limitation or reduction of their respective armaments.

(13) The signatory Powers to agree to furnish the Council with all the means and facilities required for the due discharge of its functions.

(14) The Council to deliberate in public or in private, as it thinks fit.

(15) The Council to have power to appoint committees, which may or may not be composed exclusively of its own members, to report to it on any matter within the scope of its functions.

N.B.-It will be observed that it is not proposed to confer any executive power on the Council.

Moratorium for Hostilities

(16) Every signatory Power to agree not to commence hostilities against any other signatory Power before the matter in dispute has been submitted to an arbitral tribunal, or to the Council, or within a period of twelve months thereafter; or, if the award of the arbitral tribunal or the report of the Council, as the case may be, has been published within that time, then not to commence hostilities within a period of six months after the publication of such award or report.

Limitation of Effect of Alliances

(17) The signatory Powers to agree that no signatory Power commencing hostilities against another without first complying with the provisions of the preceding clauses, shall be entitled, by virtue of any existing or future treaty of alliance or other engagement, to the material support of any other signatory Power in such hostilities.

Enforcement of Obligations by the Signatory Powers

(18) All the signatory Powers to undertake that in case any signatory Power resorts to hostilities against another signatory Power, without first having submitted its case to an arbitral tribunal, or to the Council of Conciliation, or before the expiration of the prescribed period of delay, they will support the Power so attacked by such concerted measures, diplomatic, economic or forcible, as, in the judgement of the majority of them, are most effective and appropriate to the circumstances of the case.

(19) The signatory Powers to undertake that if any Power shall fail to accept and give effect to the recommendations contained in any report of the Council, they will consider, in concert, the situation which has arisen by reason of such failure, and what collective action, if any, it is practicable to take in order to make such recommendations operative.

N.B.-The measures contemplated in the last two paragraphs would, of course, be taken by the constituent Powers acting in concert, and not by the Council of Conciliation.

Bibliography

Unpublished Primary Sources

United Kingdom
British Library
    Albert I of Belgium: Papers rel. to the War Refugees Committee:
      1914–1919
    Balfour Papers
    Bernard Shaw Papers
    The Burns Papers
    The Cecil of Chelwood Papers
    C. P. Scott Papers
    Macmillan Archive
    Mary Gladstone Papers
    Northcliffe Papers
    Stopes Papers
    Strachey Papers
    Viscount Gladstone Papers
    Wentworth Bequest
    Wickham Steed Papers
British Library of Economic and Political Science
    Beveridge Papers
    Cannan Papers
    Courtney Papers
    Dell Papers
    Dickinson Papers
    Fabian Society Archives
    Gardiner Papers
    Keen Papers
    Lloyd Papers
    Morel Papers
    Passfield Papers
    Wallas Papers
Cambridge, King's College Archives
    The Papers of Arthur Elliott Felkin
    The Papers of Charles Robert Ashbee

The Paper of Goldsworthy Lowes Dickinson
The Papers of John Maynard Keynes
Cambridge, Newnham College Archives
    Wallas Family Papers
The National Archives
    Cabinet Office Records
    Domestic Records of the Public Record Office, Gifts, Deposits,
        Notes and Transcripts
    Foreign Office Records
    Home Office Records
    Records Created or Inherited by the Central Office of Information
    Records of The National Archives
    Records of the Security Service
    War Office Records
The National Archives of Scotland
    Papers of the Kerr Family, Marquises of Lothian (Lothian
        Muniments)
The National Library of Wales
    Lord Davies of Llandinam Papers
Lambeth Palace Library
    Davidson, Randall Thomas (1848–1930), Baron Davidson
Oxford, Bodleian Library,
    The Papers of Sir Alfred Zimmern
    The Papers of Arthur Augustus William Harry Ponsonby, 1st Baron
        Ponsonby of Shulbrede
    The Papers of Francis Sydney Marvin
    The Papers of Gilbert Murray
    The Papers of Herbert Henry Asquith, 1st Earl of Oxford and
        Asquith
    The Papers of H. W. Nevinson
    The Papers of James, Viscount Bryce
    The Papers of Sir Willoughby Hyett Dickinson
Oxford, Bodleian Library of Commonwealth & African Studies at
    Rhodes House
    Political and Colonial Papers of Charles Roden Buxton
Parliamentary Archives
    Papers of John Campbell Davidson
    Papers of John St Loe Strachey
    The Lloyd George Papers
    The Whitehead Papers
Private Collection
    Arthur Ponsonby's Diary (transcript)

United States
Columbia University, Rare Book & Manuscript Library
    Carnegie Endowment for International Peace Records, 1910–1954,

Harvard University, Houghton Library
  Abbott Lawrence Lowell Peace Papers (*2005-481)
  League to Enforce Peace Records
Yale University, Manuscripts and Archives
  The Irving Fisher Papers

Italy
Historical Archives of EU, Florence
  Dwight Morrow Papers

Switzerland
The League of Nations Archives, Geneva
  IPB Correspondence, 1892–1950

Published Primary Sources

Newspapers and Magazines

Annals of the American Academy of Political and Social Science
The Fabian News
Fabian Tracts
Headway: The Monthly Progress of the L.N.U.
International Conciliation
League of Nations Society, *Monthly Report for Members*
League of Nations Society, *League of Nations Society Publications* (London)
The Manchester Guardian
The Morning Post
The Nation
The New Statesman
The New Republic
The New York Times
The Observer
The Times
War & Peace
The Westminster Gazette

Pamphlets, Diaries and Memoirs

Angell, Norman, *The Great Illusion: A Study of the Military Power to National Advantage* (William Heinemann, 1913).
Ashbee, Charles R., *The American League to Enforce Peace: An English Interpretation* (G. Allen & Unwin, 1917).

Asquith, Herbert H., *Memories and Reflections, 1852–1927: By the Earl of Oxford and Asquith, K. G.* (Cassell and Company, 1928).

Balfour, Arthur James, *Opinions and Argument from Speeches and Addresses of the Earl of Balfour* (Doran, 1928).

Bell, G. K. A., *Randall Davidson: Archbishop of Canterbury* (Oxford University Press, 1935).

Bourne, Kenneth (ed.), *British Documents on Foreign Affairs – Reports and Papers from the Foreign Office Confidential Print from the First to the Second World War, the League of Nations, 1918–1941* (University Publications of America, 1992–1995).

Brailsford, Henry Noel, *After the Peace* (T. Seltzer, 1922).

  The Covenant of Peace: An Essay on the League of Nations (B. W. Huebsch, 1919).

  A League of Nations (Macmillan, 1917).

Bryce, James, *The Attitude of Great Britain in the Present War* (Macmillan, 1918).

  Essays and Addresses in War Time (Macmillan, 1918).

  Proposals for the Prevention of Future Wars (G. Allen & Unwin, 1917).

  Studies in History and Jurisprudence (Clarendon, 1901).

  The War of Democracy: The Allies' Statement: Chapters on the Fundamental Significance of the Struggle for a New Europe (Doubleday, Page, 1917).

  et al., *The International Crisis: The Theory of the State* (H. Milford, Oxford University Press, 1916).

Cecil, Robert, *All the Way* (Hodder & Stoughton, 1949).

  A Great Experiment: An Autobiography (Jonathan Cape, 1941).

  The Moral Basis of the League of Nations (The Lindsey Press, 1923).

  The New Outlook (George Allen & Unwin, 1920).

Clausewitz, Carl von, *On War* (Start Pub. LLC, 2013).

Courtney, Kate, *Extracts from a Diary during the War* (Victor Press, 1927).

Crucé, Emeric, *The New Cyneas of Émerie Crucé* (Allen Lane and Scott, 1909).

Dickinson, G. Lowes, *After the War* (Fifield, 1915).

  'The American "League to Enforce Peace"', *War and Peace* (June 1916), pp. 134–35.

  The Autobiography of G. Lowes Dickinson and Other Unpublished Writings (Duckworth, 1973).

  Causes of International War (Swarthmore Press, 1920).

  Documents and Statements Relating to Peace Proposals & War Aims (G. Allen & Unwin, Macmillan, 1919).

  The European Anarchy (George Allen & Unwin, 1916).

  The Foundation of a League of Peace, World Peace Foundation Pamphlet Series, vol. V, no. 2 (April 1915).

  'How Can America Best Contribute to the Maintenance of the World's Peace?', *Annals of the American Academy of Political and Social Science* (September 1915), pp. 235–38.

  The International Anarchy, 1904–1914 (George Allen & Unwin, 1926).

  Towards a Lasting Settlement (George Allen & Unwin, 1916).

  The War and the Way Out (Chancery Lane Press, 1917).

Eliot, Charles W., 'An International Force Must Support an International Tribunal', *Judicial Settlement of International Disputes*, no. 19 (American Society for Judicial Settlement of International Disputes, 1914).

Erasmus, Desiderius, *The Complaint of Peace* (Open Court Publishing, 1917).

Goldsmith, Robert, *A League to Enforce Peace* (Macmillan, 1917).

Grey, Edward, *The League of Nations* (George H. Doran Company, 1918).

Speeches on Foreign Affairs, 1904–1914 (George Allen & Unwin, 1931).

Twenty-five Years, 1892–1916 (Frederick A. Stokes Company, 1925).

et al., *Great Speeches of the War* (Hazell, Watson & Viney, 1915).

Grotius, Hugo, *The Rights of War and Peace: Including the Law of Nature and of Nations*, Campbell, A. C. (trans.) (Walter Dunne, 1901).

Hugo Grotius on the Law of War and Peace, Neff, Stephen C. (ed.) (Cambridge University Press, 2012).

Hobson, John A., *Confessions of an Economic Heretic* (George Allen & Unwin, 1938).

Towards International Government (Macmillan, 1915).

Kant, Immanuel, *Perpetual Peace, and Other Essays on Politics, History, and Morals*, Humphrey, Ted (trans.) (Hackett Pub. Co., 1983).

Perpetual Peace: A Philosophical Essay, 1795 (George Allen & Unwin, 1903).

Keen, Frank N., *A League of Nations with Large Powers* (George Allen & Unwin, 1918).

The Revision of the League of Nations Covenant (Grotius Society, 1919).

The World in Alliance: A Plan for Preventing Future Wars (Walter Southwood & Co., 1915)

Keynes, John Maynard, *The Collected Writings of John Maynard Keynes* (Macmillan, 1989).

League of Nations Society, *The League of Nations Society: Explanation of the Objects of the Society* (League of Nations Society, 1917).

League to Enforce Peace, *Enforced Peace: Proceedings of the First National Annual Assemblage of the League to Enforce Peace* (League to Enforce Peace, 1916).

Win the War for Permanent Peace: Addresses Made at the National Convention of the League to Enforce Peace (League to Enforce Peace, 1918).

Lloyd George, David, *The Truth about the Peace Treaties* (Gollancz, 1938).

War Memoirs of David Lloyd George, vols. 3–5 (Ivor Nicholson & Watson, 1934–1936).

Mackinder, Halford J., *Democratic Ideals and Reality: A Study in the Politics of Reconstruction* (Constable & Co., 1919).

Marburg, Theodore, *Development of the League of Nations Idea: Documents and Correspondence of Theodore Marburg* (Macmillan, 1932).

'World Court and League of Peace', *Judicial Settlement of International Disputes*, no. 20 (American Society for Judicial Settlement of International Disputes, 1914).

Mill, John Stuart, *J. S. Mill: 'On Liberty' and Other Writings*, Collini, Stefan (ed.) (Cambridge University Press, 1989).

On Liberty (London, 1864).

Montesquieu, Charles-Louis de, *The Spirit of Laws* (London, 1758).

The Spirit of the Laws, Cohler, Anne M., Miller, Basia Carolyn, and Stone, Harold Samuel (trans. and eds.) (Cambridge University Press, 1989).

More, Thomas, *Utopia* (Oxford University Press, 1923).

Murray, Gilbert, *The Cult of Violence* (Lovat Dickson, 1934).

Murray, Gilbert, Smith, Jean, and Toynbee, Arnold (eds.), *Gilbert Murray: An Unfinished Autobiography* (George Allen & Unwin, 1960).

Nasmyth, George, *Social Progress and the Darwinian Theory: A Study of Force As a Factor in Human Relations* (G. P. Putnam's Sons, 1916).

National Liberal Club, *The National Liberal Club (Photo-lithograph of the Architect's Drawing. A Detailed Official Description of the Premises)* (London, 1884).

Parmoor, Lord, 'The League of Nations', *Transactions of the Grotius Society*, vol. 4 (Cambridge University Press, 1918), pp. xvii–xxvi.

Phillimore, Walter George Frank, *Three Centuries of Treaties of Peace and Their Teaching* (John Murray, 1919).

Rask-Ørstedfonden, *Les Origines et L'œuvre de la Société des Nations* (Gyldendalske Boghandel/Nordisk Forlag, 1923).

Russell, Bertrand, *Autobiography* (Routledge, 2009).

Justice in War-Time (Open Court Publishing, 1916).

Smuts, Jan Christiaan, *The League of Nations: A Practical Suggestion* (Hodder and Stoughton, 1918).

Smuts, Jan Christiaan, Hancock, W. K., and van der Poel, Jean (eds.), *Selections from the Smuts Papers Vol.3, June 1910–November 1918* (Cambridge University Press, 1966).

Stuart, Campbell, *Secrets of Crewe House: The Story of a Famous Campaign* (Hodder and Stoughton, 1920).

Taft, William H., *The Proposal for a League to Enforce Peace: Lake Mohonk Conference on International Arbitration, 1916* (American Association for International Conciliation, 1916).

Vattel, Emer de, *The Law of Nations: Or, Principles of the Law of Nature, Applied to the Conduct and Affairs of Nations and Sover[e]igns* (T. & J. W. Johnson, 1853).

Webb, Beatrice, *Beatrice Webb's Diaries, 1912–1924*, Cole, Margaret I. (ed.) (Longmans, Green and Co., 1952).

Wells, H. G., *Experiment in Autobiography: Discoveries and Conclusions of a Very Ordinary Brain* (Victor Gollancz Ltd., 1966).

White, Hope C., *Willoughby Hyett Dickinson, 1859–1943: A Memoir, etc. [with Plates, including Portraits]* (Privately printed, 1956)

Wilkinson, Marion, E. *Richard Cross: A Biographical Sketch with Literary Papers and Religious and Political Addresses* (J. M. Dent, 1917).

Williams, Aneurin, 'A New Basis of International Peace', delivered at the Ethical Church, Queen's Road, W., 31 January 1915.

'Proposals for a League of Peace and Mutual Protection among Nations' (reprinted from the *Contemporary Review*, November 1914), March 1915.

Wilson, Florence, *The Origins of the League Covenant: Documentary History of Its Drafting* (Leonard and Virginia Woolf, 1928).

Woolf, Leonard, and Fabian Research Department, *International Government: Two Reports* (Fabian Society, 1916).

World Peace Foundation, League to Enforce Peace, *Historical light on the League to Enforce Peace* (World Peace Foundation, 1916).

Web Sources

Avalon Project, *The Covenant of the League of Nations*, http://avalon.law.yale.edu/
20th_century/leagcov.asp.
Hague Conference of 1899 and 1907, http://avalon.law.yale.edu/subject_menus/
lawwar.asp.
HANSARD 1803–2005, http://hansard.millbanksystems.com.
House of Commons, Parliamentary Papers, http://parlipapers.chadwyck.co.uk/
hansard/fullrec.do?source=config5.cfg&area=hcpp&id=
CDS5CV0065P0–0011.
United Nations, *The Charter of the United Nations*, www.un.org/en/documents/
charter/chapter1.shtml.

Secondary Sources

Books

Abbenhuis, Maartje Maria, *An Age of Neutrals: Great Power Politics 1815–1914*
(Cambridge University Press, 2014).
The Hague Conferences and International Politics, 1898–1915 (Bloomsbury
Academic, 2019).
Adelman, Paul, *Gladstone, Disraeli and Later Victorian Politics* (Longman, 1997).
Victorian Radicalism: The Middle-class Experience 1830–1914 (Longman, 1984).
Ahlstrom, Sydney Eckman, *A Religious History of the American People* (Yale
University Press, 1972).
Alonso, Harriet Hyman, *The Women's Peace Union and the Outlawry of War,
1921–1942* (University of Tennessee Press, 1989).
Ambrosius, Lloyd E., *Wilsonianism: Woodrow Wilson and His Legacy in American
Foreign Relations* (Palgrave Macmillan, 2002).
*Wilsonian Statecraft: Theory and Practice of Liberal Internationalism during World
War I* (Scholarly Resources, 1991).
Woodrow Wilson and American Internationalism (Cambridge University Press,
2017).
*Woodrow Wilson and the American Diplomatic Tradition: The Treaty Fight in
Perspective* (Cambridge University Press, 1987).
Anderson, Benedict, *Imagined Communities: Reflections on the Origin and Spread of
Nationalism* (Verso, 2006).
Andrew, Christopher M., *The Defence of the Realm: The Authorized History of MI5*
(Penguin, 2010).
Anghie, Antony, *Imperialism, Sovereignty and the Making of International Law*
(Cambridge University Press, 2004).
Armitage, David, *Foundations of Modern International Thought* (Cambridge
University Press, 2013).
Armstrong, David, Lloyd, Lorna, and Redmond, John, *International Organisation
in World Politics* (Palgrave Macmillan, 2004).
Atkin, Jonathan, *A War of Individuals: Bloomsbury Attitudes to the Great War*
(Manchester University Press, 2002).

Bartlett, Ruhl, *The League to Enforce Peace* (University of North Carolina Press, 1944).

Batchelor, John, *H. G. Wells* (Cambridge University Press, 1985).

Baylis, John, Smith, Steve, and Owens, Patricia (eds.), *The Globalization of World Politics: An Introduction to International Relations* (Oxford University Press, 2016).

Beales, Arthur Charles Frederick, *The History of Peace: A Short Account of the Organised Movements for International Peace* (G. Bell, 1931).

Bebbington, David, and Swift, Roger (eds.), *Gladstone Centenary Essays* (Liverpool University Press, 2000).

Bell, Duncan, *The Idea of Greater Britain: Empire and the Future of World Order, 1860–1900* (Princeton University Press, 2007).
  Reordering the World: Essays on Liberalism and Empire (Princeton University Press, 2016).

Bell, Duncan, (ed.), *Victorian Visions of Global Order: Empire and International Relations in Nineteenth-Century Political Thought* (Cambridge University Press, 2007).

Bell, G. K. A., *Randall Davidson: Archbishop of Canterbury* (Oxford University Press, 1935).

Benton, Lauren A., and Ford, Lisa, *Rage for Order: The British Empire and the Origins of International Law, 1800–1850* (Harvard University Press, 2016).

Bessner, Daniel, and Guilhot, Nicolas (eds.) *The Decisionist Imagination: Democracy, Sovereignty, and Social Science in the 20th Century* (Berghahn Books, 2018).

Best, Geoffrey, *Humanity in Warfare: The Modern History of the International Law of Armed Conflicts* (Weidenfeld and Nicolson, 1980).

Bew, John, *Realpolitik: A History* (Oxford University Press, 2016).

Biagini, Eugenio F., *Gladstone* (Macmillan, 2000).

Biddel, Henrik, Sylvest, Casper, and Wilson, Peter (eds.), *Classics of International Relations: Essays in Criticism and Appreciation* (Routledge, 2013).

Birn, Donald S., *The League of Nations Union, 1918–1945* (Oxford University Press, 1981).

Boemeke, Manfred F., Feldman, Gerald D., and Glaser, Elisabeth (eds.), *The Treaty of Versailles: A Reassessment after 75 Years* (Cambridge University Press, 2006).

Bond, Brian, *The Unquiet Western Front: Britain's Role in Literature and History* (Cambridge University Press, 2002).

Borowy, Iris, *Coming to Terms with World Health: The League of Nations Health Organization, 1921–1946* (Lang, 2009).

Bosworth, Richard, and Maiolo, Joseph A. (eds.), *Cambridge History of the Second World War*, vol. 2 (Cambridge University Press, 2015).

Bouchard, Carl, *Le Citoyen et L'ordre Mondial (1914–1919). Le Rêve D'une Paix Durable au Lendemain de la Grande Guerre (France), Grande-Bretagne, États-Unis* (Pédone, 2008).

Boyle, Francis Anthony, *World Politics and International Law* (Duke University Press, 1985).

Braybon, Gali (ed.) *Evidence, History, and the Great War: Historians and the Impact of 1914–18* (Berghahn Books, 2003).

Briggs, Asa, and Clavin, Patricia, *Modern Europe, 1789–Present* (Longman, 2003).

Brock, Peter, *Twentieth-Century Pacifism* (Van Nostrand Reinhold, 1970).

Brown, Chris, and Ainley, Kirsten, *Understanding International Relations* (Palgrave Macmillan, 2009).

Brown, Chris, Nardin, Terry, and Rengger, Nicholas (eds.) *International Relations in Political Thought: Texts from the Ancient Greeks to the First World War* (Cambridge University Press, 2002).

Bull, Hedley, *The Anarchical Society: A Study of Order in World Politics* (Columbia University Press, 2002).

Burchill, Scott, and Linklater, Andrew et al., *Theories of International Relations* (Palgrave Macmillan, 2013).

Buzan, Barry, and Little, Richard, *International Systems in World History: Remaking the Study of International Relations* (Oxford University Press, 2000).

Cabanes, Bruno, *The Great War and the Origins of Humanitarianism, 1918–1924* (Cambridge University Press, 2014).

Cain, P. J., *Hobson and Imperialism: Radicalism, New Liberalism, and Finance 1887–1938* (Oxford University Press, 2002).

Carr, Edward Hallett, *The Twenty Years' Crisis, 1919–1939, an Introduction to the Study of International Relations* (Macmillan, 2001).

Carter, April, *Peace Movements: International Protest and World Politics Since 1945* (Routledge, 1992).

Cassels, Alan, *Ideology and International Relations in the Modern World* (Routledge, 1996).

Ceadel, Martin, *Living the Great Illusion: Sir Norman Angell, 1872–1967* (Oxford University Press, 2009).

The Origins of War Prevention: The British Peace Movement and International Relations 1730–1854 (Oxford University Press, 1996).

Pacifism in Britain, 1914–1945: The Defining of a Faith (Oxford University Press, 1980).

Semi-Detached Idealists: The British Peace Movement and International Relations, 1854–1945 (Oxford University Press, 2000).

Thinking about Peace and War (Oxford University Press, 1989).

Clark, Christopher M., *The Sleepwalkers: How Europe Went to War in 1914* (Allen Lane, 2012).

Clark, Ian, *The Hierarchy of States: Reform and Resistance in the International Order* (Cambridge University Press, 1989).

Legitimacy in International Society (Oxford University Press, 2005).

Clarke, I. F., *Voices Prophesying War, 1763–1984* (Oxford University Press, 1966).

Clarke, Peter F., *Liberals and Social Democrats* (Cambridge University Press, 1978).

A Question of Leadership: British Rulers: Gladstone to Thatcher (Penguin, 1991).

Claude, Inis L., *Swords into Plowshares: The Problems and Progress of International Organization* (Random House, 1971).

Clavin, Patricia, *Securing the World Economy: The Reinvention of the League of Nations, 1920–1946* (Oxford University Press, 2013).

Coates, Benjamin Allen, *Legalist Empire: International Law and American Foreign Relations in the Early Twentieth Century* (Oxford University Press, 2016).

Cohrs, Patrick O., *The Unfinished Peace after World War I: America, Britain and the Stabilisation of Europe, 1919–1932* (Cambridge University Press, 2006).

Cooper, Sandi E., *Patriotic Pacifism: Waging War on War in Europe, 1815–1914* (Oxford University Press, 1991).

Cox, Jeffrey, *The English Churches in a Secular Society: Lambeth, 1870–1930* (Oxford University Press, 1982).

Crawford, James, and Koskenniemi, Martti (eds.), *The Cambridge Companion to International Law* (Cambridge University Press, 2012).

Crook, Paul, *Darwinism, War, and History: The Debate over the Biology of War from the 'Origin of Species' to the First World War* (Cambridge University Press, 1994).

den Otter, Sandra M., *British Idealism and Social Explanation: A Study in Late Victorian Thought* (Oxford University Press, 1996).

Detter Delupis, Ingrid, *The Law of War* (Cambridge University Press, 2000).

Dickson, Lovat, *H.G. Wells: His Turbulent Life and Times* (Macmillan, 1969).

Dobson, Alan P., *Anglo-American Relations in the Twentieth Century: Of Friendship, Conflict and the Rise and Decline of Superpowers* (Routledge, 1995).

Dunne, Timothy, Cox, Michael, and Booth, Ken (eds.), *The Eighty Years' Crisis: International Relations 1919–1999* (Cambridge University Press, 1998).

Dunne, Timothy, Kurki, Milja, and Smith, Steve (eds.), *International Relations Theories* (Oxford University Press, 2013).

Duxbury, Alison, *The Participation of States in International Organisations: The Role of Human Rights and Democracy* (Cambridge University Press, 2011).

Edgerton, David, *Rise and Fall of the British Nation: A Twentieth-Century History* (Penguin Books, 2019).

Edwards, David L., *Christian England, Vol. 3: From the Eighteenth Century to the First World War* (Collins, 1984).

Egerton, George W., *Great Britain and the Creation of the League of Nations: Strategy, Politics, and International Organization, 1914–1919* (Scolar Press, 1978).

Ferrell, Robert H., *Peace in Their Time: The Origins of the Kellogg-Briand Pact* (Yale University Press, 1952).

Fisher, H. A. L., *James Bryce (Viscount Bryce of Dechmont, O.M.)* (Macmillan, 1927).

Fisher, John, Pedaliu, Effie G. H., and Smith, Richard (eds.), *The Foreign Office, Commerce and British Foreign Policy in the Twentieth Century* (Palgrave Macmillan, 2016).

Forster, Edward Morgan, *Goldsworthy Lowes Dickinson* (E. Arnold & Co., 1934). *Goldsworthy Lowes Dickinson, and Related Writings* (Edward Arnold, 1973).

French, David, *The Strategy of the Lloyd George Coalition, 1916–1918* (Clarendon, 1995).

Gerwarth, Robert, *The Vanquished: Why the First World War Failed to End* (Farrar, Straus & Giroux, 2016).

Geyer, Martin H., and Paulmann, Johannes (eds.), *The Mechanics of Internationalism: Culture, Society, and Politics from the 1840s to the First World War* (German Historical Institute; Oxford University Press, 2001).

Ghosh, Peter, and Goldman, Lawrence (eds.), *Politics and Culture in Victorian Britain: Essays in Memory of Colin Matthew* (Oxford University Press, 2006).

Gorman, Daniel, *The Emergence of International Society in the 1920s* (Cambridge University Press, 2012).

International Cooperation in the Early Twentieth Century (Bloomsbury Academic, 2017).

Graham, Gordon, *Ethics and International Relations* (Blackwell Publishers, 1997).

Gregory, Adrian, *The Last Great War: British Society and the First World War* (Cambridge University Press, 2008).

Hall, Ian, *British International Thinkers from Hobbes to Namier* (Palgrave Macmillan, 2009).

Hancock, William Keith, *Smuts* (Cambridge University Press, 1962).

Hann, Matt, *Egalitarian Rights Recognition: International Political Theory* (Palgrave Macmillan, 2016).

Hannigan, Robert E., *The Great War and American Foreign Policy, 1914–24* (University of Pennsylvania Press, 2016).

Harris, Jose (ed.), *Civil Society in British History: Ideas, Identities, Institutions* (Oxford University Press, 2003).

Hartz, Louis, *The Liberal Tradition in America: An Interpretation of American Political Thought Since the Revolution* (Harcourt, 1991).

Haslam, Jonathan, *The Vices of Integrity: E. H. Carr, 1892–1982* (Verso, 1999).

Hastings, Adrian, *A History of English Christianity 1920–2000* (SCM Press, 2001).

Hathaway, Oona A., and Shapiro, Scott J., *The Internationalists: How a Radical Plan to Outlaw War Remade the World* (Simon & Schuster, 2017).

Herman, Sondra R., *Eleven against War: Studies in American International Thought, 1898–1921* (Hoover Institution Press, 1969).

Hinsley, F. H., *Power and the Pursuit of Peace: Theory and Practice in the History of Relations between States* (Cambridge University Press, 1963).

Hobsbawm, Eric J., *Age of Extremes: The Short Twentieth Century, 1914–1991* (Michael Joseph, 1994).

Nations and Nationalism Since 1780: Programme, Myth, Reality (Cambridge University Press, 1992).

Hofstadter, Richard, *The American Political Tradition and the Men Who Made It* (Cape, 1962).

Anti-Intellectualism in American Life (Cape, 1964).

Social Darwinism in American Thought (G. Braziller, 1959).

Horne, John (ed.), *State, Society and Mobilization in Europe during the First World War* (Cambridge University Press, 1997).

Howard, Michael Eliot, *The Continental Commitment* (Ashfield Press, 1989).

The Invention of Peace: Reflections on War and International Order (Profile Books, 2000).

A Part of History: Aspects of the British Experience of the First World War (Bloomsbury Continuum, 2008).

War and the Liberal Conscience (Oxford University Press, 1981).

Ikenberry, G. John, *After Victory: Institutions, Strategic Restraint, and the Rebuilding of Order after Major Wars* (Princeton University Press, 2019).

Iriye, Akira, *War and Peace in the Twentieth Century* (Tokyo University Press, 1986) [in Japanese].

Jackson, Peter, *Beyond the Balance of Power: France and the Politics of National Security in the Era of the First World War* (Cambridge University Press 2013).

Jackson, Simon, and O'Malley, Alanna(eds.), *The Institution of International Order: From the League of Nations to the United Nations* (Routledge, 2018).

Jagger, Peter J. (ed.), *Gladstone* (Hambledon Press, 1998).

Janis, Mark Weston, *America and the Law of Nations 1776–1939* (Oxford University Press, 2010).

Johnson, Gaynor, *Lord Robert Cecil: Politician and Internationalist* (Ashgate Publishing, 2013).

Johnson, James Turner, *Can Modern War Be Just?* (Yale University Press, 1984).
   Ideology, Reason, and the Limitation of War: Religious and Secular Concepts, 1200–1740 (Princeton University Press, 1975).

Johnson, Paul (ed.), *Twentieth-Century Britain: Economic, Social, and Cultural Change* (Longman, 1994).

Joll, James, *The Origins of the First World War* (Longman, 2006).

Jones, John D., and Griesbach, Marc F. (eds.), *Just War Theory in the Nuclear Age* (University Press of America, 1985).

Jones, Raymond A., *Arthur Ponsonby: The Politics of Life* (Bromley, 1989).

Kapossy, Béla, Nikhimovsky, Isaac, and Whatmore, Richard (eds.), *Commerce and Peace in the Enlightenment* (Cambridge University Press, 2017).

Keefer, Scott Andrew, *The Law of Nations and Britain's Quest for Naval Security: International Law and Arms Control, 1898–1914* (Palgrave Macmillan, 2016).

Kennedy, David M., *Over Here: The First World War and American Society* (Oxford University Press, 1982).

Kennedy, Paul M., *The Rise and Fall of the Great Powers: Economic Change and Military Conflict from 1500 to 2000* (Fontana, 1989).

Kennedy, Ross A. (ed.), *A Companion to Woodrow Wilson* (Wiley-Blackwell, 2013).

Kennedy, Ross A. *The Will to Believe: Woodrow Wilson, World War I, and America's Strategy for Peace and Security* (Kent State University Press, 2009).

Keylor, William R., *The Twentieth-Century World and Beyond: An International History Since 1900* (Oxford University Press, 2006).

Knock, Thomas J., *To End All Wars: Woodrow Wilson and the Quest for a New World Order* (Oxford University Press, 1992).

Koch, H. W. (ed.), *The Origins of the First World War: Great Power Rivalry and German War Aims* (Macmillan, 1984).

Kosaka, Masataka, *International Politics* (Chuo Koronsha, 2017) [In Japanese].

Koskenniemi, Martti, *From Apology to Utopia: The Structure of International Legal Argument* (Cambridge University Press, 2005).
   The Gentle Civilizer of Nations: The Rise and Fall of International Law, 1870–1960 (Cambridge University Press, 2002).

Krüger, Peter, and Schroeder, Paul W. (eds.), *'The Transformation of European Politics, 1763–1848': Episode or Model in Modern History?* (Palgrave Macmillan, 2002).

Kuehl, Warren, *Seeking World Order: The United States and International Organization to 1920* (Vanderbilt University Press, 1969).

Laity, Paul, *The British Peace Movement 1870–1914* (Clarendon Press, 2001).

Laqua, Daniel (ed.), *Internationalism Reconfigured: Transnational Ideas and Movements between the World Wars* (Tauris Academic Studies, 2011).

Lemnitzer, Jan Martin, *Power, Law and the End of Privateering* (Palgrave Macmillan, 2014).

Lentin, Antony, *General Smuts: South Africa: The Peace Conferences of 1919–23 and Their Aftermath* (Haus Publishing, 2010).

Lesaffer, Randall, *Peace Treaties and International Law in European History: From the Late Middle Ages to World War One* (Cambridge University Press, 2004).

Link, Arthur S., *Woodrow Wilson and a Revolutionary World, 1913–1921* (University of North Carolina Press, 1982).

Long, David, and Wilson, Peter (eds.), *Thinkers of the Twenty Years' Crisis: Inter-War Idealism Reassessed* (Clarendon Press, 1995).

Lorca, Arnulf Becker, *Mestizo International Law: A Global Intellectual History 1842–1933* (Cambridge University Press, 2014).

Luard, Evan, *A History of the United Nations* (Macmillan, 1982).

  War in International Society: A Study in International Sociology (I.B. Tauris, 1986).

Lynch, Cecelia, *Beyond Appeasement: Interpreting Interwar Peace Movements in World Politics* (Cornell University Press, 1999).

MacKenzie, Norman Ian, *The Time Traveller: The Life of H. G. Wells* (Wiedenfeld and Nicolson, 1973).

MacMillan, Margaret, *Peacemakers: The Paris Conference of 1919 and Its Attempt to End War* (J. Murray, 2001).

Manela, Erez, *The Wilsonian Moment: Self-determination and the International Origins of Anticolonial Nationalism* (Oxford University Press, 2007).

Mangone, Gerard J. *A Short History of International Organization* (McGraw-Hill, 1954).

Marchand, C. Roland, *The American Peace Movement and Social Reform, 1898–1918* (Princeton University Press, 1972).

Marks, Sally, *The Illusion of Peace: International Relations in Europe, 1918–1933* (Macmillan, 1976).

Marrin, Albert, *The Last Crusade: The Church of England in the First World War* (Duke University Press, 1974).

Martin, Laurence W., *Peace without Victory* (Yale University Press, 1958).

Mayall, James, *Nationalism and International Society* (Cambridge University Press, 1990).

Mayer, Arno J., *Political Origins of the New Diplomacy, 1917–1918* (Yale University Press, 1959).

Mazower, Mark, *Dark Continent: Europe's Twentieth Century* (Vintage Books, 2000).

  Governing the World: The History of an Idea (Penguin Books, 2012).

  No Enchanted Palace: The End of Empire and the Ideological Origins of the United Nations (Princeton University Press, 2009).

McCarthy, Helen, *The British People and the League of Nations: Democracy, Citizenship and Internationalism, c. 1918–45* (Manchester University Press, 2011).

Merriam, Charles Edward, *American Political Ideas: Studies in the Development of American Political Thought, 1865–1917* (Macmillan, 1920).

Merriman, John M., *A History of Modern Europe: From the Renaissance to the Present* (W.W. Norton, 2004).

Millman, Brock, *Managing Domestic Dissent in First World War Britain* (Frank Cass, 2000).

Moesch, Sophia, *Augustine and the Art of Ruling in the Carolingian Imperial Period: Political Discourse in Alcuin of York and Hincmar of Rheims* (Routledge, 2019).

Mogami, Toshiki, *International Organisations* (Tokyo University Press, 2006) [in Japanese].

The United Nations and the United States (Iwanami Shoten, 2005) [in Japanese].

Monger, David, *Patriotism and Propaganda in First World War Britain: The National War Aims Committee and Civilian Morale* (Liverpool University Press, 2012).

Morefield, Jeanne, *Covenants without Swords: Idealist Liberalism and the Spirit of Empire* (Princeton University Press, 2005).

Empires without Imperialism: Anglo-American Decline and the Politics of Deflection (Oxford University Press, 2014).

Morris, A. J. Anthony (ed.), *Edwardian Radicalism, 1900–1914: Some Aspects of British Radicalism* (Routledge and Kegan Paul, 1974).

Mosse, George L., *Fallen Soldiers: Reshaping the Memory of the World Wars* (Oxford University Press, 1991).

Moyn, Samuel, *The Last Utopia: Human Rights in History* (Belknap Press of Harvard University Press, 2010).

Mueller, John E, *The Remnants of War* (Cornell University Press, 2004).

Mulder, Nicholas, *The Economic Weapon: Interwar Internationalism and the Rise of Sanctions, 1914–1945* (forthcoming).

Mulligan, William, *The Great War for Peace* (Yale University Press, 2014).

Mulligan, William, and Simms, Brendan, *The Primacy of Foreign Policy in British History, 1660–2000: How Strategic Concerns Shaped Modern Britain* (Palgrave Macmillan, 2010).

Nardin, Terry, and Mapel, David, *Traditions of International Ethics* (Cambridge University Press, 1992).

Neff, Stephen C., *War and the Law of Nations: A General History* (Cambridge University Press, 2005).

Nicholson, Peter, *The Political Philosophy of British Idealists: Selected Case Studies* (Cambridge University Press, 1990).

Nippold, Otfried, *The Development of International Law after the World War* (Read Books, 2007).

Noll, Mark A., *A History of Christianity in the United States and Canada* (Society for Promoting Christian Knowledge, 1992).

Orakhelashvili, Alexander, *Collective Security* (Oxford University Press, 2011).

Oshimura, Takashi, *International Political Thoughts: Survival, Order and Justice* (Keisou Shobou, 2010) [in Japanese].

Theory of International Justice (Kodan-sha, 2008) [in Japanese].
Parkinson, F., *The Philosophy of International Relations: A Study in the History of Thought* (SAGE Publications, 1978).
Pease, Edward R., *The History of the Fabian Society* (E. P. Dutton & Company, 1916).
Pedersen, Susan, *The Guardians: The League of Nations and the Crisis of Empire* (Oxford University Press, 2015).
Pitts, Jennifer, *Boundaries of the International: Law and Empire* (Harvard University Press, 2018).
Plumb, J. H. (ed.), *Studies in Social History: A Tribute to G. M. Trevelyan* (Longmans, 1955).
Porta, Donatella Della. and Diani, Mario, *Social Movements: An Introduction* (Wiley-Blackwell, 2005).
Powaski, Ronald E. *Toward an Entangling Alliance: American Isolationism, Internationalism, and Europe, 1901–1950* (Greenwood Press, 1991).
Qualter, Terence H., *Graham Wallas and the Great Society* (Macmillan, 1980).
Reynolds, David, *America, Empire of Liberty: A New History* (Allen Lane, 2009).
Britannia Overruled (Longman, 2000).
The Long Shadow: The Great War and the Twentieth Century (Simon & Schuster, 2014).
Roach, Steven C., Griffiths, Martin, and O'Callaghan, Terry, *International Relations: The Key Concepts* (Routledge, 2013).
Robbins, Keith, *The Abolition of War: The 'Peace Movement' in Britain, 1914–1919* (University of Wales Press, 1976).
Politicians, Diplomacy, and War in Modern British History (Hambledon Press, 1994).
Sir Edward Grey: A Biography of Lord Grey of Fallodon (Cassell, 1971).
Rodogno, Davide, *Against Massacre: Humanitarian Interventions in the Ottoman Empire, 1815–1914: The Emergence of a European Concept and International Practice* (Princeton University Press, 2012).
Rosenau, James N. (ed.), *International Politics and Foreign Policy: A Reader in Research and Theory* (Collier Macmillan, 1969).
Rosenboim, Or, *The Emergence of Globalism: Visions of World Order in Britain and the United States 1939–1950* (Princeton University Press, 2017).
Rosenthal, Lawrence (ed.), *The New Nationalism and the First World War* (Palgrave Macmillan, 2015).
Rothwell, Victor, *British War Aims and Peace Diplomacy, 1914–1918* (Clarendon, 1971).
Rousseau, Jean-Jacques, *On the Social Contract* (Dover Publications, 2012).
Sayward, Amy L., *The United Nations in International History* (Bloomsbury Academic, 2017).
Scaglia, Ilaria, *The Emotions of Internationalism: Feeling International Cooperation in the Alps in the Interwar Period* (Oxford University Press, 2020).
Schabas, William A., *The Trial of the Kaiser* (Oxford University Press, 2018).
Schroeder, Paul W., *Systems, Stability, and Statecraft: Essays on the International History of Modern Europe* (Palgrave Macmillan, 2004).

Seaman, John T., *A Citizen of the World: The Life of James Bryce* (I. B. Tauris, 2006).

Sharp, Alan, *Consequences of Peace: The Versailles Settlement: Aftermath and Legacy 1919–2010* (Haus, 2010).

The Versailles Settlement: Peacemaking after the First World War, 1919–1923 (Palgrave Macmillan, 2018).

Shaw, Caroline, *Britannia's Embrace: Modern Humanitarianism and the Imperial Origins of Refugee Relief* (Oxford University Press, 2015).

Shinohara, Hatsue, *US International Lawyers in the Interwar Years: A Forgotten Crusade* (Cambridge University Press, 2012).

Simms, Brendan, and Trim, D. J. B. (eds.), *Humanitarian Intervention: A History* (Cambridge University Press, 2011).

Sluga, Glenda, *Internationalism in the Age of Nationalism* (University of Pennsylvania Press, 2013).

Sluga, Glenda, and Clavin, Patricia (eds.), *Internationalisms: A Twentieth-Century History* (Cambridge University Press, 2017).

Smith, Leonard V., *Sovereignty at the Paris Peace Conference of 1919* (Oxford University Press, 2018).

Smith, Tony, *Why Wilson Matters: The Origin of American Liberal Internationalism and Its Crisis Today* (Princeton University Press, 2017).

Smuts, J. C., *Jan Christian Smuts: A Biography* (Cassell, 1952).

Snyder, Sarah B., *Human Rights Activism and the End of the Cold War: A Transnational History of the Helsinki Network* (Cambridge University Press, 2011).

Steiner, Zara S., *Britain and the Origins of the First World War* (Macmillan, 1977).

The Lights That Failed: European International History, 1919–1933 (Oxford University Press, 2005).

The Triumph of the Dark: European International History 1933–1939 (Oxford University Press, 2010).

Stevenson, David, *Cataclysm: The First World War As Political Tragedy* (Basic Books, 2004).

1914–1918: The History of the First World War (Penguin, 2005).

1917: War, Peace, and Revolution (Oxford University Press, 2017).

Stone, Jon R., *On the Boundaries of American Evangelicalism: The Postwar Evangelical Coalition* (St. Martin's Press, 1997).

Stoner, John E., *S. O. Levinson and the Pact of Paris: A Study in the Techniques of Influence, a Dissertation* (University of Chicago Press, 1942).

Stromberg, Roland N., *Collective Security and American Foreign Policy: From the League of Nations to NATO* (Praeger, 1963).

Redemption by War: The Intellectuals and 1914 (Regents Press of Kansas, 1982).

Suganami, Hidemi, *The Domestic Analogy and World Order Proposals* (Cambridge University Press, 1989).

Swartz, Marvin, *The Union of Democratic Control in British Politics during the First World War* (Clarendon Press, 1971).

Sylvest, Casper, *British Liberal Internationalism, 1880–1930: Making Progress?* (Manchester University Press, 2009).

Tarrow, Sidney G., *Power in Movement: Social Movements and Contentious Politics* (Cambridge University Press, 2011).

Taylor, A. J. P., *The Trouble Makers: Dissent over Foreign Policy, 1792–1939* (H. Hamilton, 1957).

Taylor, Sally J., *The Great Outsiders: Northcliffe, Rothermere and the Daily Mail* (Phoenix Giant, 1998).

Thompson, J. Lee, *Politicians, the Press, and Propaganda: Lord Northcliffe and the Great War, 1914–1919* (Kent State University Press, 1999).

Throntveit, Trygve, *Power without Victory: Woodrow Wilson and the American Internationalist Experiment* (University of Chicago Press, 2017).

Tilly, Charles, *The Rebellious Century, 1830–1930* (Dent, 1975).

Tollardo, Elisabetta, *Fascist Italy and the League of Nations, 1922–1935* (Palgrave Macmillan, 2016).

Tooze, J. Adam, *The Deluge: The Great War and the Remaking of Global Order, 1916–1931* (Allen Lane, 2014).

Trevelyan, George Macaulay, *Grey of Fallodon: Being the Life of Sir Edward Grey, afterwards Viscount Grey of Fallodon* (Longmans, 1937).

Tuck, Richard, *The Rights of War and Peace: Political Thought and the International Order from Grotius to Kant* (Oxford University Press, 2001).

Tyler, Colin, *Common Good Politics: British Idealism and Justice in the Contemporary World* (Palgrave Macmillan, 2017).

Unger, Corinna R., *International Development: A Postwar History* (Bloomsbury Academic, 2018).

Wallace, Stuart, *War and the Image of Germany: British Academics 1914–1918* (Donald, 1988).

Walters, F. P., *A History of the League of Nations* (Oxford University Press, 1952).

Watt, Donald Cameron, *Succeeding John Bull: America in Britain's Place 1900–1975: A Study of the Anglo-American Relationship and World Politics in the Context of British and American Foreign-Policy-Making in the Twentieth Century* (Cambridge University Press, 1984).

Weigall, David, *International Relations* (Arnold Publishers, 2002).

Wiener, Martin J., *Between Two Worlds: The Political Thought of Graham Wallas* (Clarendon Press, 1971).

Wight, Martin, *International Theory: The Three Traditions* (Leicester University Press, 1991).

Wilkinson, Alan, *The Church of England and the First World War* (SPCK, 1978).

Wilkinson, Paul, *International Relations: A Very Short Introduction* (Oxford University Press, 2007).

Williams, Howard L., *Kant and the End of War: A Critique of Just War Theory* (Palgrave Macmillan, 2012).

Williams, Paul, *Security Studies: An Introduction* (Taylor and Francis, 2012).

Wilson, Peter, *The International Theory of Leonard Woolf: A Study in Twentieth Century Idealism* (Palgrave Macmillan, 2003).

Wilson, Trevor, *The Myriad Faces of War: Britain and the Great War, 1914–1918* (Polity, 1986).

Wimmer, Andreas, *Waves of War: Nationalism, State Formation, and Ethnic Exclusion in the Modern World* (Cambridge University Press, 2013).

Winkler, Henry R. *The League of Nations Movement in Great Britain, 1914–1919* (Rutgers University Press, 1952).

Winter, Jay M. (ed.), *The Cambridge History of the First World War*, vols. 1–3 (Cambridge University Press, 2013).

Winter, Jay M. *Dreams of Peace and Freedom: Utopian Moments in the Twentieth Century* (Yale University Press, 2006).

  Socialism and the Challenge of War: Ideas and Politics in Britain, 1912–18 (Routledge and Kegan Paul, 1974).

Winter, J. M., and Prost, Antoine, *The Great War in History: Debates and Controversies, 1914 to the Present* (Cambridge University Press, 2005).

Wohl, Robert, *The Generation of 1914* (Harvard University Press, 1979).

Wolfe, Willard, *From Radicalism to Socialism: Men and Ideas in the Formation of Fabian Socialist Doctrines, 1881–1889* (Yale University Press, 1975).

Yearwood, Peter J., *Guarantee of Peace: The League of Nations in British Policy, 1914–1925* (Oxford University Press, 2009).

Young, Iris Marion, *Global Challenges: War, Self Determination, and Responsibility for Justice* (Polity, 2007).

Young, John W., *International Relations Since 1945* (Oxford University Press, 2013).

Web Sources

Oxford Dictionary of National Biography, www.oxforddnb.com/public/index.html.

Theses

Dackombe, Barry Patrick, 'Single-Issue Extra-Parliamentary Groups and Liberal Internationalism, 1899–1920' (The Open University, 2008).

Keefer, Scott Andrew, 'Great Britain and Naval Arms Control International Law and Security 1898–1914' (London School of Economics and Political Science, 2011).

Monger, David, 'The National War Aims Committee and British Patriotism during the First World War' (King's College London, 2009).

Mulder, Nicholas, 'The Economic Weapon: Interwar Internationalism and the Rise of Sanctions, 1914–1945' (Columbia University, 2019).

Tollardo, Elisabetta, 'Italy and the League of Nations: Nationalism and Internationalism, 1922–1935' (University of Oxford, 2014).

Wade, William Warren, 'Public Opinion in International Relations' (London School of Economics and Political Science, M.Sc. thesis, 1948).

Journal Articles

'AHR Reflections: One Hundred Years of Mandates', *American Historical Review*, vol. 124, no. 5 (December 2019), pp. 1673–731.

'Is Democracy Dying? Global Report', *Foreign Affairs*, vol. 97, no. 3 (May/June 2018).

'Ordering the World? Liberal Internationalism in Theory and Practice', *International Affairs*, vol. 94, no. 1 (January 2018), pp. 1–172.

'Out of Order? The Future of the International System', *Foreign Affairs*, vol. 96, no. 1 (January/February 2017).

'Rising Powers and the International Order', *Ethics & International Affairs*, vol. 32, no. 1 (Spring 2018), pp. 15–101.

'World Politics 100 Years after the Paris Peace Conference', *International Affairs*, vol. 95, no. 1 (January 2019), pp. 1–200.

Abbenhuis, Maartje Maria, 'A Most Useful Tool for Diplomacy and Statecraft: Neutrality and Europe in the "Long" Nineteenth Century, 1815–1914', *International History Review*, vol. 35, no. 1 (2013), pp. 1–22.

Amrith, Sunil, and Sluga, Glenda, 'New Histories of the United Nations', *Journal of World History*, vol. 19, no. 3 (September 2008), pp. 251–74.

Anderson, Perry, 'Internationalism: A Breviary', *New Left Review*, no. 14 (March–April 2002), pp. 5–6.

Antic, Ana, Conterio, Johanna, and Vargha, Dora, 'Conclusion: Beyond Liberal Internationalism', *Contemporary European History*, vol. 25, no. 2 (May 2016), pp. 359–71.

Ashworth, Lucian M., 'Did the Realist-Idealist Great Debate Really Happen? A Revisionist History of International Relations', *International Relations*, vol. 16, no. 1 (2002), pp. 33–51.

'Where Are the Idealists in Inter-War International Relations?', *Review of International Studies*, vol. 32, no. 2 (2006), pp. 291–308.

Betts, Richard K., 'Systems for Peace or Causes of War? Collective Security, Arms Control, and the New Europe', *International Security*, vol. 17, no. 1 (1992), pp. 5–43.

Ceadel, Martin, 'Enforced Pacific Settlement or Guaranteed Mutual Defence? British and US Approaches to Collective Security in the Eclectic Covenant of the League of Nations', *International History Review*, vol. 35, no. 5 (2013), pp. 993–1008.

Cecil, Hugh, 'Lord Robert Cecil, 1864–1958: A Nineteenth-Century Upbringing', *History Today*, vol. 25, no. 2 (1975), pp. 118–27.

Cello, Lorenzo, 'Jeremy Bentham's Vision of International Order', *Cambridge Review of International Affairs* (2020), pp. 1–19.

Clavin, Patricia, 'Defining Transnationalism', *Contemporary European History*, vol. 14, no. 4 (November 2005), pp. 421–39.

Clavin, Patricia, and Wessels, Jens-Wilhelm, 'Transnationalism and the League of Nations: Understanding the Work of Its Economic and Financial Organization', *Contemporary European History* (2005), pp. 465–92.

Clinton, Michael, '"The New World Will Create the New Europe": Paul-Henri d'Estournelles de Constant, the United States, and International Peace', *Proceedings of the Western Society for French History*, vol. 40 (2012), pp. 84–95.

'Wilsonians before Wilson: The French Peace Movement & the Société des Nations', *Western Society for French History Conference, Lafayette, LA* (October 2010), pp. 1–16.

Cooper, Sandi E., 'Liberal Internationalists before World War I', *Peace & Change*, vol. 1, no. 2 (April 1973), pp. 11–19.

Curry, George, 'Woodrow Wilson, Jan Smuts, and the Versailles Settlement', *American Historical Review*, vol. 66 (1961), pp. 968–86.

Dubin, Martin David, 'Toward the Concept of Collective Security: The Bryce Group's "Proposals for the Avoidance of War," 1914–1917', *International Organization*, vol. 24, pp. 288–318.

Edling, Max M., 'Peace Pact and Nation: An International Interpretation of the Constitution of the United States', *Past & Present*, vol. 240, no. 1 (August 2018), pp. 267–303.

Egerton, George W., 'The Lloyd George Government and the Creation of the League of Nations', *American Historical Review*, vol. 79, no. 2 (April 1974), pp. 419–44.

Galtung, Johan, 'An Editorial', *Journal of Peace Research*, vol. 1, no. 1 (March 1964), pp. 1–4.

Gorman, Daniel, 'Ecumenical Internationalism: Willoughby Dickinson, the League of Nations and the World Alliance for Promoting International Friendship through the Churches', *Journal of Contemporary History*, vol. 45, no. 1 (January 2010), pp. 51–73.

Hall, Ian, and Bevir, Mark, 'Traditions of British International Thought', *International History Review*, vol. 36, no. 5 (2014), pp. 823–34.

Hathaway, Oona A., and Shapiro, Scott J., "International law and Its Transformation through the Outlawry of War', *International Affairs*, vol. 95, no. 1 (January 2019), pp. 45–62.

Horne, John, 'End of a Paradigm? The Cultural History of the Great War', *Past & Present*, vol. 242, no. 1 (February 2019), pp. 155–92.

Kaymaz, Nazli Pinar, 'From Imperialism to Internationalism: British Idealism and Human Rights', *International History Review*, vol. 41, no. 6 (2019) pp. 1235–55.

Keil, André 'The National Council for Civil Liberties and the British State during the First World War, 1916–1919', *English Historical Review*, vol. 134, no. 568 (June 2019), pp. 620–45.

Kennedy, Ross A., 'Woodrow Wilson, World War I, and an American Conception of National Security', *Diplomatic History*, vol. 25, no. 1 (2001), pp. 1–31.

Langan, John, 'The Elements of St. Augustine's Just War Theory', *Journal of Religious Ethics*, vol. 12, no. 1 (Spring, 1984), pp. 19–38.

Laqua, Daniel, 'Activism in the "Students' League of Nations": International Student Politics and the Confédération Internationale des Étudiants, 1919–1939', *English Historical Review*, vol. 132, no. 556 (June 2017), pp. 605–37.

Lemnitzer, Jan Martin, '"That Moral League of Nations against the United States": The Origins of the 1856 Declaration of Paris and the Abolition of Privateering', *International History Review*, vol. 35, no. 5, pp. 1068–88.

Maiolo, Joseph Anthony, 'Systems and Boundaries in International History', *The International History Review*, vol. 40, no. 3 (2018), pp. 576–91.

Mazower, Mark, 'Violence and the State in the Twentieth Century', *The American Historical Review*, vol. 107, no. 4 (October 2002), pp. 1158–78.

McCarthy, Helen, 'Leading from the Centre: The League of Nations Union, Foreign Policy and "Political Agreement" in the 1930s', *Contemporary British History*, vol. 23, no. 4 (2009), pp. 527–42.

'The League of Nations, Public Ritual and National Identity in Britain, c. 1919–1956', *Historical Workshop Journal*, vol. 70, no. 1 (2010), pp. 108–32.

Millman, Brock, 'A Counsel of Despair: British Strategy and War Aims 1917–18', *Journal of Contemporary History*, vol. 36, no. 2 (April 2001), pp. 241–70.

Mueller, John, 'Changing Attitudes towards War: The Impact of the First World War', *British Journal of Political Science*, vol. 21 (1991), pp.1–28.

Mulder, Nicholas, 'The Trading with the Enemy: Acts in the Age of Expropriation, 1914–49', *Journal of Global History*, vol. 15, no. 1 (March 2020), pp. 81–99.

Nehring, Holger, 'National Internationalists: British and West German Protests against Nuclear Weapons, the Politics of Transnational Communications and the Social History of the Cold War, 1957–1964', *Contemporary European History*, vol. 14, no. 4 (November 2005), pp. 559–82.

Ostrower, Gary B., 'Historical Studies in American Internationalism', *International Organization*, vol. 25, no. 4 (September 1971), pp. 899–916.

Owen, John M., 'Liberalism and Its Alternatives, Again', *International Studies Review*, vol. 20, no. 2 (June 2018), pp. 309–16.

Pedersen, Susan, 'Back to the League of Nations: Review Essay', *American Historical Review*, vol. 112, no. 4 (October 2007), pp. 1091–117.

Porter, Brian, 'David Davies: A Hunter after Peace', *Review of International Studies*, vol. 15, no. 1 (January 1989), pp. 27–36.

Reinisch, Jessica, 'Introduction: Agents of Internationalism', *Contemporary European History*, vol. 25, no. 2 (May 2016), pp 195–205.

Robbins, Keith, 'Lord Bryce and The First World War', *Historical Journal*, vol. 10, no. 2 (January 1967), pp. 255–78.

Rosenberg, Emily S, 'World War I, Wilsonianism, and Challenges to U.S. Empire', *Diplomatic History*, vol. 38, no. 4 (2014), pp. 852–63.

Rosow, Stephen J. 'Commerce, Power and Justice: Montesquieu on International Politics', *The Review of Politics*, vol. 46, no. 3 (July 1984), pp 346–66.

Steeds, David, 'David Davies, Llandinam, and International Affairs', *Transactions of the Honourable Society of Cymmrodorion*, vol. 9 (2003), pp. 122–34.

Stöckmann, Jan, 'The First World War and the Democratic Control of Foreign Policy', *Past & Present* (forthcoming).

'Studying the International, Serving the Nation: The Origins of International Relations (IR) Scholarship in Germany, 1912–33', *International History Review*, vol. 38, no. 5 (2016), pp. 1055–80.

'Women, Wars, and World Affairs: Recovering Feminist International Relations, 1915–39', *Review of International Studies*, vol. 44, no. 2 (April 2018), pp. 215–35.

Stromberg, Roland N., 'Uncertainties and Obscurities about the League of Nations', *Journal of the History of Ideas*, vol. 33 (1972), pp. 139–54.

Sylvest, Casper, 'Continuity and Change in British Liberal Internationalism, c. 1900–1930', *Review of International Studies*, vol. 31, no. 2 (2005), pp. 263–83.

'Interwar Internationalism, the British Labour Party, and the Historiography of International Relations', *International Studies Quarterly*, vol. 48, no. 2 (2004), pp. 409–32.

Tomz, Michael, Weeks, Jessica L. P., and Yarhi-Milo, Keren, 'Public Opinion and Decisions about Military Force in Democracies', *International Organization*, vol. 74, no. 1 (Winter 2020), pp. 119–43.

Trachtenberg, Marc, 'Versailles after Sixty Years', *Journal of Contemporary History*, vol. 17, no. 3 (July, 1982), pp. 487–506.

Weiss, Jeremy, 'E. H. Carr, Norman Angell, and Reassessing the Realist-Utopian Debate', *International History Review*, vol. 35, no. 5 (2013), pp. 1156–84.

Wertheim, Stephen, 'Instrumental Internationalism: The American Origins of the United Nations, 1940–3', *Journal of Contemporary History*, vol. 54, no. 2 (April 2019), pp. 265–83.

'The League of Nations: A Retreat from International Law?', *Journal of Global History*, vol. 7, no. 2 (2012), pp. 210–32.

'The League That Wasn't: American Designs for a Legalist-Sanctionist League of Nations and the Intellectual Origins of International Organization, 1914–1920', *Diplomatic History*, vol. 35, no. 5 (November 2011), pp 797–836.

Wheatley, Natasha, 'Mandatory Interpretation: Legal Hermeneutics and the New International Order in Arab and Jewish Petitions to the League of Nations', *Past & Present*, vol. 227, no. 1 (May 2015), pp. 205–48.

Yearwood, Peter, '"On the Safe and Right Lines": The Lloyd George Government and the Origins of the League of Nations, 1916–1918', *Historical Journal*, vol. 32, no. 1 (1989), pp. 131–55.

'"Real Securities against New Wars": Official British Thinking and the Origins of the League of Nations, 1914–19', *Diplomacy and Statecraft*, vol. 9, no. 3 (1998), pp. 83–109.

Index

www.ingramcontent.com/pod-product-compliance
Ingram Content Group UK Ltd.
Pitfield, Milton Keynes, MK11 3LW, UK
UKHW020454010325

455719UK00016B/577